What People

"This book is a remarkable journey. It is an eye-opener that could help align an increasingly polarized American church. The misunderstanding of prosperity and suffering has left the Western church often excited and flaky or disciplined and powerless. Steve is uniquely positioned and called by God to write this book. As a pastor in Aspen, he lives in the epicenter of affluence, but he has also served in India, Haiti, and Africa, and is well acquainted with suffering throughout the globe. Steve has pastored evangelicals and charismatics, billionaires and beggars, faith-filled and faith-less. Steve demonstrates God's heart toward us and how we deal with blessing, suffering, and what we are really meant to be pursuing. Its message has the potential to bring clarity to Christians and unity to the Church. I have been blessed to visit 50 countries and meet Christians in most of them. I have observed that how we view prosperity and suffering will greatly impact what we believe, how we live, and the impact we will have. This book is a timely and needed resource for anyone wanting to walk in biblical prosperity through a world of suffering."

Clint Phillips
Founder and Chairman
2nd.MD easy access to leading doctors

"Steve has articulated so clearly what many have felt intuitively. The American Church has tried to resolve the Biblical tension between suffering and prosperity that should be managed with wisdom. His insight into Job's progression from prosperity without suffering, to suffering without prosperity, to prosperity through suffering, is brilliant! This is an important book bringing a necessary corrective to us all. I commend it to you!"

Alan Frow
Pastor Southlands Church Brea, CA
Author of *Broken for Blessing, The Underrated Potential of the Medium-sized Multiplying Church*

"This is a courageous book. Steve blends the best of a theology of suffering with the best of a theology of prosperity to produce a powerful cocktail of faith not fatalism, and realism without triumphalism. Drawing on the life of Job, his own journey, and years of pastoral experience, Steve skillfully calls for both power and perseverance in the face of suffering."

PJ Smyth
Pastor, Monument Church, Washington, D.C.
Leader of Global Advance family of churches

"No, not just another book attempting to take the suffering out of suffering. 'How to Live in Prosperity in a Suffering World' is very possibly the read from which you will grasp not only why, but what to do with agonizing troubles, lingering disappointments, and failures. Though the quest for answers goes on, Steve doesn't leave us in perplexity, but thankfully shows us that our heavenly Father has not failed us after all. It is a gratifying understanding of what true prosperity is all about…God's secret of lasting gladness. Soak in it, reflect, and prosper!"

Dr. Greg Livingstone
Founder, Frontier

How To Live
in
PROSPERITY
in a
SUFFERING
World

By
Stephen Royse
Woodrow

STEPHEN ROYSE WOODROW

How To Live In Prosperity in a Suffering World
Copyright © 2019 by Stephen Royse Woodrow
steve@stephenwoodrow.com

This title is also used in ebook format.

Requests for information should be addressed to:
Stephen Woodrow, 726 W. Francis, Aspen, Colorado 81611
www.stephenwoodrow.com

ISBN 9781099900679

All rights reserved. No part of this publication may be reproduced, stored in a retrieval system, or transmitted in any form or by any means – electronic, mechanical, photocopy, recording, or any other – except for brief quotations in printed reviews, without the prior permission of the publisher.

Cover & Interior Design: Alex Dale, loudmark.com
Author Photo: Brian Matthew, radiantlionfilms.com

Dedication

This book is dedicated to the Elders of Crossroads Church Aspen who I have had the privilege of serving with in the glorious task of loving and leading the Body of Christ. Your friendship and fellowship have been life to me and
my family.

And to my beautiful wife, Meshell whose love, devotion and tireless acts of kindness continue to inspire and encourage me.

For Grace, Growth and Greater Things

Table of Contents

Introduction: Do You Feel Prosperous?......................1

Section One: Prosperity without Suffering

Chapter One: Uber-rich: The Search for
Prosperity Without Suffering 11
Chapter Two: We Were Made to Prosper 21
Chapter Three: The Search for Contentment 39
Chapter Four: Becoming Truly Rich......................55

Through these chapters the goal is to come up with a concise biblical understanding of prosperity.

Section Two: Suffering without Prosperity

Chapter Five: The Purpose of Suffering 79
Chapter Six: Suffering and the Spiritual Realm 99
Chapter Seven: Different Kinds of Suffering........127
Chapter Eight: Big "S" and Little "s" Suffering 149

Through these chapters the goal is to come up with a concise biblical understanding of suffering.

Section Three: Prosperity through Suffering

Chapter Nine: Cultivating a Culture of Faith 171

Chapter Ten: A Faith in Tension Approach
to Poverty and Wealth 193

Chapter Eleven: A Faith in Tension
Approach to Sickness and Health 219

Chapter Twelve: A Faith in Tension
Approach to Oppression and Deliverance 241

Through these chapters we bring together our understanding of prosperity and suffering to develop a healthy and whole approach to healing and material wealth and a convergence of the two to be applied in the spiritual life as a whole.

Conclusion: Don't Lose the Plot 267
Acknowledgements 269
Notes 271

"In prosperity may Thou grant perseverance to will one thing; amid distractions, collectedness to will one thing; in suffering, patience to will one thing."

–Soren Kierkegaard

INTRODUCTION

Do You Feel Prosperous?

We all have bad days. Most of us can just push through and hold on tight to get through without having to wrestle with the deeper issues. But there are also traumatic days. These are days that bring devastating circumstances and force us to deal with the deeper issues of reality. Both bad days and traumatic days intrude upon our quest and understanding of prosperity.

One of the most traumatic days I have ever heard anyone experience took place somewhere in the Middle East. Life was going well for this Middle Eastern man. He was wealthy and successful well beyond the norm of his day. He had a wonderful family and community of friends who were all living in peaceful community. On top of all of this he was well respected as a devout man full of integrity. He was experiencing the epitome of a prosperous life, everything and more than the promises of capitalism and the American Dream. Then one day without any warning a tsunami of evil came upon him and his family. His peaceful existence and prosperity were shredded blow by blow in a day that would go down in infamy. On this evil day he lost all of his children and all of his wealth. In the days to follow he lost his health. But what was most amazing about this man was that he did not lose his faith and his trust in God. This man is famous. His name is Job and his story is recorded in the Old Testament book by the same name. This story challenges everything we know and think about prosperity and suffering.

One of the things that make this story so unique and universally profound is that it pulls the curtain back so we can get a glimpse of what was happening in the spiritual realm during Job's life. We would think that this would help shed light on all of our big questions related to prosperity and suffering. In actuality it takes us on the deepest journey of the soul that many are not willing to take. But if we are not willing to take it, we are left with a superficial spirituality removed from the intimate areas of our heart. If we are willing to take it, it will demand everything of us and at the same time lead us into true lasting prosperity.

Dealing with the issues of suffering and evil and how to live in prosperity are hard enough to understand without having to contemplate the issues that were going on behind the curtain. What do we do with the reality of a real devil that appears in heaven before God? What do we do with God asking Satan to examine Job? And what do we do with God allowing Satan to inflict Job with horrors of evil to test him? More than all that what do we do with Job 42:11 that says God is the one who brought all the evil upon Job? Is God good? Who or what is the source of evil? And what do we do with the extreme prosperity that God gave Job for most of his life and doubled it in the last part of his life? These are all critical questions that must be explored if we are going to learn to live in prosperity in a suffering world. Ultimately, it was Job's personal faith in God his Redeemer that allowed him to journey through suffering and attain a new deeper understanding and experience of prosperity.

Inside every soul is the desire to prosper. Have you spent much time thinking about what makes you feel prosperous? Is it financial security, physical security, good health, good relationships, being in control, lack of stress, or plenty of vacation time? Many people have a hard time answering these questions because they have never really stopped to consider what prosperity is and what a truly prosperous life looks and feels like.

Life moves quickly, often with little or no margin to consider what we are really working and striving for.

The world around us is constantly defining prosperity for us and subtly forming within us its vision of a prosperous life. Confusion and even disillusionment takes over when this ingrained worldly vision of prosperity clashes with the harsh realities of life. Relational trauma, health issues, economic and social unrest, and ultimately death powerfully erode this worldly vision of prosperity, which in the West has been defined as the American Dream.

There are two primary responses of our heart to this clash: Our heart will either harden to the harsh realities of life and try to hold on more tightly to the worldly vision of prosperity, or our heart will seek to find a better, more satisfying vision of prosperity. This pursuit is primarily a spiritual pursuit that seeks to find a path that can make sense of all the suffering in the world and at the same time offer a satisfying vision of prosperity.

The desire to make sense of the tension between prosperity and suffering is underlying almost every problem in life. Balance in life is elusive. Balance is something of this world. It is what we attempt to do on our own. Living in balance is impossible when the following two big questions go unanswered:

Does God have good things for me?

How do I handle evil and suffering?

Many struggle with these questions because they have neither understood nor experienced the depth and breadth of the Gospel and how faith holds together the tension between suffering and prosperity.

True prosperity is living in the tension between evil and suffering and the goodness of God by the power and promises of the Gospel.

It is fighting for prosperity and fighting against suffering at the same time. It is an embracing of prosperity and an engaging of suffering at the same time. Embracing prosperity is embracing God's heart, promises and inheritance for His children. Engaging suffering is rejecting passivity and fighting evil and suffering by faith in God's promises and principles. God's promises are guarantees because they are tied to His faithfulness. God's truth principles are connected to His promises but are not guaranteed in this lifetime, but can become promises by faith. Both require faith and both lead to true prosperity. Prosperity is about intimate relationship with the Father, Jesus and Holy Spirit and experiencing the abundant life He promises His followers even in the midst of tribulation.

Success is not the same as prosperity. Most of the time when we define success or someone who is successful we focus on their career success. Prosperity is bigger than success. It is holistic, encompassing every area of our life. It is God's heart for us to prosper. He has good things for us. He sent His only begotten Son, Jesus Christ, to save us from our destructive pursuits and give us life. He is a good God!

American Christian culture is polarized, with one camp leaning more on the prosperity theology side and another on the theology of suffering side. It is time to synergize these together without demonizing our brothers and sisters in the faith. This book is an attempt to bring about a convergence of both a theology and understanding of prosperity and a theology and understanding of suffering into a practical faith-in-tension lifestyle. We will look at the following Word and Spirit graph in detail in a later chapter. Where we fall on this graph impacts how we view prosperity and suffering. A Fan is stuck in superficial spirituality not willing to honestly explore behind the curtain. A Feeler's faith leans too far to the emotions and is lacking a solid theology of suffering. A Fundamentalist's faith leans too far to the intellectual side and is lacking a solid theology of prosperity. Only the Follower of Jesus is truly able to live faith-in-tension between evil and suffering and the goodness of God.

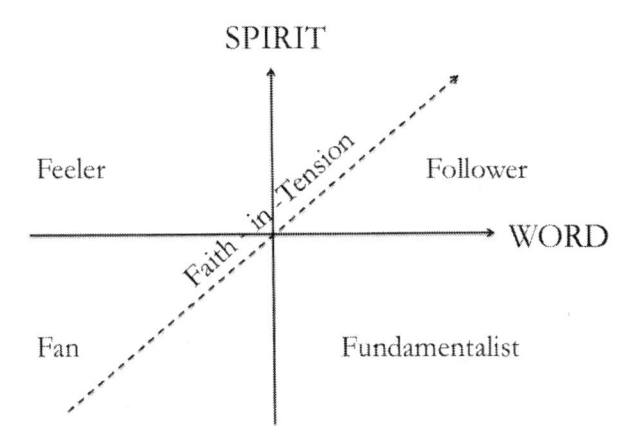

```
            SPIRIT
              ↑
              |      ↗
   Feeler     |   ⟋     Follower
              | ⟋ Tension
              ⟋
           ⟋  |
        ⟋     |————————→ WORD
     ⟋ Faith  |
   ⟋          |
   Fan        |   Fundamentalist
              |
```

One of the most vivid places in scripture we can see this faith-in-tension between prosperity and suffering is found in Hebrews 11:32-40:

> "And what more shall I say? For time would fail me to tell of Gideon, Barak, Samson, Jephthah, of David and Samuel and the prophets— who through faith conquered kingdoms, enforced justice, obtained promises, stopped the mouths of lions, quenched the power of fire, escaped the edge of the sword, were made strong out of weakness, became mighty in war, put foreign armies to flight. Women received back their dead by resurrection." (***faith-in-tension***) Some were tortured, refusing to accept release, so that they might rise again to a better life. Others suffered mocking and flogging, and even chains and imprisonment. They were stoned, they were sawn in two, they were killed with the sword. They went about in skins of sheep and goats, destitute, afflicted, mistreated— of whom the world was not worthy—wandering about in deserts and mountains, and in dens and caves of the earth. And all these, though commended through their faith, did not receive what was promised, since God had provided something better for us, that apart from us they should not be made perfect." (ESV)

From verses 32 to 35 faith is seen as victorious, with a clear vision of God's goodness and prosperity, but halfway through verse 35 things radically shift to a different side of faith, involving endurance through extreme suffering. What are we to make of this? These verses reveal a truth that is seen throughout the Scriptures. True prosperity in this life is more than just eliminating suffering. It is learning to embrace God's heart, promises, and inheritance for His children. It is also learning to endure and fight evil and suffering by faith and perseverance in God's promises and principles.

As we journey through the book of Job and wrestle with his prosperity and suffering I hope you will be willing to put your vision and definition of prosperity and suffering up for examination. Within the book of Job there is a very insightful learning progression: from the pursuit of *Prosperity without Suffering* to *Suffering without Prosperity* to *Prosperity through Suffering*.

In the first section, *Prosperity without Suffering*, we will explore what a biblical understanding of prosperity is all about.

In the second section, *Suffering without Prosperity*, we will explore what a biblical understanding of suffering looks like.

In the third section, *Prosperity through Suffering*, we will bring together our understanding of prosperity and suffering to develop a healthy and whole approach to healing, material wealth and a convergence of the two to be applied in the spiritual life as a whole.

Feel free to jump ahead to the third section where we get practical and apply our theology of prosperity and suffering. However, I hope you will take the time to work through the first two sections as they lay a biblical foundation for section three.

As we embark on this journey of faith-in-tension and learn, "How to live in prosperity in a world of suffering", we will see that Jesus' life and mission followed this same journey. Jesus existed in ultimate prosperity in union with the Father and Holy Spirit in eternity past. Jesus left this paradise of prosperity to come and suffer for us so we could enter into His eternal prosperity. While on His mission, Jesus experienced suffering without prosperity as He bore the suffering and sorrows of the world through His sacrifice, and He also experienced prosperity through suffering as He engaged and conquered suffering by the power of the Holy Spirit. After His resurrection, He again entered into prosperity without suffering where He will exist for all eternity in perfect paradise along with all the redeemed who have embraced Him as Lord and Savior of the world.

There is no greater prosperity message in all the world than the gospel of Jesus Christ!

That is a massive statement and needs to be backed up. It is my prayer that this book will help show that there is no other message in religion or philosophy that coherently and comprehensively deals with sin and death, which are the two main barriers to lasting prosperity. Without a proper understanding and experience of the promises of prosperity and the purposes of suffering we miss the fullness of God's heart for us.

Section One: Prosperity without Suffering

"There was a man in the land of Uz whose name was Job, and that man was blameless and upright, one who feared God and turned away from evil. ²There were born to him seven sons and three daughters. ³He possessed 7,000 sheep, 3,000 camels, 500 yoke of oxen, and 500 female donkeys, and very many servants, so that this man was the greatest of all the people of the east."

    Job 1:1-3, ESV

"And now, Father, glorify me in your own presence with the glory that I had with you before the world existed."

    John 17:5, ESV

SECTION ONE: PROSPERITY WITHOUT SUFFERING

CHAPTER ONE

Uber-rich: The Search for Prosperity Without Suffering

Before moving to Aspen, Colorado in July of 2000, I was serving on the staff of a large church in Atlanta, GA. The Sunday that the senior pastor announced that I was being "called" to lead a church in Aspen the congregation didn't just clap but clapped and laughed. They were sincere in their celebration, but joked by saying, "Yeah, I feel called to Aspen too." In many Christian's minds to be truly "called" you have to go somewhere like Haiti or Siberia where you would truly suffer for Jesus. I had to admit, I felt like I was going on vacation to serve Jesus. Aspen…really? But that feeling revealed something deeper within my soul, which was a questioning of God's heart. Does He want good things for me, or just suffering? I found myself bouncing back and forth between two different messages taught within the Church. On one hand, I heard and taught about all the sacrifices it took to follow Jesus and that trials and suffering were from God to make us more holy. On the other hand, I also heard and taught another message that God desires to heal, bless, and financially prosper us. These apparently contradictory versions of the gospel kept clashing in my mind and disrupted my spiritual walk with God. In some of the circles I ran in, the word "prosperity" was an evil word. In other circles, the word "suffering" was treated as an evil word. I started to see that not only was I confused, but it seemed like the Church in America was really confused about how to define "prosperity" and what the role of "suffering" was in this world. I believe many people today are deeply confused about what true prosperity is and how to attain it while dealing with the reality of suffering along the way.

Moving toward comfort and avoiding suffering drives our pursuit for prosperity far more than we realize. For most of us, when we think of success, we think of a host of "comforts" that we love and long for. Once we attain these comforts and the standard of living that goes with them we can hardly imagine living without them. The search for prosperity without suffering is built into us. The reason why we desire this utopia and prosperity without suffering is because we used to have it! We had ultimate prosperity without suffering in the Garden of Eden, and we gave it up. And ever since we gave it up we have been trying to find it once again, but because of our sinful nature we try to find it in the things of this world. But our desire for prosperity without suffering is actually good and natural. It is the primal drive for utopia and ultimately for heaven. But in our pursuit of utopia and heaven we are repeatedly confronted with the harsh reality of great sufferings. We try to satisfy ourselves with comforts, but satisfaction and contentment remain elusive. Unfortunately, way too many people do not take adequate time to dig deep and do some soul searching about what it truly means to be prosperous in this suffering world.

Richest People Ever

Living in America we have experienced a level of affluence and prosperity that has been unmatched by any other people in history.

"Economics professors Steve Corbett and Brian Fikkert observe how the standard of living essentially common among us is extremely uncommon in human history. They write, 'At no time in history has there ever been greater economic disparity in the world than at present.' Speaking specifically about present-day Americans, they conclude, 'By any measure, we are the richest people ever to walk on the planet Earth.'[i]

Did you get that? We are the "richest people to ever walk on planet earth!" What a statement about American prosperity. But there is a lingering problem. Many people do not "feel" prosperous no matter what level of success they have attained. There can be a big difference between being successful and feeling prosperous. Our default when we do not feel prosperous is to rid our lives of the things we think are keeping us from feeling prosperous and instead pursue more comforts. The problem with this approach is that it keeps us in an endless loop, where we never are able to truly enjoy our prosperity while simultaneously failing to understand, engage, or integrate the role of suffering into our lives.

A Week in the Life of the Uber-rich

Aspen, Colorado is one of the uber-rich destinations of the world. It is where I moved 19 years ago with my family to pastor Crossroads Church. We live in a duplex just a couple minutes from town that the church bought decades ago for pennies. Multi-million dollar homes surround us in our neighborhood now. We are squatters. Some are jealous and angered by all the opulence in Aspen, but this wealth infusion into our small mountain town drives an economic system that provides a good living for many people who are fortunate enough to call the Roaring Fork Valley home. This wealth infusion also brings to Aspen some of the best culture, arts, entertainment, sports and intellectual capital the world has to offer. It is not small town U.S.A., and it's also not your typical ski resort. In many ways Aspen is a utopian community. It is a small resort mountain town with four separate amazing ski mountains, the Aspen Music

Festival, the Aspen Ideas Festival, low crime, no traffic, great schools, four beautiful seasons, incredible weather, beautiful in-shape people, no bugs, no poisonous snakes, no drive thru fast food and an ethos of exploring and improving the mind, body and spirit. Aspen is a world-class resort but has a small town community feel to it that makes people want to not only vacation here, but live here and raise their kids here. It would be hard to find a place with a better quality of life to raise a child than the Aspen community - that is, if you can afford it or figure out how to make it work here. These are just a few reasons why the wealthy of the world build their dream homes here and those who live here rarely want to leave.

Here is a taste of uber-rich living in Aspen, Colorado:

- A dream second or third home of 10-20 thousand square feet made of the world's finest materials with a view most can only dream about
- Owners of these homes do not own keys to their homes, but have management companies handle everything
- "His and hers" jets, which are the ultimate status symbol - and not just any jet but a G5 or some other jet that can fly globally
- Car and driver waiting on tarmac, bags loaded for them, house prepped with groceries, personal preferences set on all hi-tech systems in the house with the right pillows, soaps, fresh flowers, and the hot tub set to 103 degrees
- All technology upgraded annually and synched to their personal preferences
- Artwork all uncovered and prepped, for it is the ultimate in disposable income
- Wine cellars "fit for a king" are inventoried and ready to go
- The pets are flown in, pampered, trained and walked
- Luxury SUVs and sports cars cleaned and prepped and the sports cars are upgraded every year and shipped straight

from Germany into a state of the art climate controlled garage
- The private chef is flown in and special reservations are made at all the right restaurants
- The snow skis have been tuned up, private ski instructors scheduled, and lunch at the private mountain club planned
- In house private massage, personal trainers, hair stylists, and even doctors scheduled
- Personal trainers and adventure guides scheduled because Aspen is known as the cardiovascular capital of the U.S.A., where grandmas kick your ass up the hill - no joke, it's happened to me!
- Parties are planned and holidays are completely prepped, even the Christmas presents are wrapped
- Plans have been made for VIP tickets to the amazing Aspen Music Festival, Aspen Institute's Ideas Fest, Jazz Aspen and Snowmass and a host of other world-class concerts, lectures, and events
- One of the great appeals of Aspen is that the uber-rich and famous can drive their own cars, for there is no need for a driver nor need for personal security because they feel safe. This is also a place where the famous can walk around and be normal - everyone wears jeans so you can't tell the difference between the billionaires, millionaire or ski bums - though I think all true ski bums have been priced out of town
- Amazingly, most only spend 2-4 weeks in their multimillion dollar mansion, where there are often times annual renovations to improve and update the house

How does that sound? Who wouldn't want this lifestyle? We truly are "the richest people to ever walk on planet earth."

Introducing Uber-rich Job

We all want to be uber-rich, unless we are in the bondage of a spirit of poverty. We all are in search of prosperity without suffering, unless we are in bondage to a spirit of religion that embraces legalism and the desire to suffer. As hard as mankind has pursued prosperity, he has constantly run into the reality of suffering, evil, and death. And this was certainly the case with uber-rich Job.

Job is the title of an Old Testament book in the Bible about a man named Job who lived in the land of Uz. Most likely "the land of Uz" was east and south of the Dead Sea in the area known from the time of the patriarchs as Edom. It was the desert country of northern Saudi Arabia or the southern edge of Jordan. We do not know much about Job nor do we know who wrote the book, though there are indications within the book that it is an autobiography. The book is attested to in the New Testament in James 5:11:

> [11] Behold, we consider those blessed who remained steadfast. You have heard of the steadfastness of Job, and you have seen the purpose of the Lord, how the Lord is compassionate and merciful.

Therefore, we know that the early church took two important things from Job's story. First, they saw Job as a model of steadfastness in faith in God even in the midst of terrible suffering. Second, and maybe even more importantly, we can see that even in light of God allowing Job to suffer terribly, they focused on the bigger picture of God's grand purpose. They never doubted His compassion or mercy. They never doubted that He is a good God. Most books and commentaries about Job primarily deal with the harsh realities of suffering without dealing also with the issue of prosperity. In reality though, Job's book has just as much to tell us about prosperity as it does about suffering. It is true that the majority of the book is spent dealing with Job's suffering, but when we look at Job's entire life the reality is that the majority of his life was spent in excessive prosperity. This should be a big indicator of God's heart toward us and His ultimate plan to end suffering and bring us into His prosperity. The book of Job forces us to wrestle with the harsh realities of suffering and to try to understand God's purpose for suffering in the world.

The book of Job presents a simple time where wealth was measured in the number of animals and servants and was most likely either during the time of the patriarchs or before. Job reflected no knowledge of any structured religion, pagan or otherwise. Most likely he lived east of the Promised Land and therefore away from the influence of the patriarchs. He had faith in the one true God and sought to please Him. He was a priest to his household and was known as a man who was "blameless and upright who feared God and turned away from evil" (Job 1:1).

The book of Job has three clear parts to it. The first part consists of chapters 1-2 and opens with a brief description of Job's character and uber-rich life. The narrative then turns to a dramatic scene in heaven where we are privy to an alarming discussion between God and Satan, where Satan is given the freedom to test Job's faith. The next part consists of chapters 3:1-42:6 where Job and his so-called "friends" try to figure out the reason for his suffering. In this large section we can see the universal human response to suffering that wants to look for causes and find solutions rather than seeing suffering as something that can draw us closer to God and give us deeper insight into His purpose and plan. The last section is the shortest (42:7-17) and it brings resolve, restoration and revelation. God breaks Job's seemingly endless season of suffering and restores his fortunes. But even more than that, God reveals that He will not stay silent and that He ultimately has eternal good in store for His children.

The book of Job begins with a description of Job's massive wealth, his piety, and his family situation.

"There was a man in the land of Uz whose name was Job, and that man was blameless and upright, one who feared God and turned away from evil. ²There were born to him seven sons and three daughters. ³He possessed 7,000 sheep, 3,000 camels, 500 yoke of oxen, and 500 female donkeys, and very many servants, so that this man was the greatest of all the people of the east." —Job 1:1-3

We have definitely raised the bar of earthly comforts and fine living, from herds of animals defining our wealth to the number of jets and houses. And Job even held a title that few in the history of the world have held no matter how hard they pursued it. He was known as the "greatest of all the people of the east." Now, that is quite a title. For some, in their pursuit of prosperity, they are not content until they are known as the "greatest." This is the greatest disillusionment and disease of all. Ages ago it got a hold of Lucifer and brought about his downfall and antagonism toward God, His creation, and His people.

This uber-rich life that Job had attained was a life of prosperity without "suffering." It was a perceived utopia on earth enjoying the comforts of the world while avoiding the harsh realities of suffering. But sooner or later there is going to be a bad day when reality strikes and the life we have been pursing escapes us. We will be hit with the reality that obsessively pursuing comfort cannot be sustainable. But, along the way, an even more enlightening event can happen: the shocking reality that the life we had been pursuing was not truly satisfying anyway.

Introducing Uber-rich Jesus

Alongside Job's story there was another, grander story that had been unfolding from eternity past in the heavenly realm, kept secret even from the angels. Very rarely do we think about Jesus' pre-incarnate existence. But we need to understand where He came from to truly understand the fullness of what He sacrificed and what He came to do in history for our eternity. Before Jesus came to earth, He existed in glory with the Father and Holy Spirit in eternity past.[ii] The Scriptures go on to tell us that because of God's love, Jesus was planning to leave "glory" and willfully suffer for us so that we too could experience the fellowship of God's glory forever.[iii] This was the "eternity in Job's heart" when he cried out:

> "For I know that my Redeemer lives, and at the last he will stand upon the earth."
> -Job 19:25

Could there be prosperity greater than anything we can experience on earth? Could it be that we were actually created for that prosperity and can experience a foretaste of it now? Could it be that God's love is so vast and glorious that He was willing to suffer for us so that we could be able to live in His eternal prosperity starting now?

There is no greater prosperity message in all the world than the gospel of Jesus Christ. And true prosperity is living in the tension between evil and suffering and the goodness of God by the power and promises of the Gospel.

To lay hold of this life of prosperity is not as simple as just believing certain biblical truths, being part of a certain religious institution, or practicing spiritual disciplines. It requires a dynamic faith that must be tested over time through many trials before it is ultimately able to lay hold of this true and ultimate prosperity we were all created to live in.

CHAPTER TWO
We Were Made to Prosper

When things are quiet and you have time to think, what do you find yourself dreaming about? What we dream about tells us a lot about what we are living for. Have you ever thought about why we have the capacity to dream and set a vision for our life? Most do not dream about suffering or failure, and if they do it is called a nightmare. Archbishop William Temple has said,

"Your religion is what you do with your solitude."

Few people today have margin in their lives for quality solitude to think deeply about what it truly means to be prosperous and the purpose of suffering. These are spiritually confusing times. If we don't have time for solitude, being alone with our thoughts, then we have a starved spiritual life. Linda Stone, who formerly worked for Apple and Microsoft has written,

"To pay continuous partial attention is to pay partial attention- continuously. It is motivated by a desire to be a live node on the network. Another way of saying this is that we want to connect and be connected. We want to effectively scan for opportunity and optimize for the best opportunities, activities, and contacts, in any given moment. To be busy, to be connected, is to be alive, to be recognized, and to matter. We pay continuous partial attention in an effort not to miss anything. It is an always-on, anywhere, anytime, any place behavior that involves an artificial sense of constant crisis." [iv]

Today in our tech savvy culture we are continuously connected in an effort "not to miss anything" but maybe we are in danger of missing everything. If our heart, soul and mind are "always-on" and preoccupied with what is happening in cyberspace then we are completely disconnected to what is happening in spiritual space. This kills our ability to dream, connect and hear from God.

When people do have time to dream they usually dream about success and prosperous things. The Bible tells us that God had us on His mind before the foundation of the earth. God dreams, but unlike us, He has the ability to bring about His dream. And since we are created in the image of God, we are created with the amazing ability to dream. The scriptures from beginning to end reveal a good God who desires to bless and prosper His people. Do you believe that you were created to prosper?

"I don't feel prosperous at all," was the response I recently heard from a Christian when asked about their view of prosperity. What is interesting is that this person is a seasoned believer, lives an upper middle class lifestyle, and enjoys comforts of which many in the majority world only dream. This believer is not alone in how they feel. They are just being brutally honest. Feelings come and go and this statement could be the result of going through a difficult time. So, is there a "feeling" of prosperity that transcends one's circumstances? Is it possible to "feel" prosperous even without an upper middle class or uber-rich lifestyle? This all hinges on how we define and experience prosperity.

In the Beginning Prosperity

Did you grow up believing you were special? I have heard story after story of childhood experiences where nothing was special and therefore not feeling special was reinforced. Of course, it is possible to overcompensate and try to make everything special which has the same affect of making nothing truly special. There is great power in growing up believing that you are special, not an unhealthy entitlement mentality but a healthy sense of personal value. It helps birth a healthy life and healthy relationships. Without this experience people rarely are able to develop a healthy perspective on life. And they are often driven to accomplishments to prove something and leave a trail of brokenness behind them. It is one thing to feel special, but it is a much greater thing to know and feel that you are special in your Creator's eyes. This is often the missing foundation to understanding what true prosperity is all about.

God's desire from the beginning was for the pinnacle of His creation, those who are special in his eyes, to thrive and prosper. Genesis 1:26-28 (ESV) reveals this truth.

> "The God said, 'Let us make man in our image after our likeness. And let them have dominion over the fish of the sea and over the birds of the heavens and over the livestock and over all the earth and over every creeping thing that creeps on the earth. So God created man in his own image, in the image of God he created him; male and female he created them. And God blessed them. And God said to them, 'Be fruitful and multiply and fill the earth and subdue it, and have dominion over the fish of the sea and over the birds of the heavens and over every living thing that moves on the earth."

There is so much more within these verses and the first few chapters of Genesis than merely the creation story. We can see here the heart of God toward his children and that He desires for them to rule and reign over His creation. God desires for His children to flourish in relationships and family, in vocation, in health and in purpose. Just as God brought *shalom* (peace) to the chaos of the earth, so Adam and Eve were to expand the peace and prosperity of the Garden of Eden out into the rest of the world. But something went terribly wrong. Adam and Eve believed the lie that still impacts all humanity. They trusted Satan's lie that God was holding back on them and that there was a greater prosperity waiting for the taking. With this tragedy of all tragedies, the peace and prosperity of the Garden were lost.

> "The Lord God took the man and put him in the garden of Eden to work it and keep it. And the Lord God commanded the man, saying, 'You may surely eat of every tree of the garden, but of the tree of the knowledge of good and evil you shall not eat, for in the day that you eat of it you shall surely die.'" (Genesis 2:15-17)

By the way, we would have made the same decision Adam and Eve did – and we have! By their decision they lost their authority and much of their capacity to dream. And by rejecting God's blessings they came under a curse of death. But all was not lost, for this was part of God's sovereign plan which He continued by restoring peace and prosperity through one man, Abraham, so he in turn could bring that blessing to the rest of the world. This promise of prosperity is seen in Genesis 12 when God called Abraham.

> "Now the Lord said to Abram, 'Go from your country and your kindred and your father's house to the land that I will show you. And I will make of you a great nation, and I will bless you and make your name great, so that you will be a blessing. I will bless those who bless you, and him who dishonors you I will curse, and in you all the families of the earth shall be blessed." (Genesis 12:1-3)

All through the Old Testament we can see the promises of God and the blessing and cursing principle as it is lived out in

Israel's history. It is especially revealed in Deuteronomy chapters 27-30, where Moses is renewing the blessing and cursing principle with Israel. It basically states that if they walk with God and obey Him that God will bless them abundantly, but if they walk away from God and disobey Him that they will greatly suffer. The word "Israel" actually means "to wrestle." And Israel's wrestling with God is to reveal a deeper revelation of our great need for a Savior to redeem us from our unwillingness to obey and our inability to earn our salvation. This wrestling is further illustrated in the life of Job. Many scholars believe that the account of Job's life took place during the time of the Patriarchs while like Abraham Job was experiencing great prosperity and dominion over much of the earth. The story of Job was shocking to people because it seemed to go against God's blessing and cursing principle. For it seemed that all the suffering that came upon Job was not justified and that God was breaking His blessing and cursing principle. This explains why Job, his wife and friends were so mystified by his great suffering. The vast majority of the book of Job reveals his friends coming to Job based on God's blessing and cursing principle. If Job would just repent of his wrong, they reasoned, the blessings would be restored. But God was revealing something much deeper here. Even if people did their best to obey God they were ultimately unable to earn by their good deeds a new justified relationship with God. This is why Job proclaimed,

"For I know that my Redeemer lives, and at the last he will stand upon the earth." (Job 19:25)

At the center of the promises of God is the gospel itself. The gospel is based on God's grace, which saves us, not God's law, which condemns us. 2 Corinthians 1:20 says, "For all the promises of God find their Yes in him…" Jesus neither changed the blessing and cursing principle nor God's plan of salvation, but actually fulfilled them. He saves us by grace, which means we can't obey the law to earn our salvation; we have to receive it freely by faith. And Jesus empowers us with the Holy Spirit so we can obey the law and experience all the blessings of God by faith. The new covenant is superior to the Old Testament covenant because of what Jesus has done for us.

> "Do not think I came to abolish the Law or the Prophets; I have not come to abolish them but to fulfill them. For truly, I say to you, until heaven and earth pass away, not an iota, not a dot, will pass from the Law until all is accomplished. Therefore whoever relaxes one of the least of these commandments and teaches others to do the same will be called least in the kingdom of heaven, but whoever does them and teaches them will be called great in the kingdom of heaven. For I tell you, unless your righteousness exceeds that of the scribes and Pharisees, you will never enter the kingdom of heaven." (Matthew 5:17-20)

> "Christ redeemed us from the curse of the law by becoming a curse for us – for it is written, 'Cursed is everyone who is hanged on a tree'- so that in Christ Jesus the blessing of Abraham might come to the Gentiles, so that we might receive the promised Spirit through faith." (Galatians 3:13-14)

Jesus has done for us what we are incapable of doing for ourselves. Dallas Willard has said, "Depravity does not, properly refer to the inability to act, but to the unwillingness to act and clearly the inability to earn."ᵛ Jesus has changed our hearts by giving us the Holy Spirit so we can prosper under the blessings of God found in both the Old Testament and the New Testament. So, in summary, we are saved by grace through the promise of God and we therefore are then capable of experiencing God's blessings through learning obedience to the Word of God.

Today, we do not hear much about the idea of blessing and cursing. That is because we live in a man-centered culture where the discussion is primarily about success and failure. Terms that most of the time leave out the influence of God in our world and lives. When people talk about being successful they most of the time are speaking about their personal accomplishments. However, to be blessed is to have supernatural power working for you. And therefore, to be cursed is to have supernatural power working against you. God's heart is to be for us, working not just alongside us but also inside us so that we can walk in His blessings. A success and failure perspective on prosperity comes with a drive for approval that can be crippling. It is crippling in the sense that no matter what level of success is attained there can never be the deep satisfaction that you are truly special in God's eyes. For we know that no number of fans or followers or awards can ever fill the heart void of needing the approval of our heavenly Father.

    I am privileged to have several Jewish friends and I live in a city with a vibrant Jewish community. One of the consistent things I have noticed among Jewish people is that they know they are special. No matter whether they are orthodox, reformed, conservative or even secular there is built into them a sense of knowing – they are special. This sense of specialness is what has enabled them to withstand some of the worst persecution and abuse history has doled out. There is even a word for this worldwide persecution – anti-Semitism. This specialness has been with them from the beginning when God called and blessed Abraham and promised to bless the nations through him. It is the reason Israel is the longest lasting nation in the history of the world. It is the reason this little nation continues to strive and thrive even while it is surrounded on all sides by enemies who have sworn to destroy her. It is also the reason why so many Jewish people are wealthy. They are blessed. They have supernatural power working for them. However, they have also been cursed and have had supernatural power working against them because of their disobedience as well. The history of Israel reveals the blessing and cursing principle and ultimately God's heart to bless and prosper His people. He chose Israel to bless so they in turn could bring that blessing to the world. Their history should be a wake up call to the rest of the world that walking away from God brings cursing and walking with God brings blessings.

Ultimately the blessing of the Jews to the world was the Messiah, Jesus Christ, God's Son who became a curse so all people, not just the Jewish people, could walk in the blessings and prosperity of God. True prosperity begins with the heart knowledge that you are special in the eyes of God and that you have His supernatural power working for you.

Freedom from the Spirit of Poverty

Most people in the world have not been told they were created to prosper nor do they believe they were created to prosper because they get too hung up on themselves, their circumstances and the problems in the world. Poverty is not just the lack of resources, but is the lack of heart, the lack of a dream, the lack of vision and hope for a preferred future. And poverty is not just a state of material need that one finds oneself in, but can become a spiritual state that oppresses with a spirit of poverty. Bryant Myers, author of *Walking with the Poor* puts it this way,

> "Poverty is the result of relationships that do not work, that are not just, that are not for life, that are not harmonious or enjoyable. Poverty is the absence of *shalom* in all its meanings."

I have seen this spirit of poverty oppress not just the poor but also the wealthy. When it gets a hold of the wealthy it usually takes the form of a growing bondage to the fear of losing money and going to the poor house. When it gets a hold of the poor it keeps them in a poverty state no matter how much ministry, help and resource are thrown at the problem. One of the biggest examples of this I have observed is Haiti. Billions of dollars of relief and aid have been given to this tiny country with very little lasting impact in the lives of Haitians to set them free from the spirit of poverty. Government corruption not only feeds the spirit of poverty but also takes advantage of it. This is the plight of so many stuck in the majority world.

"Poverty isn't just a lack of material things – it's rooted in broken relationships with God, self, others, and the rest of creation. We were created to glorify God, reflect His image, love one another, and steward the rest of creation. But the fall and sin marred what God originally created. As a result, none of us are experiencing the fullness of what God intended for us."[vi]

I remember a few years ago our church family rallied behind a young couple with young children. The father was in and out of jail, but we were eventually able to help them stabilize with jobs and housing. We believe they grew some in the faith along the way but the spirit of poverty was never broken off. They never were able to see themselves as God saw them. They were never able to change the state of their home or dress even when funds and help were provided. It only took a few days before chaos and junk took over. The spirit of poverty cuts down our identity and expectation. It robs hope and vision for a preferred future.

In the minds of many Christians today is a deep wrestling with the idea that the possession of material things and money is evil. Often there is an underlying feeling of condemnation and guilt for having so much when so much of the world has nothing. Gordon Fee puts it this way,

"Anyone with even a surface acquaintance with the New Testament has come to recognize that the Christian faith is decidedly on the side of 'the poor' and that 'the rich' seem regularly to 'come in for it.' Thus Jesus says, 'Blessed are you who are poor' and 'woe to you who are rich' (Luke 6:20, 24, NIV). His messianic credentials are vindicated by the fact that 'the good news is preached to the poor' (Matt. 11:5; see Luke 4:18), while of the rich He says, 'It is easier for a camel to go through the eye of a needle than for a rich man to enter the kingdom of God' (Mark 10:25). In his parable of the Sower He warns of 'the deceitfulness of wealth and the desire for other things' that choke out the Word of God (Mark 4:19), while elsewhere He says that one cannot serve God and money – they are mutually exclusive masters. (Matt. 6:24)…In light of such texts it is no wonder that affluent Christians sometimes experience guilt, as though wealth, or being wealthy, in itself were evil. But such is not the case. As we shall see, it is the abuse or accumulation of wealth while others are in need that is called into question."[vii]

We have been taught, and seem to believe, that we would be more spiritual and freer if we had less material things and money. But is this what Jesus was teaching and would this line up with the heart of God found in the Old Testament for His people? Dallas Willard says,

"The idealization of poverty is one of the most dangerous illusions of Christians in the contemporary world. Stewardship – which requires possessions and includes giving – is the true spiritual discipline in relation to wealth."[viii]

Often along with the idealization of poverty comes an unhealthy teaching and embracing of suffering which is void of the promises of God that can be laid hold of to radically change one's life circumstances. Many well-meaning writers and teachers today criticize the health wealth movement and others for telling the poor that if they seek the Lord He will provide for them. Dallas Willard addresses this when he says,

"The truly poor of the earth know poverty for what it is: it is crushing deprivation and helplessness."[ix]

The poor know the harshness and darkness of the reality of poverty. So, does the Gospel, which prospers the soul, have anything to offer when it comes to the reality of poverty? The Bible is packed full of amazing promises of getting set free from a spirit of poverty and seeing not just our hearts radically transformed but our physical circumstances as well.

Unfortunately, much of the modern prosperity gospel message embraces more of an American dream pursuit of wealth than freedom from the spirit of poverty. This has the adverse affect of making formulas out of faith and not lovingly walking with people through suffering. In evangelical mainstream's harsh treatment of the prosperity gospel (and rightfully so part of the time) we have developed what I will call "faith-angst", which swings us away from a vibrant "expect greater things" attitude. This faith-angst resides hidden in our souls as anxiety resulting from a real lack of confidence and assurance of how we can practically trust in God's Word and promises. American culture for the most part (and much of religious scholarship) has rejected a biblical worldview of "spiritual warfare." Therefore, we are left in an intellectual loop wondering about the "why" questions rather than engaging suffering the New Testament way. The intellectual loop keeps us from pursuing supernatural causes and solutions. This is because the idea of spiritual warfare and the reality of a real devil are seen as ole-time religion and anti-intellectual. But there is no way to avoid it if we are going to take Jesus seriously as well as what the bible says about suffering and prosperity seriously. Also, when a large part of American Christianity (especially religious scholarship) minimalizes the present and very active power of the Holy Spirit and His very specific spiritual gifts that He gave the Church to fight suffering then yes, we are left with "faith angst" and miss the prosperity aspect of the Gospel. And even worse, the Church has not taught nor encouraged its people to pursue these things. They are left "harassed" and "helpless" (Matt. 9:35-38) just like Jesus defined them in a spiritual war with no weapons to fight and engage suffering and at the same time embrace the promises of prosperity.

Here are some big promises of prosperity that I believe are true whether you are one of the few uber –rich in Aspen, CO, or one of the many poor in the majority world. 2 Chronicles 16:9 is one of my personal favorites.

> "For the eyes of the Lord run to and fro
> throughout the whole earth, to give strong support
> to those whose heart is blameless toward him…"

What an amazing promise and what a great loving and looking God we have. This is a promise about who God is and what He does and God does not change. So, can a poor person in a poor and desperate situation take hold of this promise and expect to get God's attention and expect God to move and change their circumstances? I believe yes!

Now I know, there will be some reading this who will immediately say that I have taken this verse out of context and applied it to my personal life and made a universal promise out of it. This is one of the main arguments against the health and wealth gospel that many use. Yes, it is true that often scriptures are taken out of context and mishandled. But this raises an important aspect of how we are to apply the Word of God. Yes, we are to do good exegesis and study the original meaning and context of the scripture, but we are not to eliminate the fact that it is the "living and active" word of God and that God desires to speak to us personally through it. It is to be personalized by faith, for it is not just written for its context but written for many contexts as the children of God listen to God and walk with God. This personalization must always be "fenced in" as such by 1) the original intention of the human author, 2) the texts application to the life, ministry and work of Christ Jesus and 3) the texts transformation along redemptive-historical lines into the New Covenant. Without this personalization we would have no intimate walking-talking relationship with God. What could happen if a poor person in bondage to the spirit of poverty took hold of this promise by faith in our loving and looking God?

Let's now look at Matthew 6:25-33,

> "Therefore I tell you, do not be anxious about your life, what you will eat or what you will drink, nor about your body, what you will put on. Is not life more than food, and the body more than clothing? Look at the birds of the air: they neither sow nor reap nor gather into barns, and yet your heavenly Father feeds them. Are you not of more value than they? And which of you by being anxious can add a single hour to his span of life? And why are you anxious about clothing? Consider the lilies of the field, how they grow: they neither toil nor spin, yet I tell you, even Solomon in all his glory was not arrayed like one of these. But if God so clothes the grass of the field, which today is alive and tomorrow is thrown into the oven, will he not much more clothe you, O you of little faith? Therefore do not be anxious, saying, 'What shall we eat? or 'What shall we drink? or 'What shall we wear? For the Gentiles seek after all these things, and your heavenly Father knows that you need them all. But seek first the kingdom of God and his righteousness, and all these things will be added to you."

These verses are not promising riches, but they are promising provision! When "faith-angst" takes over we lose sight of the radical promise of provision found in these verses for anyone anywhere who will lay hold of them by faith. In the next chapter we will talk about the difference between promises of provision versus promises of riches.

Finally, let's look at Matthew 7:7-11,

> "Ask and it will be given to you; seek, and you will find; knock, and it will be opened to you. For everyone who asks receives, and the one who

seeks finds, and to the one who knocks it will be opened. Or which one of you, if his son asks him for bread, will give him a stone? Or if he ask for a fish, will give him a serpent? If you then, who are evil, know how to give good gifts to your children, how much more will your Father who is in heaven give good things to those who ask him!"

The context of this massive promise is seeking first the kingdom of God. However, Jesus illustrates here the general giving nature of our heavenly Father who desires good things for his children. He desires to "much more" bless us with "good things." And these "good things" we can put no limit on. At the same time we must constantly check our heart motive and make sure our primary pursuit is God Himself. John Piper said it well,

> "By nature we get more pleasure from God's gifts than from himself."
> –John Piper

Here are four aspects of a biblical theology of prosperity that we will explore further later in this book:

1.) God desires that we seek Him for who He is, not simply for what He gives.

2.) Poverty in all its forms is bondage and to be engaged with the promises of God.

3.) God is a good God who desires good things for His children, even material things.

4.) The blessing-cursing principle has not changed: God blesses those who seek Him.

A spirit of poverty adversely affects our dreams and expectations. Jesus came to set us free from the bondage of a spirit of poverty. You were made to prosper.

Freedom from the Spirit of Religion

Not only does the gospel free us from the spirit of poverty so we can embrace the "good things" (Matt. 7:11) God has for us, it frees us from the spirit of religion so we can embrace the "greater things" (John 14:12) God has for us. What is the spirit of religion? A spirit of religion is opposed to grace. It is a spirit of earning, guilt, shame and self-righteousness, which quenches the Spirit's work of expecting great things. The spirit of religion also can embrace suffering rather than engage suffering with faith and God's promises.

We can see a form of this spirit of religion upon Job's friends who were trying to help Job, but in the process they actually were heaping a burden upon his already terrible suffering. They approached Job's suffering with a fix-it mentality, void of deep empathy and listening. Their attitude came across as dogmatic with a quid pro quo formulaic approach to faith and suffering, which manifested as one thing in return for another rather than ministering the grace of God. They were reducing God to their own understanding in this process. We see this same spirit of religion upon the New Testament Pharisees who created laws and systems to try and put everything into a neat box and force people to conform to it rather than journey with them so the grace of God can transform them. There is a more subtle manifestation of the spirit of religion that has occurred throughout Church history where suffering is embraced rather than engaged with faith and reliance on the power and gifts of the Holy Spirit. This manifestation of the spirit of religion focuses on the spiritual benefits of suffering without or with minimal expectation of supernatural deliverance from suffering. Often Job's sufferings are mentioned, but Job's deliverance is minimalized. This can skew our view of God's heart and intention in the midst of a season of suffering and kill our fight of faith for healing and deliverance. Yes, God is transforming us in the midst of suffering (Romans 5:3, James 1:2-3), but He also desires to strengthen our faith muscles by harnessing His promises and the gifts of the Spirit to fight the suffering. In Luke chapters 11 and

18 Jesus tells parables about prayer with the point of never giving up in our expectation for God's deliverance. John 16:33 makes clear that we will have tribulation in this world, but we have been given spiritual resources (Luke 10:19; Acts 1:8; 1 Cor. 12:1-11) to engage and fight suffering in the world, because Jesus has overcome the world.

A main part of Jesus and His disciples' ministry was healing and deliverance. And it would appear from the Great Commission (Matt. 28:18-20) and the book of Acts that the disciples were to pass this on to other disciples. When Jesus states in the Great Commission, "teaching them all that I have commanded you," this does not mean just head knowledge, but includes healing the sick and the ministry of deliverance. God has not promised physical healing for everyone in this life. Christ's death, burial and resurrection though guarantee ultimate healing and glorification at His return. God has not promised spiritual maturity in this life, but again through Christ's work we will be made holy at His return. The extent of sanctification we experience in this life is determined by the application of our faith in obedience to His Word. If we obey His Word, we experience the sanctifying power of the Spirit and become more like Him. So, our healing and sanctification are not guaranteed in this life, but God has made provision for both through Jesus' death, burial and resurrection. Healing is not guaranteed in the atonement, but provision has been made for it. This means that by faith we can pursue both healing and sanctification (Matt. 8:14-17). Many look to Christ and His work only for what will happen in eternity and miss the immediate blessings and power that can be ours through faith now. God's heart is to save, heal and deliver. In 1 Timothy 2:4, Paul describes God's heart as being one, "who desires all people to be saved and to come to the knowledge of the truth." If He desires all men to be saved, then He must desire them to be ultimately healthy both spiritually and physically. The Greek word for salvation is a big word, "sozo" that encompasses the aspects of healing and deliverance. We know that not all will be saved nor delivered or healed. As we know that not all will "mature" in the Lord. But we must never doubt the good heart of God. Yes, He does allow suffering and sickness and the enemy to wreak havoc as in Job's situation, but His ultimate desire is to heal and deliver, which is why He sent Jesus and why both Jesus and the Father sent forth the Holy Spirit and power for the Church. Gordon Fee states well the current state of much of the Church in relation to the great promises found in the scriptures:

> "In fact, these texts on faith (passages on healing and deliverance) have regularly been a bit of an embarrassment to the church. They are all clearly there in the biblical text, yet seldom does one see them "at work" – except in rare instances. One must ruefully admit that evangelical Christianity by and large does not expect much from God. He is given credit for all ordinary things in our lives – as well He should be – but most Christians' expectation level, when it comes to the miraculous, is somewhere between zero and minus five."[x]

Here are four more aspects of a biblical theology of prosperity that we will explore further later in this book:

1.) God's heart is to save, heal and deliver – always.

2.) God does not guarantee healing or spiritual maturity in this life, but has made provision for both to be pursued by faith.

3.) God has given spiritual gifts to be pursued so we can set the harassed and helpless free.

4.) God expects us to engage suffering the way Jesus and the early church did.

A spirit of religion adversely affects our dreams and expectation level. Jesus came to set us free from the bondage of a spirit of religion. You were made to prosper.

CHAPTER THREE

The Search for Contentment

Contentment is necessary to live in true prosperity. What is contentment? King David reveals the essence of contentment when he expresses his heart in Psalm 131,

> "O Lord, my heart is not lifted up; my eyes are not raised too high; I do not occupy myself with things too great and too marvelous for me. But I have calmed and quieted my soul, like a weaned child with its mother; like a weaned child is my soul within me." (Psalm 131:1-2)

David uses the image of a weaned child to define the experience of contentment. He is saying that he has reached a place of being satisfied with just God Himself, regardless of what God provides for him. Contentment is impossible without a divine move upon our heart. So contentment is divine contentment, there is no such thing as a purely human experience of contentment. Charles Spurgeon said of Psalm 131 that it was, "one of the shortest Psalms to read, but one of the longest to learn." Paul gives us a picture of this divine contentment when he says,

> "Not that I am speaking of being in need, for I have learned in whatever situation I am to be content. I know how to be brought low, and I know how to abound. In any and every circumstance, I have learned the secret of facing plenty and hunger, abundance and need. I can do all things through him who strengthens me."
> (Philippians 4:11-12)

Terry Virgo says of this passage, "Paul's secret of contentment wasn't passive acceptance of events but an active pursuit of experiencing Christ in everything." But, who today is truly seeking contentment or who even understands what it is? We live in a culture that is heavily in bondage to consumerism. We are so in bondage to it that we rely upon it for the very existence of our economy. We have no vision for our culture and nation without promoting a culture of consumerism. Being a consumer is not bad and is somewhat necessary for a healthy economy, but bondage to consumerism is actually destructive to the very foundation of a healthy culture and nation. Our exponentially expanding national debt is just one indication of the death grip this beast of bondage to consumerism has upon us. And we are now a global economy and so our out of control consumerism affects the stability of the entire world. Like any bondage, it seeks to destroy and take down as many as it can. How do we go from a healthy sense of being a consumer to a destructive bondage to consumerism? It all begins with a lack of vision for the importance of contentment and that true prosperity is impossible without pursuing and experiencing contentment. Contentment is a lot more than simply satisfaction, happiness or pleasure. It is a state of the heart, a mature place where active faith resides. Contentment is impossible to achieve without the supernatural power of God working within us. The first step toward bondage to consumerism is coveting. Coveting leads to comparison, which leads to competition, which puts us in bondage to consumerism. It takes a supernatural work of the Holy Spirit on our heart to bring us to contrition. Contrition starts the inner process of breaking off the bondage to consumerism so we can be free to live in contentment. Here are the 6 C's of our journey to contentment:

> Coveting
> Comparison
> Competition
> Consumerism
> Contrition
> Contentment

It seems that the more material things we acquire the more we desire. This is for sure the case without some divine intervention into our souls. We all have experienced the law of diminishing returns. We all know what it is like to deeply long for something only to experience a diminishing satisfaction with it after we acquired it. All parents are familiar with this law of diminishing returns especially a few weeks after Christmas. Those new toys that sparked so much excitement in the kids quickly lost their appeal. This experience does not change with age unless we experience significant heart change.

Bondage to consumerism creates an ever-increasing desire for more, but results in an ever-decreasing satisfaction along the path of acquiring more.

History testifies to story after story of those who lived in absolute material abundance and yet never experienced happiness or a sense of fulfillment. There is probably no greater example in all of antiquity than King Solomon. He had history making power, fame and fortune beyond the imagination. And on top of that he had hundreds of wives and concubines (1 Kings 10-11). But, even with the divine gift of wisdom none of this fortune created contentment or satisfaction. In all of this his heart was ultimately led away from the Lord, the only one who could bring fulfillment. Near the end of his life he wrote,

> "He who loves money will not be satisfied with money, nor he who loves wealth with his income, this is vanity...There is an evil that I have seen under the sun, and it lies heavy on mankind: a man to whom God gives wealth, possessions, and honor, so that he lacks nothing of all that he desires, yet God does not give him power to enjoy them, but a stranger enjoys them." (Ecclesiastes 5:10; 6:1-2)

Another great example is Abd-ar-Rahman III.

Abd-ar-Rahman III was born in 891 AD. He became the emir of Cordoba in his early twenties and spent the next five decades becoming one of the most powerful rulers of his time. He built incredible palaces and stunning mosques. He raised a powerful navy, subdued rebellions, and consolidated Muslim power in Spain that lasted for centuries. He grew so powerful that he was able to claim the title caliph – leader of all Muslims in the world...This absolute ruler lived in opulence and luxury. It is said that his harem included six thousand women. In terms of money, power, fame, and pleasure, nothing was denied him. He must have been in bliss, right? Here is his own testimony: *I have now reigned about fifty years in victory or peace; beloved by my subjects, dreaded by my enemies, and respected by my allies. Riches and honors, power and pleasure, have waited on my call, nor does any earthly blessing appear to have been wanting to my felicity*...Sounds great, right? Ay, but hold on. Abd-ar Rahman continued his thought: *In this situation, I have diligently numbered the days of pure and genuine happiness which have fallen to my lot: They amount to fourteen.*" [xi]

Neither Solomon nor Abd-ar-Rahman died happy and feeling prosperous. Neither experienced the peace and blessing of contentment. True prosperity is found in contentment. The search for contentment does not mean we have to lower expectations of the level of blessing we can receive. But it does mean that we have to find the strength to learn both contentment for times of abundance and times of need.

Coveting, Comparison & Competition

The tenth commandment is, "You shall not covet your neighbor's house. You shall not covet your neighbor's wife, or his manservant or maidservant, his ox or donkey, or anything that belongs to your neighbor." (Exodus 20:17) In Romans 7 Paul states he would not have known what coveting really was if the law had not said, "Do not covet." He means that he would not have been aware of the inner tendency we all have to look at things we don't have and develop an unhealthy craving for them. This craving generates within us a comparison mentality with other people. And once we get stuck in a comparison mentality we subtly start to move into competition with others. It reveals its ugly head every Christmas season when there are more and more reports of fights breaking out in stores over the next new gadget or toy. Black Friday has overtaken Thanksgiving in emphasis and importance. These two things radically oppose each other. Black Friday is all about buy, buy, buy, while Thanksgiving is supposed to be a time with family focusing on everything we are thankful for. Thanksgiving is supposed to be a time to step back and reflect on all the things we have, not the things we do not have. Ubiquitous social media is also magnifying the struggle to be content. It is hard to read all the social media stories and maintain a peaceful content attitude toward life. We are constantly being encouraged to sell ourselves, acquire more "followers" and "likes" and to compete with everyone else on the world-wide-web. We are in desperate need of recovering the divine blessing of contentment, which remains so elusive today even for the affluent. Contentment is one of the key ingredients for truly experiencing a prosperous life.

I am a pastor and I am blessed every time I get the chance to spend time with other pastors. One of the things I know about pastors is that we all to some extent struggle with coveting, comparing and competing with each other. Unless the Church's leadership learns to walk in contentment there is very little hope for the larger Christian community to walk in it. Unfortunately, too many pastors are in the grip of general discontentment as they covet and compare the 4 B's: Buildings, Budgets, Baptisms and Books. Not only do pastors often stack their worth on these things, but most Christians value a Christian leader by these as well. The bigger the church building must mean that it is a healthy more successful church- right? The bigger the budget, the more they can do for the kingdom and the more impact they can have – right? The more baptisms they have the more truly successful they are, for these represent changed lives- right? And if the pastor sells lots of books and even best sellers he is successful for the kingdom and spiritually mature – right? It is the age-old problem – we equate outward success with prosperity all the while minimizing inward transformation. The result of all this is competition rather than a supernatural unity which expresses the Kingdom of God on earth. With all these forces constantly against us how are we to attain contentment? And if we are not as the church's leaders experiencing contentment how can we possibly lead others into it? We need contentment to break the strife of coveting, comparing and competing. The Church cannot embrace true prosperity and be the shining city on the hill and engage the bondage of consumerism to set people free without the supernatural experience of contentment.

Freedom from Consumerism

The enemies of contentment are coveting, comparing and competing, which all work to put us in bondage to consumerism. Can you imagine life free from these things? It might be that most people do not even know they are in bondage to consumerism along with its corollaries, joylessness and lack of peace. People are naturally more attracted to consumerism than contentment because materialism is accepted without question in most areas of our culture today. Recently, our Community Coordinator at the church came into my office to share a phone conversation she had just had with a man asking about our services. He asked her if our church had a view of the mountains, and if not, is there one in Aspen that has such a view. She told him about our beautiful view and then asked more specifically if the service was important to him or just the view? He said it was important that it be a non-denominational church. He then asked how long the service was and how many services there were and if there was a good brunch close by that he could make after the service. This is just one illustration of how rampant this bondage to consumerism is in our culture and even in our pursuit of God.

Being a consumer is necessary for a healthy economy. But as we have stated, it becomes destructive when it turns into bondage to consumerism. Arthur Brooks articulates a possible solution this way,

> "First, we should concentrate each day on the happiness portfolio: *faith, family, community,* and *earned success through work*. Teach it to those around you, and fight against the barriers to these things…Secondly, resist the worldly formula of misery, which is to use people and love things. Instead, remember your core values and live by the true formula: Love people and use things…Third,

celebrate the free enterprise system, which creates abundance for the most people – especially the poor. But always remember that the love of money is the root of all evil, and that the ideal life requires *abundance without attachment.*"[xii]

But is this right? Is the ideal life 'abundance without attachment'? Would Jesus agree with this statement? He did say, "…I came that they may have life and have it abundantly." (John 10:10b) We first have to define what we mean by abundance and also what we mean by having no attachment. Is 'abundance without attachment' even possible? And if so, how?

In defining what we mean by abundance we need to have a proper perspective on possessions. There are differing views on how the New Testament speaks about material possessions and how Jesus saw them. Gordon Fee states,

> "…for Jesus wealth and possessions were a zero value. In the new age they simply do not count. The standard is sufficiency: and surplus is called into question. The one with two tunics should share with him who has none (Luke 3:11); 'possessions' are to be sold and given to the poor (Luke 12:33). Indeed, in the new age – unshared wealth is contrary to the Kingdom breaking in as good news to the poor."[xiii]

But does seeing material possessions as "zero value" go a bit too far? God does not need our money; he needs our hearts and will set them on fire to do great things. But when He transforms our lives, He transforms how we use our resources. I can't go so far as to say that our possessions are zero value. Yes, they all just go "back in the box" in the end, but what we do with them can have a redeeming value in people's lives. We can't learn to be good stewards if we have nothing to steward. So, rather than a zero-value approach I believe the path to abundance is learning divine contentment. It is here we embrace the heart of God, Who desires to give us good things to enjoy but Who also calls us to steward well our possessions by giving and sharing as to remain unattached to our possessions.

Learning divine contentment keeps us from the extremes of a legalism that sees "stuff" as zero-value or evil on one side and a legalism that sees "stuff" as reward and a result of godliness on the other side.

What is interesting is that both of these extremes are in bondage to coveting, comparing and competition. A legalism that sees possessions as zero-value or evil often is driven by guilt for having possessions when so many in the world don't and by imposing that guilt on others. This approach builds barriers to gracious giving hearts and the freedom to enjoy the gifts of God. While on the other side a legalism that sees possessions as a result of some form of godliness is driven by materialism and greed. This approach emphasizes God's promises of material blessings while minimalizing His spiritual blessings and mission. Both of these approaches are in opposition to experiencing divine contentment because they instill guilt and greed rather than grace and gratitude. If we look at church history, it would appear that most denominations and church movements tend to be defined by one of these approaches. This is one main reason the true experience of prosperity is so evasive.

Bondage to consumerism is idolatry. And bondage to legalism is religiosity, which is just another form of idolatry where man's traditions and rules supersede the gospel. Whether these rules see possessions as evil or as reward, both extremes keep us from living in contentment and experiencing true prosperity. In them is a seeking, valuing and even worshiping anyone or anything more than God and His will and ways. However, the gospel itself frees us from bondage to consumerism and makes possible living in abundance without attachment. How does the gospel of Jesus Christ free us from consumerism? *First*, as we see Jesus for Who He is and what He has done for us our hearts begin to treasure Him above all and the true value of our idols and possessions are exposed. *Secondly*, the gospel empowers us with the Holy Spirit who instills the blessing of divine contentment in our hearts so we can properly enjoy God's gifts and creation. *Thirdly*, as this divine contentment works within our hearts we become more aware and available to meet others needs with all of our resources. We begin to truly believe what Jesus said, "It is more blessed to give than to receive." (Acts 20:35). One of the key elements in experiencing the freedom of this transformation is contrition.

Contrition

Contrition is a word we don't often use much today, but neither is repentance and that is what contrition means. The bondage of consumerism has grown in our culture as the topic of repentance has been minimalized within the church. When we are coveting, comparing and competing we are not contrite. But, when the gospel begins to free us from bondage to consumerism our hearts begin to go through a transformation of contrition. This supernatural process is initiated by God, but we are responsible to nurture it by treasuring Jesus more than any-*thing*.

Have you ever wondered how to get God's attention? There is an answer to this important question that runs consistently throughout Scripture. Two passages that have convicted and encouraged me throughout my life are:

> "…But this is the one to whom I will look: he who is humble and contrite in spirit and trembles at my word." (Isaiah 66:2)

> "...God opposes the proud, but gives grace to the humble. Humble yourselves, therefore, under the mighty hand of God so that at the proper time he may exalt you, casting all your anxieties on him, because he cares for you. Be sober minded; be watchful. Your adversary the devil prowls around like a roaring lion, seeking someone to devour." (1 Peter 5:5b-8)

The bondage of consumerism that comes from coveting, comparing and competing stokes both anxiety and pride in our soul. Anxiety thrives in the absence of contentment. And pride is fueled by treasuring things more than God. When we are in bondage to consumerism things are not just "things". Things become idols, and idols have evil supernatural power behind them. One of the greatest tactics of the devil is to keep us in this bondage to consumerism, the incubator for anxiety, fear and pride. This is why Peter exhorts us to be humble, watchful and sober-minded lest our souls are devoured by the enemy. Jesus put it this way,

> "For whoever would save his life will lose it, but whoever loses his life for my sake will find it. For what will it profit a man if he gains the whole world and forfeits his soul? Or what shall a man give in return for his soul?" (Matthew 16:25-26)

The temptation to covet, compare, and compete is real in our lives. It must be fought with nurturing contrition in our hearts by learning to treasure Jesus more than any-*thing*. The Old Testament recounts Israel's history, one in which they frequently trusted in unholy alliances rather than God.

> "Ah, stubborn children, declares the Lord, who carry out a plan, but not mine, and who make an alliance, but not of my Spirit, that they may add sin to sin; who set out to go down to Egypt, without asking for my direction, to take refuge in the

protection of Pharaoh and to seek shelter in the shadow of Egypt." (Isaiah 30:1-2)

We are all stubborn children, we all have carried out our own plans, and we all have made evil alliances. God in His grace has provided a way through Jesus to be free from these alliances while developing a heart attitude of contrition.

Job was exemplary in this area. God allowed the devil to destroy all the people and possessions in his life for apparently no reason at all. Job did not curse God, but remained contrite. And even in the onslaught of pressure from his friends to make an unholy alliance, he remained steadfast, contrite and waiting on God. It was the consistent contrition of Job that took him deeper into relationship with God through his sufferings and brought him to a place of restoration and greater blessing. For some of us it takes a Job like experience to break the bonds of consumerism, and to awaken us to the freedom of contrition. This is true prosperity.

Contentment

Coveting leads to comparison, comparison leads to competition and these three together put us into bondage to consumerism. Consumerism opposes contentment, and discontentment blocks the experience of true prosperity. Real prosperity is living in the tension between evil and suffering and the goodness of God by faith. It is an abundant way of living free from the extremes of a legalism that sees "stuff" as zero-value or evil on one side and a legalism that sees "stuff" as reward and a result of godliness on the other side. Either our "stuff" will keep us from experiencing contentment or contentment will transform the way we see and use our "stuff."

Is it harder to experience contentment in times of loss or abundance? Is it harder to trust in God during bad times or good times? John Piper has insightfully said, "God is most glorified in you when you are most satisfied in him." This statement deserves our study and meditation. But he added to this statement in an assessment of the Health and Wealth Gospel by saying, "God is most glorified in you when you are most satisfied in him – in the midst of loss not prosperity."[xiv] But for Paul it would seem that God is most glorified in him in the midst of divine contentment regardless of whether he was in loss or abundance.

> "Not that I am speaking of being in need, for I have learned in whatever situation I am to be content. I know how to be brought low, and I know how to abound. In any and every circumstance, I have learned the secret of facing plenty and hunger, abundance and need. I can do all things through him who strengthens me." (Philippians 4:11-13)

Experiencing divine contentment is being most satisfied in God in times of both loss and abundance. God is most glorified in us when we are most satisfied in him whether in times of loss *or times of abundance*. If our chief end is to glorify God, we should seek to do it fully in times of loss and abundance. Sufferings and loss are used to bring us to a place of contentment. However, the true test of contentment might just be in times of great abundance. Are we able to stay satisfied with God and not need more "stuff"? Does our zeal for God waiver with abundance? There are few in history, who like Paul, have been able to attain his level of satisfaction with God. But it is achievable by the power of the Holy Spirit. When was the last time you heard someone say in the midst of great abundance, "I have remained most satisfied with God because – I can do all things through Christ who strengthens me?" Was God most glorified in the midst of Job's sufferings or his restoration and abundance? Was Job "most satisfied" in God in the midst of his sufferings or were the sufferings used to get him to a place of "contentment"? Are we to think that Job was not "most satisfied" in God at the end of his life when God restored Job's fortune? Thankfully God is at work through Christ and the power of the Holy Spirit to get us to a place of contentment in the midst of loss and abundance.

What is your benchmark of contentment? Or what are the bare necessities that you need to be content? Paul writes to Timothy on these matters saying,

> "But godliness with contentment is great gain, for we brought nothing into the world, and we cannot take anything out of the world. But if we have food and clothing, with these we will be content. But those who desire to be rich fall into temptation, into a snare, into many senseless and harmful desires that plunge people into ruin and destruction. For the love of money is a root of all kinds of evils. It is through this craving that some have wandered away from the faith and pierced themselves with many pangs." (1 Timothy 6:6-10)

We are all living far above this benchmark and our expectations for living are even farther above this benchmark. Jesus upholds this benchmark when He says,

> "Therefore I tell you, do not be anxious about your life, what you will eat or what you will drink, nor about your body, what you will put on. Is not life more than food, and the body more than clothing?" (Matthew 6:25)

Life is more than food and clothing, but what about houses, cars and vacations? That is what most of us are asking. There is nothing wrong with houses, cars and vacations as long as we do not require them to be content. Because as we have seen "stuff" does not and never will bring divine contentment, even if you are King Solomon or Caliph (leader of the Muslim world) Abd-ar-Rahman III with his harem of six thousand women. God does not promise riches, He warns against the love of money and the desire to get rich. God does promise provision for our needs as Paul says in Philippians 4:19, "And my God will supply every need of yours according to his riches in glory in Christ Jesus." But this does not mean that God does not desire to bless us with good things far above our needs. For Paul says,

> "As for the rich in this present age, charge them not to be haughty, nor to set their hopes on the uncertainty of riches, but on God, who richly provides us with everything to enjoy."(1 Timothy 6:17)

So contentment is a divine blessing ignited by the Holy Spirit and accompanies living in the fruit of the Spirit; love, joy, peace, patience, kindness, goodness, faithfulness, gentleness and self-control. (Galatians 5:22) Interesting that the last of the nine fruit of the Spirit is "self-control." It is necessary if the bondage to consumerism is going to be broken and a life of abundant giving is unleashed. Contentment is what it means to live by faith-in tension, it is not a place of passivity or low expectation. It is passionate and full of faith. It is what Jesus showed us to pray for from our heavenly Father on a daily basis, because it is something we cannot attain without His supernatural working in our hearts. Jesus said to pray, "Give us this day our daily bread." (Matthew 6:11)

Here are four more aspects of a biblical theology of prosperity that we will apply to real life situations along with a biblical theology of suffering in later chapters.

1.) Divine contentment is necessary to live in true prosperity.

2.) Divine Contentment keeps us from the extremes of a legalism that sees "stuff" as zero-value or evil on one side and a legalism that sees "stuff" as reward and a result of godliness on the other side.

3.) The gospel frees us from bondage to consumerism and makes possible living in "abundance without attachment."

4.) Experiencing divine contentment is being satisfied whether through loss or gain.

I started writing this chapter thinking I had a pretty good handle on contentment, but it was revealed to me along the way that I had more going on in this area than I thought. As I wrote this chapter I experienced a real sense of peace in my soul of the great gain that comes with embracing contentment. Also, I felt the Lord lead me to do some very specific simplifying things in my life and release some "stuff" as a spiritual discipline to help my soul rest and be content and thankful. Do not interpret this as releasing a dream or giving up something – it actually was a process of making room for greater things! May these words and God's truth free you as well to live in the incredible blessing of contentment.

CHAPTER FOUR

Becoming Truly Rich

One of the greatest chasms between human beings is between those who see the material world as most important and those who see the spiritual world as most important. Our Western culture finds its ultimate priority in the material world. The Bible affirms the goodness of both the material and the spiritual worlds. God has been in the process of redeeming both. From the beginning of creation God affirmed the goodness of His creation. The ultimate affirmation of the material world was Jesus coming in the flesh and His physical body rising on the third day. But there is a biblical priority of the spiritual world over the material world. The material world is subject to the spiritual world. In Job 1:21, he states, "Naked I came from my mother's womb and naked shall I return." We come into this world with nothing but our perishable physical bodies and we leave this world with nothing but a spiritual body until our physical body is resurrected and given a new spiritual body. (1 Corinthians 15: 35-58) Jesus tells us that our heavenly Father is spirit and that we are to worship Him in spirit and truth. (John 4:23-24) He also tells us that we are to love Him with all our heart. (Matthew 22:37) Neither God nor our hearts or minds are visible. We primarily meet God in the invisible of the spiritual world. Jesus entered our material world and took upon Himself a material body to rescue us from our preoccupation and bondage to the material world. He saved us that we might learn to live in this material world with spiritual reality. In this new life we begin to lay hold of the true riches of Christ and His kingdom while stewarding and leveraging our material riches for treasures in heaven. Jesus said,

> "Do not lay up for yourselves treasures on earth, where moth and rust destroy and where thieves break in and steal, but lay up for yourselves treasures in heaven, where neither moth nor rust destroys and where thieves do not break in and steal. For where your treasure is, there your heart will be also." (Matthew 6:19-21)

The influence and temptation of the material world is to make it a priority over the spiritual. There are many people who believe the spiritual world is more important but live like the material world is more important. This would represent what Jesus said about how the Word of God was received among a certain group of people, "As for what was sown among thorns, this is the one who hears the word, but the cares of the world and the deceitfulness of riches choke the word, and it proves unfruitful." (Matthew 13:22)

We don't talk much today about what it means to be truly rich. We live in a culture that sees the material world as the only one that really matters. The prophets were perplexed when they observed the unrighteous and unjust prospering and their own people suffering. Job's story of suffering has sparked much discussion on the philosophy of riches and suffering throughout history. The early philosophers debated often about the proper view and role of riches in this life. The Old Testament and Rabbinical tradition saw riches as a sign and blessing of God's favor. This Old Testament tradition carried over into the time of Jesus and was embraced by the Jewish religious leaders and the Jewish people. Just as Jesus brought a fullness and depth to the Old Testament Law, He also brought a fuller, deeper, and more radical view of riches that shocked many. The New Testament offers amazing promises to those who would follow Him in search of true riches,

> "For you know the grace of our Lord Jesus Christ, that though he was rich, yet for your sake he became poor, *so that you by his poverty might become rich.*"
> (2 Corinthians 8:9, italics mine)

Jesus desires us to be rich as He is rich. He desires us to live in prosperity as He lives in prosperity. So, just what does this wealth look like? There are four approaches to "riches" found in the Scriptures. You can be a pauper or a billionaire but everyone is living by one of these approaches.

Money is god
God but not my money
God is a means to money
God is my money

Money is god

Very few people, if any, will say that money is their god, but everyone in one way or another has struggled with serving money as god. Money becomes our god when our thinking and dreaming come into agreement with the lie that more money is the answer to our problems. Jim Carrey has wisely commented,

> "I think everybody should get rich and famous and do everything they ever dreamed of, so they can see that it's not the answer."

If we falsely believe that riches are the answer we will find ourselves enslaved to the ever-increasing desire for more. We are serving money when we think or say things like, "if I just had more money" we could do this or that. Our eyes get set on the power of money rather than on the power of God. The tragedy is that our hopes and dreams become selfish and in bondage to money. A biblical principle I have learned the hard way, but seen to be true time and time again is, *"provision follows vision."* Jesus calls us to a life of faith; "we walk by faith, not by sight." (2 Corinthians 5:7) When we are resting and walking with Him money is never a barrier. God can move money and resources at a whim to meet any need or any vision. We are to actively break our false and unholy agreements with money and learn to rest in God's provision, "And my God will supply every need of yours according to his riches in glory in Christ Jesus." (Philippians 4:19)

It is impossible to break the yoke of materialism if we are not learning to give our tithes and offerings on a regular basis to the household of God and other charities. We do not have to look past the stats on American Christian giving to see that bondage to money seems to have won the day. It would appear that we treasure money more than we treasure Christ. The main point of giving our first to the Lord is that it is to be an act of worship and gratitude to God who gives us all things. The point of the tithe was not that it is giving 10% to the Church, though that is a great place to start, but that we honor God and the Body of Christ first and thereby trust Him with our resources. Another indication that money is god for so many believers is how upset they get when teachers and preachers talk about money and giving. Jesus talked about money a lot! And when Paul talked about it much of the church rejoiced in the opportunity to give. Yes, there are abuses within the church that need to be healed, but they should not be used as an excuse for not delighting in giving to God's work.

Money is not evil. It is the love of money that is evil. (1 Timothy 6:10) We have all heard that a thousand times, but how do we know when we are loving money more than God? This is a question that rarely is investigated. This is because it gets to the root of our soul and the true state of our heart. Another reason this question is rarely pursued is because we have not done a very good job within the Christian community in creating an environment of grace where we can be honest with the state of our heart. If a believer came out and said, "I don't feel much love for God right now, but I am excited and loving my business and hobbies," there would probably be an awkward silence and even surprise. We all have been there in one way or another, but we will never really move forward unless we can be honest with our heart and be with others who will help us move toward experiencing greater affection for Jesus than anything else. I think the parable of the rich fool (Luke 12:13-21) gives us insight into how we know we are loving money more than God. A crowd gathered around Jesus and someone from the crowd said, "Teacher, tell my brother to divide the inheritance with me."

The *first* indication that we are on the road to loving money more than God is if we are asking God for money. I was recently convicted about this. Our giving was down at the church and I was praying that God would bring in more money. The Lord gently revealed to me that I was praying for the wrong thing. I should have prayed for people's hearts to grow in their love of God and their knowledge of God's love for them. When this happens there are no giving or money issues. We never see a prayer to God in the New Testament strictly asking for money. Jesus responded to the voice in the crowd, "Take care, and be on your guard against all covetousness, for one's life does not consist in the abundance of his possessions." (Luke 12:15) Do not covet is the tenth commandment and it represents the constant temptation that life is fulfilled by having more possessions.

The *second* indication we love money more than God is when we embrace the material world over the spiritual world. But how do we know when we are embracing the material world over the spiritual world? One way to get in touch with this aspect of our soul is to reflect upon what primarily occupies our thoughts and dreams. What grips our mind and heart first thing in the morning? Jesus goes on to tell the crowd a parable,

> "…The land of a rich man produced plentifully, and he thought to himself, 'What shall I do, for I have nowhere to store my crops?' And he said, 'I will do this: I will tear down my barns and build larger ones, and there I will store all my grain and my goods. And I will say to my soul, "Soul, you have ample goods laid up for many years; relax,

eat, drink, be merry.'" But God said to him, 'Fool! This night your soul is required of you, and the things you have prepared, whose will they be?' So is the one who lays up treasure for himself and is not rich toward God." (Luke 12:16-21)

The *third* indication that we love money more than God is our soul's satisfaction with material abundance. This is exposed in what we do with our excess resources. The rich man's motives were the problem, not his desire for bigger barns. He was laying up treasures for himself rather than asking God how to invest them.

The lure and power of money is that it has the capacity to temporarily satisfy us and make us happy. The danger of money is when we start to serve it and love it. It is then that we can subtly and suddenly fall into an ever-increasing craving for more money and possessions where *money is god* producing an ever-decreasing soul satisfaction.

God but not my money

There is an old religious cartoon that often circulates around showing a man getting baptized. He is completely under the water but he is holding his wallet up out of the water. We laugh because we can relate, but it exposes a certain deceived state of the soul – a pursuit of God that doesn't mess with our money. This cartoon depicts the deep struggle between God and money found in our soul, which was powerfully illustrated in Jesus' exchange with a certain rich young ruler.

The story of the rich young ruler is found in three of the four Gospels. Jesus' teaching on money in this exchange with this young man astonished His listeners. The text tells us that a young man approached Jesus, knelt before Him, and asked, "Good Teacher, what must I do to inherit eternal life?" (Mark 10:17) Jesus replied, "Why do you call me good? No one is good except

God alone." (Mark 10:18) Before Jesus gets into this deep discussion about money and God, He lays out the ultimate question behind every money and God discussion, "Is God good and can He be trusted or do we trust in money?" If we are going to follow Jesus, we must believe that the Father, Son and Holy Spirit are good and can be fully trusted with everything in this life and in eternity. We cannot please God without faith and faith requires both belief and trust. Next, Jesus answered the young man's question by telling him to obey the commandments. The young man responded, "Teacher, all these I have kept from my youth." (Mark 10:20) Jesus knowing the young man's heart, lovingly says to him, "You lack one thing: go, sell all that you have and give to the poor, and you will have treasure in heaven; and come, follow me." (Mark 10:21) This is the only instance in the scriptures that I know of where Jesus asked someone to follow him and they chose not to! Many asked to follow Him, but after hearing the requirements chose not to. But here, the text says that Jesus "loved him" and asked him to sell his stuff and come follow him and be part of His traveling community. We can see that there was a deep struggle within this rich young person's soul as he departed with great sorrow because he had great possessions. (Mark 10:22) It was this dynamic that set up the bombshell Jesus stated next,

> "How difficult it will be for those who have wealth to enter the kingdom of God!...Children, how difficult it is to enter the kingdom of God! It is easier for a camel to go through the eye of a needle than for a rich person to enter the kingdom of God." (Mark 10:23-25)

The reaction of the disciples and crowd was exceeding astonishment. They were still holding the Rabbinical view that material wealth revealed God's favor in a person's life and wondered who then could be saved. Jesus responded,

> "With man it is impossible, but not with God. For all things are possible with God." (Mark 10:28)

Jesus was making three profound points. *First*, our relationship with God is far more important than money. *Second*, money can be a detriment to our relationship with God and is limited in its possibilities. *Third*, God is good and the source of all true riches with unlimited possibilities. The rich young ruler's soul was entangled with his riches. He had abundance but with destructive attachments. He had riches but no contentment. Dallas Willard gives some important insight when he says,

> It is crucial to note here what Jesus did not say. He did not say that the rich cannot enter the kingdom. In fact he said they could, with God's help, which is the only way anyone can do it. Nor did he say that the poor have, on the whole, any advantage over the rich so far as 'being saved' is concerned. By using the case at hand, he simply upset the prevailing general assumption about God and riches. For how could God favor a person, however rich, who loves him less than wealth?"[xv]

After Jesus' bombshell sets in, Peter pipes up and points out to Jesus that he and the other disciples had "left everything" to follow Him. Jesus responds with an often overlooked promise for those who love God more than money,

> "Truly, I say to you, there is no one who has left house or brothers or sisters or mother or father or children or lands, for my sake and for the gospel, who will not receive a hundredfold now in this time, houses and brothers and sisters and mothers and children and lands, with persecutions, and in the age to come eternal life. But many who are first will be last, and the last first." (Mark 10:29-31)

In this passage we learn divine economics, which are considerably different than the economics of the world. When we are saved and come into a relationship with God, Jesus begins to transform our view of money and wealth. We are saved out of the limited possibilities of the economics of the world and saved into a new life under the economics of God. Jesus promises that those who live according to the economics of God will be blessed hundredfold in this life and in eternity – because He is a good God. When he describes the blessing as "houses and brothers, and sisters and mothers and children and lands, with persecutions," He means there is relational and material blessing in this life and the next, and that it is based upon God's riches not the world's. But why are "persecutions" included in the hundredfold blessing for this life? Persecution is inevitable in this life because those who love money more than God eventually are threatened by those who don't. The economics of the world are at war with the economics of God. Satan is ultimately in charge of the powers behind the economics of the world. Just like Jesus loved the rich young ruler so are followers of Jesus to love those caught up in the economics of the world and present to them and model the good news of God's economics.

In the end, *God but not my money* is not a viable option. Jesus says, "No servant can serve two masters, for either he will hate the one and love the other, or he will be devoted to the one and despise the other. You cannot serve God and money." (Luke 16:13)

God is a means to money

I just finished watching a special on CNN about the eighties. It had video clip after video clip of flashy tele-evangelists pleading for money to keep their ministries and their lavish lifestyles going. And then it showed indictment after indictment as many of them were exposed. As we entered into the 21st century the pleas for money by the tele-evangelists increased and the message went global and infected the majority world with a deceptive message – *God is a means to money*.

I was taught in my formal theological training to despise the Health and Wealth Gospel. The problem is that the Health and Wealth Gospel covers a wide spectrum of churches and ministries not just the emotional tele-evangelists pleading for money. Through a set of circumstances I was invited several years ago to go to a conference sponsored by one of the Health and Wealth Gospel preachers whom I had learned to despise. I actually accepted the invitation but inside I had the attitude of a mean reporter trying to force a story of corruption. Coming out of that weekend I learned several important biblical principles, many of which are the genesis of this book. *First*, we can always learn from different streams and we should intentionally read and interact with things outside our stream. *Second*, we can all learn from the Health and Wealth stream the importance of expectant faith and hope in the promises of God for this life not just for eternity. *Third*, we can all learn from the Health and Wealth stream that when God becomes a means to money, money becomes god. It is very important to realize that it is not just the Health and Wealth gospel preachers who are susceptible to making God a means to money. This temptation permeates all theological streams and cultures. Paul warns Timothy that when the Gospel of Jesus Christ is corrupted that one result is that people will imagine that "godliness is a means of gain" and that "...those who desire to get rich fall into temptation, into a snare, into many senseless and harmful desires that plunge people into ruin and destruction." (1Timothy 6:5-9)

Those who fall prey to the God is a means to money message are also prey to the reverse message of money can buy God and His blessings. One feeds the other in a soul killing cycle. In Acts 8 we are introduced to a shadowy character named Simon who was a famous practitioner of magic in Samaria. The people said of him, "This man is the power of God that is called Great" (Acts 8:10). After the persecution broke out against the church in Jerusalem we are told that Philip went to Samaria preaching the good news and many miracles and deliverances were being experienced. It was during Philip's ministry there that Simon made a profession of faith and was baptized. He continued to follow Philip and was amazed by the signs and great miracles performed. In time Peter and John came to Samaria from Jerusalem. They ministered to the people and laid their hands on them and prayed for them. As they did this, the people received the Holy Spirit. When Simon saw that the Spirit was imparted by the laying on of hands he offered money to Peter and John to have this power. Simon was fully in the grip of the false gospel of money can buy God and God is a means to money. Simon wanted to buy the power first so he could use it to gain money, fame and power. The term "simony" comes from this story to refer to anyone who uses money to secure a role in church or a place of privilege. The term can be used of any attempt to manipulate God for personal gain.

How do we know if we are trying to manipulate God, His Word or His promises? *First*, we have to be careful not to over emphasize signs, wonders and miracles compared to receiving God's Word and obeying it. From this account of Simon it would appear that his response was more because of the signs, wonders and miracles than the gospel in his heart. The danger is becoming a "spiritual groupy" that spends hours on the internet seeking the next big revival or traveling to the next hot spiritual spot for more goose bumps. These tendencies can lead to mimicking what other spiritual leaders say and do in hopes of receiving the same spiritual and material results they report to have received.

Second, we have to be careful not to distill down the Word of God into simple formulas with a quid pro quo (if we do this we get that). Examples of this would be certain name-it-claim-it statements and seeing faith as a means of manipulation rather than a personal growing relationship with God.

Third, we have to be careful not to fall into the trap of believing that God promises material riches in this life. God promises material provision in this life, not material riches in this life and there is a big difference. Jesus nowhere promises material riches, but instead encourages His followers to "seek first the kingdom of God and his righteousness". (Matthew 6:33) He does offer spiritual riches in this life by faith, which we are to seek. The by-product of this pursuit can be material blessings, but these are not to be our main focus.

Fourth, we have to make sure that our agenda is submitted to God's agenda. God desires us to have dreams, plans, goals and agendas. But He wants us to bring them to Him both for refinement and confirmation.

Judas Iscariot is the greatest example we have of one who was under the illusion that God is a means to money. In the Gospel of John chapter 12 we find the story of Jesus and his disciples at a party with Lazarus, Martha and Mary. Jesus and Lazarus are the special guests and Martha is serving. In comes Mary with some expensive perfume, with which she begins to anoint Jesus' feet wiping them with her hair. In response to Mary's extravagant offering Judas says,

> "Why was this ointment not sold for three hundred denarii and given to the poor? He said this, not because he cared about the poor, but because he was a thief, and having charge of the moneybag he used to help himself to what was put into it." (John 12:5-6)

Jesus loved Judas. Judas had every opportunity that the other disciples had to experience intimacy with Jesus. The problem was Judas had his own agenda that opposed Jesus' agenda and he was never able to surrender his plan to Jesus' mission. One of the reasons Judas was not able to surrender his agenda was because he was deeply in bondage to the idea that God was a means to money and power and this opened his heart to the devastating demonic activity of manipulation. Eventually Judas betrayed Jesus for a small amount of money.

God is my money

What is money? According to the dictionary it is basically a convertible asset and a medium of exchange. It is the thing that makes the economics of the world run. It provides power to acquire things and make things happen in the world. Those who put a higher priority on the material world than the spiritual world are bound to the power and possibilities of money. Those who put a higher priority on the spiritual world than on the material world are not limited by the power and possibilities of money. They can live under the economics of God where the convertible asset is a vibrant personal relationship with God where all things are possible and all power is available. When God is our treasure we are free from the bondage of coveting, comparing and competing. Greed is behind all these things and we should know by now that greed is sin. It is impossible for the economics of the world to ever be free from greed, coveting, comparing and competition. The economics of the world will eventually be "hell" where people are separated from God because they desired money more than God. This hell of the economics of the world is the result of the rejection of the economics of God. Interesting that money and hell were two of Jesus' main topics.

Jesus came to rescue us out of the economics of the world and bring us into the Kingdom of God, which operates by the economics of God. One of the main ways we know that we have been saved is that we start seeing and treating money differently. As we'll see below, when people come to faith in the gospel it radically changes their use of resources and riches. This should be a wake up call for the Church in America who has in some ways embraced the American dream over the mission of God in the world. Fight the good fight of faith has faded into live long and prosper in some circles. So, what does it look like to be saved out of the economics of the world into the economics of God?

Luke's story of Zachaeus beautifully portrays what it looks like to be saved out of the economics of the world and into the economics of God. Jesus was traveling through Jericho with a large crowd following Him. Zacchaeus was a chief tax collector who was rich and known as a sinner and swindler. He was a small man and not able to get to Jesus because of the crowd so he ran ahead and climbed a sycamore tree to get a look. We know from the culture of the day that for a grown man to run and climb a tree was considered undignified, so this strongly indicates that more was going on in Zacchaeus than mere curiosity. Jesus noticed Zacchaeus in the tree and called out to him, "Zacchaeus, hurry and come down, for I must stay at your house today." (Luke 19:5) We are not told how Jesus knew Zacchaeus' name, but what we do know is what Jesus' heart and mission was, "For the Son of Man came to seek and to save the lost." (Luk19:10) This was a divine appointment for Zacchaeus to meet God. Not only did Jesus enter Zacchaeus' home, but He entered Zacchaeus' heart. And the proof of his salvation was his radical response, "And Zacchaeus stood and said to the Lord, 'Behold, Lord, the half of my goods I give to the poor. And if I have defrauded anyone of anything, I restore it fourfold. And Jesus said to him, 'Today salvation has come to this house…'" (Luke 19:8-9) The Old Testament only required a 20% increase in repaying those who were defrauded, but Zacchaeus went well beyond that and gave half of everything he had to the poor in his community! He was getting free from the economics of the world. He had a new treasure – Jesus! God was his money. Jesus came to save not just the poor, but all who recognize the emptiness of the economics of the world and all who are willing to repent and live under the economics of God. This is why Paul exhorts Timothy to teach the rich,

> "As for the rich in this present age, charge them not to be haughty, nor to set their hopes on the uncertainty of riches, but on God, who richly provides us with everything to enjoy. They are to do good, to be rich in good works, to be generous and ready to share, thus storing up treasure for themselves as a good foundation for the future, so that they may take hold of that which is truly life." (1Timothy 6:17-19)

We can see this same transformation from the economics of the world to the economics of God within the early church. It was not socialism or communism; those are man's attempts at correcting the abuses of the economics of the world. They sold things and shared things as there was need within the church family. They did not see their possessions as zero-value or evil, but as blessings that they could share and help meet the needs of others. This generous modeling of the economics of God set them apart from the culture and world and made their community attractive. They had a different kind of money, a different kind of treasure – Jesus! Acts 2:42-47 is a beautiful picture of the economics of God at work,

> "And they devoted themselves to the apostles' teaching and the fellowship, to the breaking of bread and the prayers. And awe came upon every soul and many wonders and signs were being done through the apostles. And all who believed were together and had all things in common. And they were selling their possessions and belongings and distributing the proceeds to all, as any had need. And day by day, attending the temple together and breaking bread in their homes, they received their food with glad and generous hearts, praising God and having favor with all the people. And the Lord added to their number day by day those who were being saved." (Acts 2:42-47)

The Riches of Health

We rarely understand the riches of health until our health is threatened. Monetary wealth can pay for better health services but it can never guarantee the riches of health. If we lose our health we lose much of our ability to enjoy everything that the economics of the world provide for us. This is not so with the economics of God. We can lose our health but still enjoy life with purpose and hope. Historically, the economics of the world create a wide gap between the rich and the poor. Research by epidemiologists (study of disease development) reveals that societies where there is a significant gap between rich and poor have more crime, mental illness, infant mortalities, illiteracy and other social ills. In these nations even the rich have lower life expectancy. Throughout the scriptures divine health is seen as a blessing from God. Sickness and disease are seen as a result of a fallen world, attack from the devil or discipline from God. We will work through the nuances of these in the third section of this book. For now, we need to see that good health is a huge blessing that should not be squandered but taken advantage of to maximize our calling. Yes there is a role for sickness and disease in our spiritual journey, but sickness and disease should never be embraced but engaged with faith to lay hold of the provision Jesus has made for our healing. Sickness and disease most of the time radically limit our abilities to carry out our purpose and calling. There are a few exceptions when God uses sickness of some kind to enhance our effectiveness. Job was afflicted for a period of time that he might know and experience that it is God ultimately who justifies and makes people righteous before Him. Another instance might be the thorn given to Paul. We are not sure it was an illness, but we are sure it was a messenger from the devil that was used to humble Paul. But whatever it specifically was, it did not kill him nor did it paralyze him from his mission. It actually made him more spiritually effective and that is why he was able to say,

> "But he said to me, 'My grace is sufficient for you, for my power is made perfect in weakness.' Therefore I will boast all the more gladly of my weaknesses, so that the power of Christ may rest upon me. For the sake of Christ, then, I am content with weaknesses, insults, hardships, persecutions, and calamities. For when I am weak, then I am strong."
> (2 Corinthians 12:9-10)

We talk a lot about "quality of life." Under the economics of the world there is no vision of quality of life without good health. And aging is seen as losing quality of life. However, under the economics of God, where the spiritual world takes priority over the physical world, "quality of life" takes on a deeper meaning. Within the economics of God, aging is not seen as losing life or the end of life, but the transition into new eternal life. Jesus has given us provision for healing in the "now" of today to be a pointer toward the ultimate healing He will bring about for us in the "not yet" of eternity. God desires us to prosper and health is a key part of that prosperity.

The Key to Riches

The key to riches and prosperity is "knowing" we are "right" with God. Mother Teresa has said, "Loneliness is the leprosy of the modern world." The experience of loneliness ultimately is not being sure God is there for us or loves us and that we are all alone in the world. Aloneness is a killer. We were not created to be alone. Aloneness is a result of the fall when Adam and Eve believed the lie that God was holding back on them and that they could better prosper on their own. Wrong thinking leads to wrong living. Wrong thinking begins by believing a lie and once a person has lived with a lie for a period of time the lie settles into their soul as an agreement. At this point, a person is in bondage to that agreement and to change is not as easy as just changing how one thinks. There must be a breaking of that old agreement, a renouncing of the lie and an embracing of the truth. The scriptures tell us that the devil is the father of lies and that Jesus is the truth. Lies put us in bondage. It is the truth that sets us free. We cannot truly prosper if we are in agreement with lies in our soul. We can maintain somewhat of an outward appearance of success, but the inside will remain in turmoil and aloneness until we "know" we are "right" with God. So, how do we "know" we are "right" with God?

Do you believe that God owes you something? How we answer this question will radically impact our experience with God. If you answer yes to this question then – what does God owe you? This line of thinking will lead you into further aloneness where you will remain in an endless loop of blaming God and making demands upon Him. Pride will take over and you will find yourself in opposition to God. Even worse, God will be opposed to you. "God opposes the proud, but gives grace to the humble." (1 Peter 5:5) To answer "no" to this question takes a lot of soul searching and perseverance, but can eventually lead to the experience of "knowing" we are "right" with God.

If anyone had a right to question God and to believe that God owed him something it would be Job. The book of Job begins, "There was a man in the land of Uz whose name was Job, and that man was blameless and upright, one who feared God and turned away from evil." (Job 1:1) The Hebrew words for "blameless" and "upright" do not mean that Job was perfect like God or that he was free from sin. They mean that Job honored God and was not guilty of clear observable sins. In chapter 31 Job tries to defend himself before God by denying any wrongdoing in the areas of honesty, marital fidelity, treatment of servants, generosity to the poor and avoidance of idolatry. But was it his good works and attempts at honoring God that allowed him to experience the deep prosperity of "knowing" he was "right" with God? This is exactly where his wife and friends went wrong. They held to the position that Job's actions or lack of actions are what justified him before God. What eventually vindicated Job and opened the door for his great experience and blessing with God was his perseverance and humility. He never bought the soul-killing lie that God owed him something – even if he lived blameless and upright before Him. We can see inside Job's heart of humility and faith when he states, "For I know that my Redeemer lives, and at the last he will stand upon the earth." (Job 19:25) Job was a rich and successful man by all standards of the world, but he never truly "knew" he was "right" with God until he experienced the grace of God. If we think God owes us anything we stifle the work of God's grace in our lives. For it is God's grace in our lives that justifies and makes us right before Him. Jesus came to make us truly rich. He suffered and died and rose on the third day so that we can "know" we are "right" with God through a relationship with Him. The economics of the world are never free from the death grip of loneliness. It is only under the economics of God that loneliness is defeated and we can truly prosper by "knowing" we are right with God. We cannot love

God nor receive His love without first "knowing" we are right with God.

In preparation for this book and during the writing process I kept coming back to the question, "What makes me feel prosperous?" As I have thought about this question and tried to peel back the layers I have come down to a pretty simple but profound answer – "knowing" I am loved by my heavenly Father under the grace of my Savior Jesus and experiencing the fellowship of Holy Spirit. When I keep this as my priority I can better enjoy and steward blessings and trials. Now that I am a parent of adult children, this has come into greater focus. When I think of what I truly desire for them I realize that everything, and I mean everything, falls into place when they too learn what truly makes them rich. It is pure joy to see my children walking in the truth. This truth will show them how to live in prosperity in a suffering world.

A Summary Theology of Prosperity

This ends section one, "Prosperity without Suffering". In this section we have explored the meaning of true prosperity. Listed below is a summary of what we have been exploring so far. In the next section, "Suffering without Prosperity" we will explore the meaning and purpose of suffering and then in the third section we will bring together what we have explored about prosperity and suffering and apply them to real life situations as we learn about "Prosperity through Suffering."

A brief theology of prosperity:

1.) God desires that we seek Him for who He is, not simply for what He gives.

2.) Poverty in all its forms is bondage and to be engaged with the promises of God.

3.) God is a good God who desires good things for His children, even material things.

4.) The blessing-cursing principle has not changed: God blesses those who seek Him.

5.) God's heart is to save, heal and deliver – always.

6.) God does not guarantee healing or spiritual maturity in this life, but has made provision for both to be pursued by faith.

7.) God has given spiritual gifts to be pursued so we can set the harassed and helpless free.

8.) God expects us to engage suffering the way Jesus and the early church did.

9.) Divine Contentment is necessary to live in true prosperity.

10.) Divine contentment keeps us from the extremes of a legalism that sees "stuff" as zero-value or evil on one side and a legalism that sees "stuff" as reward and a result of godliness on the other side.

11.) The gospel frees us from bondage to consumerism and makes possible living in "abundance without attachment".

12.) Experiencing divine contentment is being satisfied whether through loss or gain.

13.) Money can be a detriment to our relationship with God and is limited in its possibilities.

14.) God is good and the source of all true riches with unlimited possibilities.

15.) The economics of the world are at war with the economics of God.

16.) The key to riches and prosperity is knowing we are right with God.

Section Two: Suffering without Prosperity

"Then Job arose and tore his robe and shaved his head and fell on the ground and worshiped. And he said, 'Naked I came from my mother's womb, and naked shall I return. The Lord gave, and the Lord has taken away, blessed be the name of the Lord.'"

Job 1:20-21

"He was despised and rejected by men; a man of sorrows, and acquainted with grief; and as one from whom men hide their faces he was despised, and we esteemed him not. Surely he has borne our griefs and carried our sorrows; yet we esteemed him stricken, smitten by God, and afflicted. But he was pierced for our transgressions; he was crushed for our iniquities; upon him was the chastisement that brought peace, and with his wounds we are healed."

Isaiah 53:3-5

SECTION TWO: SUFFERING WITHOUT PROSPERITY

CHAPTER FIVE

The Purpose of Suffering

There is no way to avoid suffering in this world. C.S Lewis has stated well, "Try to exclude the possibility of suffering…and you find that you have excluded life itself." Instead of trying to understand the purpose of suffering many are driven by fear into embracing a comfortable life void of purpose and true adventure. Many people use suffering in the world to discount a good God and never contemplate why there is so much order and beauty in the world. Even now as I sit here writing I am looking out my window at the beautiful mountains that surround Aspen, Colorado just after watching the news report of yet another horrific terrorist attack. How is one to make sense of such evil and suffering in the world? How is one to explain and make sense of such beauty in the world?

> Suffering will either move us toward God or it will move us away from God.

The two primary things that move the human soul from its apathetic and lethargic state are suffering and beauty. We can overlook beauty, but we cannot overlook pain and suffering. C. S. Lewis again states,

> "We can ignore even pleasure. But pain insists upon being attended to. God whispers to us in our pleasures, speaks in our conscience, but shouts in

our pains: it is his megaphone to rouse a deaf world."[xvi]

Suffering changes the human heart. When trauma and tragedy strike it creates a crisis of faith that will either move us deeper into relationship with God or it will harden our hearts. When a heart hardens it becomes numb to both suffering and beauty. The hardened heart will end up worshiping the beauty of creation while being blind to the Creator. God's megaphone of allowing suffering is His primary plan to grow us to become the people we are meant to be. If we want to understand suffering we must allow it to move us toward God. When our lives are disrupted by pain and sorrow, the purpose of spiritual formation is rarely embraced. If we are not willing to move toward God in the midst of our pain and suffering we will miss the joy and delight of fully becoming the person our heavenly Father created us to be. Frederick Buechner has said,

> "We are never more alive to life than when it hurts – more aware both of our own powerlessness to save ourselves and of at least the possibility of a power beyond ourselves to save us and heal us if we can only open ourselves to it."[xvii]

The big question in reference to suffering is; "Are we willing to open ourselves to God's purpose and power to bring understanding and healing?" When we do take steps of faith to open our heart, God starts to empower us to engage suffering for the purpose of strengthening our faith, building our character and powerfully ministering to others. There is a big difference between engaging suffering versus embracing suffering. We embrace things we love and cherish. We engage things for the purpose of seeing something change. We are never to embrace our suffering. Yes, the scriptures tell us we are blessed when we suffer for 'righteousness sake' and on account of Jesus. (Matthew 5:9-10) And 1 Peter 4:13-14 says we are to "rejoice insofar as you share in Christ's sufferings." These verses are not telling us to embrace suffering, but to embrace Jesus and the privilege to serve and suffer for Kingdom purposes. It is a subtle but important distinction. We are to engage not embrace suffering by faith in God's promises to see evil defeated and the glory of God manifested. We are to embrace the prosperity of an abundant life our Savior promises. As we learn to do both of these things we will begin to truly live in prosperity in a suffering world. The definition of prosperity we are working with in this book is:

> True prosperity is living in the tension between evil and suffering and the goodness of God by faith.

Living in this tension by faith requires a proper theology of prosperity and suffering. Proper theology should lead to proper practice. This lifestyle sees beauty as an expression of God's goodness that should drive us to embrace God's Word so we may experience His abundant blessings. Also, this lifestyle sees suffering as something to be engaged for the purpose of strengthening our faith, building our character and empowering us to powerful ministry to others. I agree with Randy Alcorn who says, "Suffering is, in the end, God's invitation to trust him." However, I want to clarify that to trust God in the midst of all different forms of suffering is never to be passive, but an active agent. If we do not learn to properly engage suffering, our faith will not strengthen and grow. And if we do not learn to embrace God's prosperity, our hope and love will not deepen and grow.

In this section we will be developing a brief theology of suffering. In this chapter we will wrestle with the purpose of suffering, then we will look at the connection between suffering and the spiritual realm then we will look to understand the different kinds of sufferings and finally the difference between Big "S" suffering and Little "s" suffering.

A Really Bad Day

I can remember the moment vividly. It was a Friday night and some of my High School buddies and I had plans to go out. I was getting ready to leave to pick everyone up for a night of fun, when my Dad and Mom asked if they could talk with me before I left. They both started to cry and said they had just gotten off the phone with the doctor. There was a long pause and then they told me that Mom had breast cancer. This was long before many of the great medical options available today and her mother, my grandmother, died when she was just thirty years old from the same disease. This was my first major awakening to deep pain and suffering. I didn't feel like going out. I didn't feel like doing anything, but my parents insisted. The rest of that night I was struggling to engage my friends and the world around me because of the battle with pain and suffering going on inside me. I could relate with C.S. Lewis' words describing his internal battle after losing his wife Joy to cancer,

> "An overdose of sleeping pills would do it. I am more afraid that we are really rats in a trap. Or, worse yet, rats in a laboratory. Sooner or later I must face the question in plain language. What reason have we, except our own desperate wishes to believe that God is, by any standard we can conceive, 'good'? Doesn't all the prima facie evidence suggest exactly the opposite?" Read on to get his conclusion about suffering.[xviii]

There is no way to avoid having a really bad day. The question is, "Are we going to be willing to face the hard internal questions?" Of all the myriad of questions that are conjured up in the midst of deep suffering, none are more important than, "Is God good and does He have good things for us, even in the midst of unexplainable pain and suffering?"

No one had to wrestle with these questions more than Job. Most of us have never had as bad a day as Job. Job's bad day consisted of four different messengers coming to him one after another with increasing bad news of the loss of almost everything. The fourth messenger brought the most devastating news of all, that all of Job's sons and daughters had been killed by a sudden storm. How would you respond to a day like that? How have you responded to bad news? Job's response was shockingly humble and insightful.

> "Then Job arose and tore his robe and shaved his head and fell on the ground and worshiped. And he said, "Naked I came from my mother's womb, and naked shall I return. The LORD gave, and the LORD has taken away; blessed be the name of the LORD." (Job 2:20-21)

There is no indication that Job gave even a thought to questioning God's goodness, but he did question God's purpose, and there is a big difference. The majority of the rest of the book deals with Job questioning God not whether He is a good God, but questioning the purpose for his suffering and the justice of it all. Verse 22 confirms Job's steadfast faith in God saying, "In all this Job did not sin or charge God with wrong." His response is all the more astonishing in that he immediately took a position of humility and repentance and worshiped God. One of the main indicators of a vibrant, strong faith is a position of humility and worship in response to pain and tragedy. Job's mourning for his kids and his grief over great material loss was not separated from worshiping God. There is a worldly sorrow and there is a godly sorrow. (2 Cor. 7:10) In the midst of his worship was the acknowledgement of God's great blessings and great loss and his heart was able to say either way, "Blessed be the name of the Lord." And when we thought it could not get any worse another bad day comes in the midst of his mourning. It seems there is some truth to the old saying, "When it rains, it pours." But the greater truth is that God has a purpose for our suffering, even if we don't see it at first, and sometimes things have to get worse for His purpose to be accomplished. Job's next bad day came with an affliction of painful sores all over his body. (Job 2:7) We will deal with the issues surrounding the fact that the messenger of this sickness was Satan in the next chapter. To add insult to injury his wife responds with one of the most harsh and condemning statements possible.

> "Then his wife said to him, "Do you still hold fast your integrity? Curse God and die." But he said to her, "You speak as one of the foolish women would speak. Shall we receive good from God, and shall we not receive evil?" In all this Job did not sin with his lips." (Job 2:9-10)

Obviously, Job's wife did not share his level of faith and trust in God. She had "had it" with God and was not interested in worshiping God and waiting on His purpose. Her heart had hardened and she was lashing out by attributing blame to God. She was at a standstill in her healing and understanding journey. But again, we see an astonishing response from Job to his wife. First, he calls her out for her foolishness in blaming and cursing God. Secondly, his statement of utter abandonment to God's sovereignty over his own understanding is staggering. However, Job's statement, "Shall we receive good from God, and shall we not receive evil?" requires a lot of explaining. How can we hold our integrity to the goodness of God while believing that we might receive evil from Him? How can He be a good God and allow evil to fall to His children?

First, we have to understand the origin and nature of evil. We live in a fallen world where God created mankind and angelic beings to possess a "free will" with the potential of evil. We will go into more detail about this in the next chapter.

Secondly, we need to realize the dangerous thinking process that is rooted in pride that makes us think we can define what "good" truly is. Let's say we come to the conclusion God is not good, then what; is He evil? This will only harden our heart and leave us stuck in our pursuit of God, either trying to ignore Him or appease Him through religion. This kind of decision has not turned out "good" for anyone.

Thirdly, only the heart of God revealed through the cross and resurrection adequately can satisfy our questions about the goodness of God and the source and purpose of suffering. Romans 8:32 says, "He who did not spare his own Son but gave him up for us all, how will he not also with him graciously give us all things?"

The Lord's Prayer, or more accurately, the Disciple's Prayer shows us that we are to pray for the Lord's Kingdom to come and His will to be done. (Matt. 6:9-10; Luke 11:2-4) This reveals that there is a battle of wills going on and that there are wills that are opposed to God's will. Specifically, the devil and his demons and our own will oppose God's will. This has created a fallen world that is at war and desperately needs saving. In the Disciple's Prayer Jesus commands us to pray, "And lead us not into temptation, but deliver us from evil." (Matt. 6:13) Because of Jesus' death and resurrection we are not defenseless in this spiritual battle.

We are not able to understand nor start learning the purposes of suffering until we get past the "goodness" of God questions. If we get hung up questioning the "goodness" of God like Job's wife and his friends we put ourselves into an adversarial position with God. We are stuck in this position until there is repentance and recognition of our deep sin in questioning the character of God.

This is why at the end of Job, God's anger burned against Job's friends for their folly and required them to offer a sacrifice and have Job pray for them. (Job 42:8) Job's faith even in the midst of unexplainable suffering never questioned the "goodness" of God. Job had big questions for God and His purposes but never questioned the character of God. In the middle of his season of suffering he stated, "For I know my Redeemer lives, and at the last he will stand upon the earth and after my skin has been thus destroyed yet in my flesh I shall see God."(Job 19:25-26) This is a key aspect to a proper theology of suffering.

One of our daughters went through a tough season in her life and when she started seeking God again she received the words, "In the beginning God…" during one of her prayer times. She knew these were the first four words of the Bible, but did not yet understand what it meant for her personally. She had a few friends praying for her during this time who encouraged her with other words. It was several months later as she had made steps forward in learning to trust God again that she heard God speak with greater clarity saying to her, "Unless you begin with Me, I will not walk and work with you." This was the word she needed to help her recognize where she had stepped out without God. She needed to be willing to revisit that and start with God rather than ask Him to bless her situation, which resulted from her wrong start. This is a critical piece in our quest to understand suffering. If we do not start with God as a good God worthy of our trust we will never grow in our understanding of suffering and our ability to engage it for the strengthening of our faith, the building of our character and empowered ministry to others. God is opposed to the proud. We are proud when we question God's goodness. We can be humble and trusting like Job wrestling deeply with our suffering without questioning God's goodness.

> "God opposes the proud but gives grace to the humble. Humble yourselves, therefore, under the mighty hand of God so that at the proper time he may exalt you, casting all your anxieties on him, because he cares for you." (footnote, James 5:5-7)

Questioning God's goodness is a major problem today, especially among western Christians. Too much of the Church Body today is getting hung up with life's trials and is not coming through them stronger and bolder, but often times losing faith altogether.

Without surrender to His sovereignty, we cannot grow in our understanding of the purposes for suffering.

My mom's struggle with cancer went on for decades. It was full of seasons of victory and seasons of pain. But I can say with all honesty, that even in the darkest hour, I never struggled with the goodness of God. This was partly because my mother never struggled with His goodness, but sought His purposes in the midst of her battle with cancer.

This faith she passed on to me that I eventually made my own. But I did struggle greatly. My struggle was a struggle with the healing power of faith. In light of the spiritual gifts available to God's people and God's command to his Church to pray for the sick, why were we not able to bring about healing? Do we just throw our hands up and say things like, "It must not be God's will for her to be healed?" No, we learn from these lost battles that there is always another level of faith we can pursue in our lives so we can better engage suffering with greater empowerment and greater trust in God's sovereignty. Yes, there will always be unanswered questions and lost battles, but we cannot let them have a faith-numbing affect upon our soul.

Faith and Doubt

There is no room in faith's definition for doubt. Doubt is dangerous. To understand the purposes behind suffering we must have faith, which does not doubt God, but does at times question God's purposes and silence. It is critically important to understand the difference between doubting God and doubting His purposes. It is a fine line within the soul. It is the difference between an orphan questioning the motives of a father he never knew and a child asking his father why he had to discipline him. Some will push back on the idea that doubt is dangerous by pointing to Jesus' so-called reward of Thomas's disbelief in John 20:24-29. I do not think we can build from this text a positive picture of doubt. First, Thomas was one of the unique 12 apostles and a requirement of being one of this special group of apostles was seeing the resurrected Lord. (1 Cor. 9:1, 15:3-9; 1 John 1:1) Second, it would be very dis-unifying for the band of 12 if not all of them had seen Jesus after His death. And thirdly, Jesus does not commend in any way the idea of doubt, but actually condemns it. He says in John 20:27, "Do not disbelieve, but believe." And He goes on to say in verse 29, "Have you believed because you have seen me? Blessed are those who have not seen and yet have believed." Paul builds upon this in 2 Corinthians 5:7, "for we walk by faith, not by sight."

It is not just the skeptic and non-believer whose soul is bound by doubt. It is those who call themselves Christians, but are bound more by doubt in their soul than faith. Doubt is not good. Some Christian teachers today are more concerned for people that they don't get let down when they pray and apply faith rather than push them on to fight for greater things and expectation.

These same teachers would teach that much of Jesus' teaching on faith as accomplishing greater things is just hyperbole. Faith is trusting in God for greater things regardless of our circumstances or the outcome. This is best illustrated in Hebrews chapter 11 by what some call the "Hall of Faith." In verses 32 through the first half of verse 35 we see some extraordinary things happen because of faith. But in the second half of verse 35, we see others who were commended for their faith who went through severe persecution.

So faith is maintaining our trust in God through the victories and the defeats of life. The most popular biblical definition of faith is found in Hebrews 11:1, "Now faith is the assurance of things hoped for, the conviction of things not seen." Verse 6 goes on to say, "And without faith it is impossible to please him, for whoever would draw near to God must believe that he exists and that he rewards those who seek him." There is no room for doubt within these verses. But James 1:5-8 makes this even clearer,

> "If any of you lacks wisdom, let him ask God, who gives generously to all without reproach, and it will be given him. But let him ask in faith, with no doubting, for the one who doubts is like a wave of the sea that is driven and tossed by the wind. For that person must not suppose that he will receive anything from the Lord; he is a double-minded man, unstable in all his ways."

One of the main purposes of suffering is to test the genuineness of our faith and refine it. And it is during these tests and trials that doubt is exposed. Either doubt will gain territory in our heart during these times of suffering or faith will be strengthened. There is no neutral ground in the heart between doubt and faith. And if there is not a healthy spiritual formation process to root out doubt then as James says we become "double-minded" and "unstable" in all our ways. The ultimate purpose of suffering in the believer's life is to strengthen faith for the building of character, which exudes the kind of person God desires us to become. This can be seen in James 1:2-4;

> "Count it all joy, my brothers, when you meet trials of various kinds, for you know that the testing of your faith produces steadfastness. And let steadfastness have its full effect, that you may be perfect and complete, lacking in nothing."

Doubt is fleshed out in the midst of suffering and "trials of various kinds." Again, either our heart moves toward seeing these trials as refinement and a strengthening of faith or our heart hardens with doubt. It is impossible for the fruit of joy to manifest in a soul that is bound with doubt. Faith must be tested to be genuine and for it to be strengthened. Someone has said, "There is no testimony without a test." Paul addresses this in Romans 5:1-5;

> "Therefore, since we have been justified by faith, we have peace with God through our Lord Jesus Christ. Through him we have also obtained access

by faith into this grace in which we stand, and we rejoice in hope of the glory of God. Not only that, but we rejoice in our sufferings, knowing that suffering produces endurance, and endurance produces character, and character produces hope, and hope does not put us to shame, because God's love has been poured into our hearts through the Holy Spirit who has been given to us."

The strengthening of our faith builds character, which brings hope alive. And with hope comes greater expectation for this life and for eternity. Doubt kills hope. Only faith has the ability to put suffering into perspective for this life and eternity. Faith and hope are linked inseparably. When tragedy hits it tries to knock the air of faith and hope out of our soul.

No one probably has felt that struggle more than Job. Yet in all of his suffering he never gave up his faith and hope in God to come to his rescue. He did not curse God, but he did question God about His purposes and struggled with His silence. Suffering is the refiner's fire for faith and hope if we are willing to trust God and wait on Him to bring us through.

A common saying in the midst of trials and suffering is, "It will all work out." It all depends on "who" we are depending on to work things out. In the midst of suffering ourselves or journeying with others who are suffering it is important we do not flippantly make empty optimistic statements, but that we listen to God and allow Him to lead the process. All things do "work together for good," but only for those "who love God and who are called according to his purpose." (Romans 8:28) To love God is to trust God and have faith in Him. To be called according to His purpose is to trust God even in the midst of unexplainable suffering as we learn to share in His mission for the world.

The third purpose for suffering is that we would be empowered to minister to others as we share in God's mission for the world. This purpose is directly dependent upon the strengthening of our faith and building of our character. If we do not learn to properly engage suffering, our faith will not strengthen and grow. And if we do not learn to embrace God's prosperity, our hope and love will not deepen and grow. In Matthew 9:35-38, Jesus says,

> "And Jesus went throughout all the cities and villages, teaching in their synagogues and proclaiming the gospel of the kingdom and healing every disease and every affliction. When he saw the crowds, he had compassion for them, because they were harassed and helpless, like sheep without a shepherd. Then he said to his disciples, 'The harvest is plentiful, but the laborers are few; therefore pray earnestly to the Lord of the harvest to send out laborers into his harvest."

Jesus engaged the suffering around Him by preaching the gospel of the kingdom as well as ministering healing and deliverance. It was His compassion for their state of being "harassed and helpless" that led Him to action. This state of being describes everyone before they encounter Jesus. It was in the context of His compassion and the reality of people's suffering that He commanded the disciples to pray for laborers who could step into people's great suffering and bring the power of the gospel of the kingdom to them.

These laborers that Jesus is looking for are not just evangelists who will go into the world and share the gospel and lead people to Jesus. Much of Christian teaching has taught just that. Jesus is looking for laborers who are empowered by the Holy Spirit who not only preach the kingdom of God, but who are also gifted to bring supernatural deliverance to people who are in bondage.

This is integral to a healthy theology of prosperity. Proof of this is seen in the next verse, Matthew 10:1, "And he called to him his twelve disciples and gave them authority over unclean spirits, to cast them out, and to heal every disease and every affliction." As followers of Jesus we are called to engage suffering in this world by the truth of His Word and the power of the Holy Spirit.

So, one of the key purposes of suffering in the world is that followers of Jesus would grow in compassion and power to engage suffering to set the captives free. The scriptures define this as suffering with Christ for His ongoing mission. In Romans 8:16-17 Paul says, "The Spirit himself bears witness with our spirit that we are children of God, and if children, then heirs – heirs of God and fellow heirs with Christ, provided we suffer with him in order that we may also be glorified with him."

Not only does God use suffering to strengthen our faith and build our character, but He also uses suffering to equip His children to minister in power like His Son Jesus. He says a similar thing in Philippians 3:10, "that I may know him and the power of his resurrection, and may share his sufferings, becoming like him in his death." We suffer as we engage the suffering of others as Christ did.

Too much of our western Christian discipleship focuses just on building character and service and not enough on empowered ministry. The result of this is that we have an unbalanced approach to suffering. On one side suffering is highlighted too much and on the other it is not highlighted enough. On one side suffering is embraced rather than engaged, while on the other side the value of suffering is ignored. It would be of great benefit to the Church at large if those streams with a good theology of suffering came together with those streams that have a good theology of prosperity.

What for not Why

Justice does not reign in this world – yet. We live in an unjust world that is not fair, but this does not mean that God is unjust or unfair. We all from time to time have become discontent with God and have questioned how He runs things. We have had open debates with God about why He allows certain things to happen and why He doesn't make other things happen. No book deals with the depth of this struggle like the book of Job.

The message of the book of Job is not intended to tell us why we suffer. The book is not so much about Job as it is about God and how we are to think about God especially in times of suffering. Can we truly believe God's ways are the best ways, even in the worst of suffering? Job did eventually get his debate with God. God did break His silence and Job got a lot more than he was expecting. As far as we know Job never received any answers to his or his friends "why" questions. Job was hoping that God would come to His senses and see that he did not deserve to suffer like he was suffering. Instead, he received a powerful humbling encounter with the living God.

> "And the Lord said to Job: 'Shall a faultfinder contend with the Almighty? He who argues with God, let him answer it.' Then Job answered the Lord and said: 'Behold, I am of small account; what shall I answer you? I lay my hand on my mouth. I have spoken once, and I will not answer; twice, but I will proceed no further.'" (Job 40:1-5)

The real issue within Job is the question of who is ultimately "good" and "righteous"? Does man have any right to question God on these things? God's answer to Job is no. Man has no ability on his own to change his status of "goodness" and "righteousness" before God. The history of the world is full of mankind attempting to gain "goodness" and "righteousness" by his efforts and religious practice.

Here is where the death and resurrection of Christ our Redeemer shines. For God in His unfathomable mercy and grace did for us what we could never do for ourselves; "For our sake he made him to be sin who knew no sin, so that in him we might become the righteousness of God." (2 Corinthians 5:21) Job's faith was tested and he kept his trust in the "goodness" and "righteousness" of God through all of his sufferings learning that there is a purpose for the righteous to suffer in this world. And Job received a reward for his faith and steadfastness through his sufferings.

But Job also received something else. He received the blessing of being able to intercede for his friends and see them set free from a wrong view of God, suffering and righteousness. (Job 42:7-8) For his friends had fallen prey to an unbiblical pagan view of God. This view technically is called the retribution principle. It manifested through his friend's counsel that believed suffering was the consequence of sin only. They believed the righteous should not suffer.

The complementary assumption of this view was that prosperity was the reward for right living. So, his friend's argument after they had questioned Job was that he must have sinned and that it must be a secret sin since no one could pinpoint exactly what it was. They believed that Job just had to confess his secret sin to get fixed and get his life and stuff back. Job's wife and his friends were still under the pagan retribution principle and not faith in God even in the midst of suffering and trials.

God has a greater concern for us than our comfort and that we have a bunch of material stuff. God's main concern is our "righteousness," through which we can have eternal fellowship with Him in His presence. God desires to bless us richly in every way, just like He restored Job's fortunes. His ability to keep blessing us is dependent upon our "righteousness," which comes by faith in the completed work of Christ. Jesus had to deal with remnants of this retribution principle that existed in some rabbinical traditions and within the disciples. In John 9:2-3, we are told of a time when the disciples passed by a man born blind from birth. When they saw him they asked Jesus, "'Rabbi, who sinned, this man or his parents, that he was born blind?' Jesus answered, 'It was not that this man sinned, or his parents, but that the works of God might be displayed in him.'" Jesus was correcting their wrong ideas of suffering away from the "why" questions to the "what for" questions. God has greater purposes for suffering in this world than we will ever realize. A key piece of a healthy understanding of suffering is:

> We cannot start to understand the purpose for suffering until we get over the "why" questions and open our hearts to the "what for" questions.

The unhelpful words of Job's friends were bound up with a wrong understanding of God and His purposes for suffering in this world. These same wrong ideas permeate throughout the church and counseling offices today. Job was not set free to help his friends get free until he got past the "why" questions and opened his heart to the "what for" questions.

Again, one of the main purposes for suffering is that we would be empowered to minister to others by stepping into their pain and suffering not trying to fix them but set them truly free. We can do more damage to a person's heart in the midst of suffering if our own view of God is not right.

On the opposite side of the retribution principle is another dangerous approach. Dan Allender has said, "Optimism is the comfort zone of those who want to distance themselves from pain."[xix] Just positive encouraging language alone is not adequate. Without the willingness to wrestle deeply with the reality of pain and suffering we are left with just a "fix it" mentality that is not so much about knowing God, but about reclaiming the good comfortable life with plenty of stuff.

I sometimes have people say things like this to me: "I have been reading my bible and going to church, so why has God not given me that ideal job or ideal mate I have been praying for?" A.W. Tozer highlighted this issue several decades ago:

"Here again is seen the glaring discrepancy between biblical Christianity and that of present-day evangelicals, particularly in the United States...I speak not of such as they, but of the multitudes of religious weaklings within our evangelical fold here in America. To make converts here, we are forced to play down the difficulties and play up the peace of mind and worldly success enjoyed by those who accept Christ. We must assure our hearers that Christianity is now a proper and respectable thing, and that Christ has become quite popular with political bigwigs, well-to-do business tycoons, and the Hollywood swimming pool set. Thus assured, hell-deserving sinners are coming in droves to 'accept' Christ for what they can get out of Him; and though one now and again may drop a tear as proof of his sincerity, it is hard to escape the conclusion that most of them are stooping to patronize the Lord of glory much as a young couple might fawn on a boresome but rich old uncle in order to be mentioned in his will later on...Those first believers turned to Christ with the full understanding that they were espousing an unpopular cause that could cost them everything. They knew they would henceforth be members of a hated minority group with life and liberty always in jeopardy."[xx]

It would appear that Tozer's critique, highlighting a weak faith, which does not have the ability to engage suffering with a vibrant faith is still accurate today. We are too bound up with the "why" questions and therefore are missing the great fellowship of having God lead us in understanding the "what for" questions of suffering.

Here is a summary of some initial key aspects to a biblical understanding of suffering:

1.) Suffering either moves us toward God or it moves us away from God.

2.) Only faith has the ability to put suffering into perspective for this life and eternity.

3.) We cannot understand nor learn the purposes of suffering until we settle the "goodness" of God question in our heart.

4.) We cannot understand nor learn the purposes of suffering until we get over the "why" questions and open our hearts to the "what for" questions.

5.) Suffering is used to strengthen our faith, build our character and equip us to minister in power like Jesus.

CHAPTER SIX
Suffering and the Spiritual Realm

I had the great privilege recently to spend time with a Navy Seal. A friend and I were given the honor to help guide him on an archery hunt for elk in the beautiful mountains close to our home in Aspen, Colorado. The hunting and the shared experience were great, but the thing that impacted me most was getting to know this brave soul and hearing about some of the behind the scenes missions – at least the ones he could tell us about. I was overwhelmed by the reality of a whole secret battle going on that most of us are unaware of and take for granted. We live our daily lives without any thought to what it took and continues to take to secure our freedoms. While we are sipping our coffee and carrying on with our work, hobbies and entertainment there are a few who are risking their lives in intense battles to secure our freedom and stability in this increasingly dangerous world.

    This experience also made me think about how blind we are today to the reality of a spiritual realm that is just as real as the physical realm. Our western culture today denies or at best only gives lip service to the spiritual realm. This can be observed especially in how our media deals with tragedy. We are quick to blame someone or something, for in blaming we think we have found the cause of evil and therefore can control it. Here is a string of tragic events that have occurred just in the last few weeks. A child falls into a gorilla cage and there is a national smearing of the mother's lack of responsibility. Another child was taken by an alligator at a Disney park and the cause was attributed to not having enough signs posted. 50 people were massacred at a gay nightclub in Orlando and it is primarily blamed on hatred of the gay lifestyle. A five-year-old boy is attacked by a mountain lion near my home in Aspen, Colorado, and the media struggled to find someone or something to blame. Multiple inner city conflicts erupted causing several deaths with the media primarily blaming racism within the police departments. Several shootings occurred with the media blaming terrorism and lack of gun control. It is also interesting what we do not talk about publically. A gun does not influence anyone but all we seem to talk about is gun control, which is an important topic. But, we know that pornography and violent video games directly influence violent behavior and an unhealthy view of women. So, why are we not blaming those things? Simply put, we are not willing as a culture to truly uncover the source of evil and then deal with the suffering it brings forth. This is ultimately the role of the church, to be a lighthouse in the community and culture by shedding light upon the darkness and offering the real solution of the Gospel of Jesus Christ to the real problem of evil and suffering in the world. The Bible describes this ministry as a spiritual battle. Paul defines it very specifically in Ephesians 6:12,

> "For we do not wrestle against flesh and blood, but against the rulers, against the authorities against the cosmic powers over this present darkness, against the spiritual forces of evil in the heavenly places."

What happens when the Church becomes blind to the reality of the battle in the spiritual realm? Many within the Church today are ignoring this battle and the spiritual resources given by Jesus to fight against the evil behind all the suffering. Could it be that the Church has been influenced by the culture to see the world as a playground rather than a battleground? A.W. Tozer has said,

"How different today. The fact remains the same, but the interpretation has changed completely. Men think of the world not as a battleground but as a playground. We are not here to fight we are here to frolic. We are not in a foreign land we are at home. We are not getting ready to live but we are already living and the best we can do is rid ourselves of our inhibitions and our frustrations and live this life to the full. This we believe is a fair summary of the religious philosophy of modern man."[xxi]

The Church can only be the Church when it is Christ-exalting and counter-cultural. When the Church drifts to adopt a playground rather than a battleground view of the world it loses its transformative power. Evidence of this drift is when the Church is more captivated by its reputation and relevance in the culture than pleasing and honoring God. This is especially clear when the media asks the Church about an issue where the culture is embracing something opposite of what the Bible clearly teaches. Sadly, we see some leaders more committed to pleasing the culture than honoring God. This reveals the consequences and tragedies of a spiritual battle raging in our culture. When the Church forfeits a spiritual warfare worldview it loses its ability to view suffering properly and loses its power to address suffering in the world.

In the last chapter we saw that without faith we cannot attain a proper perspective on suffering. In this chapter we are going to see that faith can only help us attain a proper perspective on suffering when it is lived out in the context of spiritual warfare.

The Devil

If we don't believe in the reality of the devil and his demons, we can never fully understand evil and suffering. If we focus too much on the devil we become too occupied with evil and suffering. Tozer again has great insight here,

"Human nature tends to excesses by a kind of evil magnetic attraction. We instinctively run to one of two extremes, and that is why we are so often in error. A proof of this propensity to extremes is seen in the attitude of the average Christian toward the devil. I have observed among spiritual persons a tendency either to ignore him altogether or to make too much of him. Both are wrong…There is in the world an enemy whom we dare not ignore."[xxii]

The first time the devil clearly shows up is as a serpent in the Garden of Eden. We do not know much of how he got there or why he is described as a serpent but there are several scriptures that give us some insight. It is clear that the New Testament writers believed that the serpent in Genesis chapter three was the devil, also called Satan. (2 Cor. 11:3; 1 Thess. 3:5; Rev. 12:9) "Satan" is the Greek transliteration of the Hebrew term used to describe the enemy of God and humanity (Job 1:6–12; 2:1–7). It is usually translated into Greek by the term "devil," though in Luke and Acts "Satan" is also used. The first five verses of the Bible possibly open the door to the beginning of this cosmic battle between the rebellious forces of Satan and the host of heaven.

> [1]In the beginning, God created the heavens and the earth. [2]The earth was without form and void, and darkness was over the face of the deep. And the Spirit of God was hovering over the face of the waters. [3]And God said, "Let there be light," and there was light. [4]And God saw that the light was good. And God separated the light from the darkness. [5]God called the light Day, and the darkness he called Night. And there was evening and there was morning, the first day.
> (Genesis 1:1-5, ESV)

The Hebrew words used in verse two to describe the earth are used elsewhere to describe chaos and it is clear that darkness is not good compared to the light. So, what happened between verse one and verse two to bring this chaos and darkness upon God's creation? This very well could be an indicator of the fall of Satan from heaven to the earth and along with him was his horde of fallen spirits wreaking chaos and bringing darkness to the earth. It is interesting to note that God did not create the sun, moon or stars until the fourth day. So what was this light that He created on the first day separating it from darkness? There was obviously something much bigger going on that first day than the physical creation of light. The theme of light and darkness flows throughout the entire Bible telling the story of God's redemption plan. 1 John 1:5 tells us, "This is the message we have heard from him and proclaim to you, that God is light, and in him is no darkness at all." So, if there is no darkness in him at all where did the darkness come from in Genesis 2:2? Colossians 1:13 tells us the good news of the Gospel of Jesus Christ, "He has delivered us from the domain of darkness and transferred us to the kingdom of his beloved Son." The devil is darkness and the presence of darkness reveals rebellion against God. The devil traffics within darkness and where there is spiritual darkness there is the works of the devil. Revelation 22:5, gives us a glorious picture of the end when night and darkness will be no more, "And night will be no more. They will need no light of lamp or sun, for the Lord God will be their light, and they will reign forever and ever."

    Two other verses that give us great insight into the devil's identity and the cause of his fall are Ezekiel 28 and Isaiah 14. In the beginning of Ezekiel 28 God is chastising the prince of Tyre for extreme arrogance and pride. Later in the chapter the writer refers to the Garden of Eden and describes the prince of Tyre's downfall in reference to the ancient downfall of Satan in the beginning because of his pride and arrogance. In chapter 14 of Isaiah, the prophet is told by God to chastise the king of Babylon. And just like Ezekiel 28, the writer describes the king's downfall in terms of the ancient downfall of Satan who desired to make himself like the Most High. Michael Heiser gives us further insight into the serpent's identity,

"The pivotal character of Genesis 3 is the serpent. The Hebrew word translated *serpent* is *nachash*. The word is both plain and elastic. The most straightforward meaning is the one virtually all translators and interpreters opt for: *serpent*. When the Hebrew root letters n-ch-sh are a noun, that's the meaning. But n-ch-sh are also the consonants of a verb. If we changed the vowels to a verbal form (recall that Hebrew originally had no vowels), we would have *nochesh*, which means 'the diviner.' Divination refers to communication with the supernatural world. A diviner in the ancient world was one who foretold omens or gave out divine information (oracles). We can see that element in the story. Eve is getting information from this being…The serpent (*nachash*) was an image commonly used in reference to a divine throne guardian. Given the context of Eden, that helps identify the villain as a divine being. The divine adversary dispenses divine information, using it to goad Eve. He gives her an oracle (or, an omen!): You won't really die. God knows when you eat you will be like one of the elohim."[xxiii]

    The Garden of Eden was God's temple, His house where He planned to walk and have fellowship with His image bearers. It was the epitome of peace and prosperity until the devil got to Adam and Eve's mind and things took a turn for the worst. But not all was lost, for God had a plan all along to redeem His image bearers back into an everlasting prosperity. There is nothing new under the sun as the writer of Ecclesiastes has written. And behind all of the devil's schemes is the same lie he used from the beginning. The lie that tries to get us to doubt the Words and Ways of God and that somehow He is holding us back from the best. The consequences of believing these lies have brought about great evil and suffering in this world. The vision of prosperity the devil sells has wreaked great havoc throughout history. Deep inside every human soul is a yearning for Eden and Prosperity. We have an inner desire to restore something that was lost and to create utopia. This prosperity we are looking for that explains and heals the suffering of the world cannot be accomplished by human means alone. The devil is behind every worldly vision of prosperity. His goal is to enslave God's image bearers and cover His creation with darkness. The good news is that Jesus came to "destroy the works of the devil," (1 John 3:8). And He came to empower His image bearers to bring light to the darkness through a life of faith that embraces God's prosperity and engages the suffering in the world with the love and power of Jesus.

The Source of Evil

One of the big questions modern people ask is, "Why all the evil and suffering if God is good?" For us to adequately answer this question we have to go back and uncover the source of evil itself and see how it has been propagated throughout history. It would be easy and a cop out to blame the devil for all the evil and suffering in the world. The old adage, "The devil made me do it," is not a biblical option. The devil cannot make anyone do anything. He did not make Adam and Eve sin. He did, however, tempt them relentlessly. The source of evil lies deep within our soul. It is something we have in common with the angelic realm. Its origin is the fact that God created us with "free will." He created us to be His image-bearers who possess a mind, emotions and a will with the capacity to make real decisions.

There are a lot of unanswered questions about the story of creation in the first three chapters of Genesis. However, there is much that we can mine from these three incredible chapters. In chapter two we see that God created man and placed him in the Garden of Eden, which He had planted. In verse nine of chapter two we can see that the tree of life and the tree of the knowledge of good and evil were in the garden, but were unlike the other trees. Genesis 2:16-18 says, "And the LORD God commanded the man, saying, 'You may surely eat of every tree of the garden, but of the tree of the knowledge of good and evil you shall not eat, for in the day that you eat of it you shall surely die.'" Adam and Eve lived in the garden in the presence of God enjoying all that He had created and did not experience any evil and suffering. They did not know good and evil. However, it is important to realize that Adam and Eve possessed "free will" the capability of good and evil. They were not perfect beings, because they possessed the capability to "know good and evil."

We know from Genesis chapter three that not only was the "tree of the knowledge of good and evil" present in the garden, but the devil was in the garden and closely associated with this tree. Adam and Eve seemed completely comfortable conversing with the devil and comfortable that he was in God's garden. Since they did not "know good and evil" they were at this time oblivious as far as we know to the sinister purposes of the serpent. We do not know how many conversations or how much interaction they had with the devil. Genesis 3:1-5 says,

> [1] Now the serpent was more crafty than any other beast of the field that the LORD God had made. He said to the woman, "Did God actually say, 'You shall not eat of any tree in the garden'?" [2] And the woman said to the serpent, "We may eat of the fruit of the trees in the garden, [3] but God said, 'You shall not eat of the fruit of the tree that is in the midst of the garden, neither shall you touch it, lest you die.' " [4] But the serpent said to the woman, "You will not surely die. [5] For God knows that when you eat of it your eyes will be opened, and you will be like God, knowing good and evil.

This is the first crisis of faith moment for Adam and Eve. Were they going to believe and trust God or allow the devil's temptation and deception to lead them away from God? This was the first true test of what they were going to do with their "free will." The next few verses reveal the loss of innocence, the awareness of evil and the bondage of sin.

⁶ So when the woman saw that the tree was good for food, and that it was a delight to the eyes, and that the tree was to be desired to make one wise, she took of its fruit and ate, and she also gave some to her husband who was with her, and he ate. ⁷ Then the eyes of both were opened, and they knew that they were naked. And they sewed fig leaves together and made themselves loincloths.

The devil's motive was to make Adam and Eve like him so he could put them under his control and destiny. With this first abuse of their "free will" they forfeited their innocence. They both for the first time were experiencing guilt and shame, which was revealed in the fact that they no longer where comfortable in their skin. They also were no longer just capable of good and evil, but now experienced evil and forfeited the ability to live in the presence of God. But it gets worse. By sinning, they gave the devil access and control to their lives and the rest of humanity to put them in bondage to sin. The rest of human history reflects the inability to use our "free will" to restore abundant life with God and restore Eden.

The same strategy used to tempt and deceive Adam and Eve is used everyday in our lives by the devil and his army and their influence over the world. It begins with a lie or a half- truth, which is also a lie. Behind every temptation is a lie and deception. Can you imagine the devil saying to Eve, "Did God actually say, 'You shall not eat of any tree in the garden?' (Genesis 3:1, ESV) The devil began by drawing Eve and silent Adam (Adam forsook his spiritual leadership, which has been the plight of manhood. Genesis 2:15-17) into a discussion questioning what God said. Then he at the right time proposes an alternative to God's word - a lie to contemplate. "You will not surely die. For God knows that when you eat of it your eyes will be opened, and you will be like God, knowing good and evil." (Genesis 3:4-5, ESV) At this point, if the lie is not rejected by faith in God's truth and goodness, we pass the point of no return. For the purpose of the lie is for us to come into agreement with it and reject the word of God. But this did not happen with Eve and silent Adam. They started embracing the lie. The devil is not stupid. He knows that to get people to embrace his lies he has to present them as attractive. He is the deceiver and comes as an angel of light. (John 8:44; 2 Cor 11:14) The devil vamps things up by offering Eve and silent Adam an alternative way of life, which really was the path to death. Genesis 3:4-5 records it, "But the serpent said to the woman, 'You will not surely die. For God knows that when you eat of it your eyes will be opened, and you will be like God, knowing good and evil.'" Instead of fighting the serpent's lie with faith and the Word of God, Eve and silent Adam started embracing the lie and coming into agreement with it. They did not take it captive to obedience to God. (Luke 4:1-15, 2 Cor. 10:3-5) They passed the point of no return and came into agreement with the devil's lie.

Being tempted is not a sin; it is part of everyday life. Questioning the truth of an option or idea is not sin; it also is part of everyday life. Coming into agreement in our mind with something that is contradictory to God's Word and then acting upon it is sin. Genesis 3:6 reveals the path toward bondage to sin, "So when the woman saw that the tree was good for food, and that it was a delight to the eyes, and that the tree was to be desired to make one wise, she took of its fruit and ate, and she also gave some to her husband who was with her, and he ate." Eve and silent Adam did not fight the lie with faith and the Word of God, therefore, they came into agreement with their minds with the lie. They made a mental alignment with the devil, which led to taking action according to the lie. Immediately upon their disobedience, they came into alignment with the devil, for they were now like him in "knowing good and evil." They did not immediately die physically, but they immediately died spiritually. They were now in bondage to sin, shame and guilt. And now the rest of their posterity, all of humanity, was bound by sin, shame and guilt.

Lies lead to agreements. Agreements lead to strongholds. Strongholds lead to death. Evil and all forms of suffering in the world are the result of lies, agreements and strongholds. The front line of this spiritual battle is fought primarily in the mind. Once the mind comes into agreement with a lie of the enemy, territory is taken and strongholds set in with devastating consequences.

We were created to be God's image-bearers. The devil's purpose has been to corrupt that image and destroy God's purposes. That God allowed the devil into the Garden is not a problem when we realize that the devil is under God's control and ultimate purposes. Eve and silent Adam's sin did not surprise God. He has a glorious plan, an eternal covenant He has made to save and redeem His image-bearers so they can bring His light to the darkness and suffering in this world. The tree of the knowledge of good and evil is never mentioned again in the bible, but the tree of life is (Rev 2:7; 22:2, 14, 19). And the tree of life is the eternal destiny of everyone who trusts in God's provision of His Son, Jesus Christ.

Sin, Evil and Suffering

The devil and his army of demons use evil and suffering to destroy faith, hope and love. Jesus said in John 10:10, that the devil "comes only to steal and kill and destroy."

The serpent's first line of attack on Eve and silent Adam was to breach their faith. This begins with getting them to question the truthfulness of God's Word and their trust in Him. Once faith was breached, the door was open for rebellion against God's Words and Ways. Sin ushered in the soul devastating forces of guilt and shame, which put a relational chasm between them and God. Though they didn't physically die at this time, they did experience spiritual death. Once there is a breach in faith and an act of disobedience there is a loss of hope. This can be seen from Eve and silent Adam's immediate response after eating the apple they hid from God. Sin, shame and guilt drive us into hiding. The place of hiding is dark and hopeless. It is in this hopeless place where silent Adam blamed his wife for the whole thing instead of seeing it primarily as a result of a failure in his spiritual leadership. And the woman in turn blames the serpent for deceiving her instead of taking responsibility for not trusting God's commands. Where hope is destroyed there is blame. Where there is blame love is corrupted. The enemy's ability to drive this devastating process once he gets a foothold has been manifested throughout history. We can see in the next chapter of Genesis that Cain kills his brother Abel, the first murder. Eve and silent Adam are experiencing the consequences of their sin, which destroys faith, hope and love and ushers in all forms of suffering into their family and the world. The evidence of the work of the devil is darkness, barrenness and wasteland, which are at war with the fruit of the Spirit; love, joy, peace, patience, kindness, goodness, faithfulness, gentleness and self-control. There is no real prosperity without the fruit of the Spirit. The devil uses lies and suffering in this world to destroy faith, hope and love.

All is not lost. Even in the midst of Eve and silent Adam's rebellion, God is at work using even evil and suffering for His grander purposes of salvation and renewal. It is God who makes the first sacrifice and provides Eve and silent Adam with covering for their shame and nakedness foreshadowing what He intends to do for the sin of the world through Jesus. (Genesis 3:21) It is God who graciously removes them from the garden so that they will not eat the tree of life and live forever in a hopeless and unredeemable state. (Genesis 3:22-24) And it is God who ultimately will use the suffering caused by evil to redeem and restore. (1 Peter 2:24) God will restore His prosperity to His people and this earth again.

The devil is evil. And the devil causes suffering. We have inherited evil from silent Adam and therefore, we can cause evil as well. God allowed evil for His purposes. He is not the cause of evil for He is perfect. Though God created the angels and humans with the capacity to choose evil, He did not choose or cause evil. Just because God foreknew that we would choose evil does not mean He predestined it. Michael Heiser helps us with this difficult but extremely important point:

> *Foreknowledge does not necessitate predestination – they are separable.*
>
> *Some events God foreknows do not happen. (1 Samuel 23:1-13)*
>
> *That which never happens can be foreknown by God, but it is not predestined since it never happened.*
>
> *Since foreknowledge doesn't require predestination, foreknown events that happen may or may not have been predestined.*[xxiv]

This can be seen in Romans 8:28-30. God foreknew sinners who had caused great evil. But He predestined that they would be conformed to the image of His Son. And those He predestined He called, justified and glorified. He foreknew the evil and suffering caused by the abuse of our "free will," but He predestined the fullness of our salvation. God foreknew evil; He did not create evil. We can never completely resolve the issue of God's sovereignty and evil. However, we must make sure that we do not drift toward Open Theism where God is not all knowing or drift toward an Augustinian predestination that does not allow room for a difference between foreknowledge and predestination which would eliminate our free will.

We can see that the devil brought evil and suffering into Job's life. He asked God permission to sift Job so that he could destroy his faith, hope and love. Satan also asked to sift Peter. We are in a spiritual battle and we have an adversary the devil "who prowls around like a roaring lion, seeking someone to devour"? (1 Peter 5:8) Some have said we are safe from sifting, but that is not completely accurate and fits into the devil's schemes. The reason for Job and Peter's siftings are different and similar. They both were leaders and exemplars of faith so they had a bigger target on them. But in some ways they are different. The reason for Job's sifting was not clear and it was not dealt with within Job's story. Some try to point to Job 1:5 and 3:25 to show that Job had a stronghold of fear that gave access to the devil to sift him, but there is not enough scriptural evidence and it does not contribute to the larger purpose of the book. The reason for Peter's sifting could be primarily because he was the leader of the disciples or his pride.

If a follower of Christ tolerates sin in their life through continued willful disobedience to the Word of God, they leave themselves vulnerable to demonic attack. This is why Paul exhorts the Church in Ephesians 4:26-27, "do not let the sun go down on your anger, and give no opportunity to the devil." This is one example where we can see that believers can give access to demonic activity in their lives if they tolerate sin.

Satan had asked to sift Peter like wheat so he could destroy Peter's faith, hope and love and disqualify him as the leader of the Apostles. (Luke 22:31-32) But Jesus' purpose for allowing Satan to sift Peter was to strengthen him and conquer his pride so he could be used powerfully for God's purposes. We can first see evidence of Peter's pride in Matthew 16 where Jesus tells Peter that upon his faith confession He will build His church and He will give him the keys to the kingdom. Immediately after this Jesus began to tell them He must go to Jerusalem and suffer many things. In response to this Peter pulled Jesus aside and began to rebuke Him. This would be almost comical to think about anyone rebuking the Lord, but Jesus' response reveals the magnitude of Peter's sin. Jesus responds in Matthew 16:23, "But he turned and said to Peter, 'Get behind me, Satan! You are a hindrance to me. For you are not setting your mind on the things of God, but on the things of man.'" Francis Frangipane sheds light on this;

> "Pride caused Satan's fall, and pride was the very same darkness manipulated by Satan to cause Peter's fall. Lucifer, from experience, knew well the judgment of God against religious pride and envy. He knew personally that pride goes 'before the fall' (Proverbs 16:18 KJV). Satan did not have a right to indiscriminately assault and destroy

Peter. He had to secure permission from Peter's Lord before he could come against the young apostle. But the fact is, the devil demanded permission to sift Peter, and he received it."[xxxv]

Peter was sifted and he did deny his Lord three times just like Jesus said he would. (Luke 22:31-34) Peter's sin of pride exposed him to the enemy's attack and brought detrimental consequences for Peter's life as well as the rest of the disciples he was suppose to be leading. One result of Peter's sifting and denial was that he lost confidence and clarity in his calling. After Jesus' resurrection John gives us insight into Peter's state in chapter 21. Apparently, Peter had lost confidence and clarity in his calling because we see him rallying several of the disciples to go fishing with no mention of the mission Jesus had given them. A matter of fact, Jesus had called them away from the vocation of fishing and called them to be "fishers of men." In this encounter Jesus graciously restores Peter's confidence and clarity in his calling by removing the guilt of Peter's three denials with three affirmations. (John 21)

The good news is that in the midst of evil spiritual attack and suffering we have an advocate in Jesus Christ. We can see this in the Old Testament and New Testament.

"For I know that my Redeemer lives, and at the last he will stand upon the earth."(Job 19:25)

"My little children, I am writing these things to you so that you may not sin. But if anyone does sin, we have an advocate with the Father, Jesus Christ the righteous. He is the propitiation for our sins, and not for ours only but also for the sins of the whole world."
(1 John 2:1-2)

And there is more good news. Not only do we have an Advocate in Jesus who intercedes to the Father for us, we also have a Helper in the Holy Spirit who intercedes for us.

> "Likewise the Spirit helps us in our weakness. For we do not know what to pray for as we ought, but the Spirit himself intercedes for us with groanings too deep for words. And he who searches hearts knows what is the mind of the Spirit, because the Spirit intercedes for the saints according to the will of God."(Romans 8: 26-27)

> "Who is to condemn? Christ Jesus is the one who died – more than that, who was raised – who is at the right hand of God, who indeed is interceding for us."(Romans 8:34)

Christus Victor

The New Testament repeatedly proclaims the good news that the death and resurrection of Jesus Christ has defeated the powers of the devil and his evil kingdom of demons. The disciples and the early church operated from a spiritual warfare worldview. They regularly engaged evil and suffering with the power of the Holy Spirit in a spiritual conflict defeating the supernatural powers of the enemy and bringing freedom and salvation to those in bondage to darkness. One of the primary themes of Jesus' ministry was ushering in the kingdom of God to conquer the kingdom of this world under the devil's power. Jesus' deliverance ministry was unique in all of biblical history and it revealed the evidence of spiritual victory over the devil and his demons. Exorcism was common among both Jews and Greeks in the first-century. What was so unique and shocking about Jesus' and the early church's ministry was just how powerful and successful they were at setting people free.

Often the only aspect of the victorious work of Christ on the cross that is taught is the substitutionary atonement view. This view teaches that the main thing God was accomplishing in sending Jesus to die on the cross was the satisfaction of His perfect justice and the forgiveness of our sins. This is a critically important aspect of understanding what Jesus accomplished on the cross, but there is more. The scriptures clearly communicate that God through Jesus was defeating the power of the devil and his evil kingdom.

"…The reason the Son of God appeared was to destroy the works of the devil." (1 John 3:8)

"He disarmed the rulers and authorities and put them to open shame, by triumphing over them in him." (Colossians 2:15)

"When he ascended on high he led a host of captives, and he gave gifts to men."(Ephesians 4:8)

"…that through death he might destroy the one who has the power of death, that is, the devil, and deliver all those who through fear of death were subject to lifelong slavery."(Hebrews 2:14)

Christ's substitutionary death for us so we can be free from the power of sin and death is possible because He defeated the devil and his kingdom of darkness. This spiritual warfare worldview is essential to understanding evil and suffering. It is essential to understanding how to resist the devil and his temptations and engage suffering with divine weapons of warfare. Christ's death and resurrection have won the war against Satan and his dark kingdom but there are battles yet to fight until the final war is realized in the end when Christ returns. Theologians call this "the already-not yet" aspect of the Kingdom of God. Jesus has ushered in His kingdom and empowered the Church to fight the darkness, but the fullness of His kingdom has "not yet" been realized. So, until Jesus returns He has commissioned His Church and empowered His Church to battle evil and suffering through spiritual warfare.

Jesus began His ministry by defeating Satan in a spiritual warfare showdown in the wilderness. Right after His baptism and filling of the Holy Spirit, Jesus was led into the desert by the Spirit for forty days. The three temptations as recorded in Luke chapter 4 foreshadow the ultimate victory Jesus would win over Satan in His death and resurrection. Satan first tempts Jesus by saying to Him, "If you are the Son of God, command this stone to become bread. And Jesus answered him, 'It is written, Man shall not live by bread alone.'" (Luke 4:3-4) Jesus was quoting Deuteronomy 8:3 and the rest of the verse reads, "…but man lives by every word that comes from the mouth of the Lord." The essence of this temptation is behind every temptation and sin, which is to listen and obey a voice other than God's voice. This same temptation was behind Satan's temptation of Eve in the beginning that caused all mankind to fall into sin. Jesus' victory here over Satan foreshadowed His victory over the power of sin, which Satan used to keep humanity in bondage. Jesus perfectly fulfilled the law for us and died as a perfect sacrifice so we could be free to walk in righteousness. So what does this victory specifically mean for us in our battle against evil and suffering and our ability to embrace the abundant prosperous life Jesus has for us? If we are not confident in our standing and relationship with God we will not be able to stand in battle against evil and suffering. In Jesus' victory over Satan we are set free from the power of sin; free from guilt, shame and condemnation; free from the power of the law; and free from the power of death. These are all part of our new inheritance as children of God and are foundational to what it means to live in true prosperity. It is living in radical freedom that Jesus has won for us. It is when we start walking in the freedom of these blessings that we become dangerous to the devil and the kingdom of darkness. The sad reality is that there are too many believers today who are not walking in the freedom that is available to them and are regularly losing spiritual battles and are not empowered to fight for other's freedom.

The second temptation has the devil taking Jesus to a high point and showing Him all the kingdoms of the world. He said to Jesus, "To you I will give all this authority and their glory, for it has been delivered to me, and I give it to whom I will. If you, then, will worship me, it will all be yours." (Luke 4:6-7) First, we need to take note of the fact that Satan has been given authority over this earth. In Adam and Eve's sin they forfeited their authority to rule over the earth and put themselves captive to the devil. Paul defines humanity's plight after the garden in Ephesians 2:1-3,

> "And you were dead in the trespasses and sins in which you once walked, following the course of this world, following the prince of the power of the air, the spirit that is now at work in the sons of disobedience – among whom we all once lived in the passions of our flesh, carrying out the desires of the body and the mind, and were by nature children of wrath, like the rest of mankind."

Satan was tempting Jesus with access to power and authority. And it was a level of temptation that no one but Jesus will ever be tempted with. Someone has said that power corrupts and absolute power corrupts absolutely. Man has always coveted power and authority. And Satan is more than willing to give any person his earthly power and authority if they will just worship him. The tricky thing is that most do not know they are worshiping him. Jesus responds to Satan's temptation by answering him, "It is written, 'You shall worship the Lord your God, and him only shall you serve.'" (Luke 4:8) Jesus' victory over Satan's second temptation foreshadows Jesus' reclaiming of authority and power on the earth for His church to fight against the gates of hell. So what does this victory specifically mean for us in our battle against evil and suffering and our ability to embrace the abundant prosperous life Jesus has for us? It means that we have authority and power available to us to minister the kingdom of God into this dark world. This authority and power was a defining mark for Jesus and His disciples as it was for the early church. And it should again be a defining mark of the church today. Jesus in His commission to the Church starts by encouraging His followers that "all authority in heaven and on earth has been given to me." (Matthew 28:18) And since Jesus has won back the authority on earth over mankind He commissions His followers to "Go therefore and make disciples of all nations, baptizing them in the name of the Father and of the Son and of the Holy Spirit, teaching them to observe all that I have commanded you. And behold I am with you always, to the end of the age." (Matthew 28:19-20) To be faithful to His commission we too need to teach others to obey all that Jesus commanded the disciples. And one of the main things He taught them was to battle evil and darkness with His authority and power to set people free from the bondage of the enemy.

The third temptation has Satan taking Jesus to Jerusalem on top of the Temple. He said to Jesus, "If you are the Son of God, throw yourself down from here, for it is written, 'He will command his angels concerning you, to guard you,' and 'On their hands they will bear you up, lest you strike your foot against a stone.'" (Luke 4:9-11) Jesus replied, "It is said, 'You shall not put the Lord your God to the test.'" (Luke 4:12) Satan was tempting

Jesus with the most powerful thing he had, the power of death. Back in Eden, the devil had lied to Adam and Eve that if they ate of the tree of the knowledge of good and evil they would not die. But once they ate it they didn't immediately physically die but they spiritually died with the result of death entering into the world. This third temptation foreshadows Jesus' defeat of the power of death at His resurrection. He redeemed us from the fear and power of death. So what does this victory specifically mean for us in our battle against evil and suffering and our ability to embrace the abundant prosperous life Jesus has for us? If the fear and power of death no longer holds us captive we are free from the bondage of any and all fears. What an amazing prosperity – to live without any fear – to be fearless. This is why Jesus said in Matthew 10:28, "And do not fear those who kill the body but cannot kill the soul. Rather fear him who can destroy both soul and body in hell." If we fear God we are free from the destructive bondage of all fears, especially the fear of death. We can see this was the essence of Paul's radical life when he said, "For me to live is Christ, and to die is gain." (Philippians 1:21) We cannot truly live for Christ embracing His abundant prosperous life and fighting evil and suffering if we are not free from the power of death. We still physically die, but are spiritually alive and immediately with our Lord when we die. (2 Corinthians 5:8) When Jesus returns He will give us a new eternal body. The reason we still physically die is because there is a close association between sin and death and that there is time for many others to hear the Good News of Jesus and be saved before the final judgment.

The Weapons of Our Warfare

Even though Jesus' death and resurrection dealt Satan and his kingdom a deathblow, the New Testament affirms the ongoing influence of Satan and his kingdom in the world until the end. The devil is still seen as the "prince of the power of the air," (Eph 2:2) and the "god of this world." (2 Cor 4:4) He is our present adversary who is constantly seeking someone to devour. (1 Pt 5:8) He is still "blinding the eyes of unbelievers." (2 Cor 4:4) And the whole world still "lies in the power of the evil one." (1 Jn 5:19). All of this sheds light on why Jesus commands His followers at the end of the Lord's Prayer to pray, "And lead us not into temptation, but deliver us from evil." (Matt 6:13) In our western culture and in our western church these realities have been minimized in our teaching and in our ministry. The reality is that to follow Jesus is to step into a life that is at war with the god of this "present darkness." Without this emphasis Christianity is left powerless and hopeless and harassed in dealing with evil. It is left with only an intellectual interaction with evil and a ministry that is no different or more powerful than the world's methods.

But Jesus has not left His Church powerless or helpless in the midst of this "present darkness" (Eph 6:12) He has not left His people in a state of confusion about how to handle evil and suffering in the world. He has given authority and power to His Church through the Holy Spirit.

> "The seventy-two returned with joy, saying; 'Lord, even the demons are subject to us in your name!' And he said to them, 'I saw Satan fall like lightning from heaven. Behold, I have given you authority to tread on serpents and scorpions, and over all the power of the enemy, and nothing shall hurt you. Nevertheless, do not rejoice in this, that the spirits are subject to you, but rejoice that your names are written in heaven." (Luke 11:17-20)

This verse as well as many others reveals that Jesus desires His Church to be operating in authority to take the fight against evil and darkness to the very "gates of hell."(Matt 16:18) He desires a Church that is praying for and equipping "laborers" for the harvest. (Matt 9:37-38) The kind of "laborer" Jesus is referring to is illustrated in the verses above and the verses below. Jesus is looking for co-laborers to engage the evil and suffering that afflicts the whole person.

> "And Jesus went throughout all the cities and villages, teaching in their synagogues and proclaiming the gospel of the kingdom and healing every disease and every affliction…And he called to him his twelve disciples and gave them authority over unclean spirits, to cast them out, and to heal every disease and every affliction." (Matt 9:35; 10:1)

When Jesus looked upon the crowds, which represented all unredeemed humanity, He had compassion on them and described them as harassed and helpless and sheep without a shepherd. (Matt 9:36) In other words, He saw them as enslaved to the devil and open to the affliction of demons and utterly helpless in and of themselves to get free. This is not the way most of the western church sees the unbelieving world around it today. It is politically incorrect and culturally insensitive to talk like this about unbelievers and there is no tolerance for it in the public square and in many churches. Any wonder why too much of the church's ministry today is powerless?

The main battleground in this spiritual battle is the mind where the devil deceives and tempts and where our Savior has come to set us free so we can take captive every thought.

> "For though we walk in the flesh, we are not waging war according to the flesh. For the weapons of our warfare are not of the flesh but have divine power to destroy strongholds. We destroy arguments and every lofty opinion raised against the knowledge of God, and take every thought captive to obey Christ." (2 Cor 10:3-5)

Paul describes here the dynamic of spiritual warfare and that the primary battlefield is our mind and our thoughts. The devil "prowls around like a roaring lion, seeking someone to devour." (1 Peter 5:8) His tactic is to get us first to buy his lie. Once he has our thoughts captivated with his lie he can start his destructive work. Lies lead to agreements. Agreements lead to strongholds. Strongholds lead to death. Death in the bible does not just refer to physical death. It refers to spiritual death and a break in fellowship with God. The destructive path begins with believing a lie. So, what are these weapons of warfare that Paul speaks of?

The weapons of spiritual warfare we can see in the bible are the armor of our identity in Christ (Eph 6:10-18), the sword of the Spirit, the Word of God (Eph 6:17), the spiritual disciplines, the spiritual gifts (1 Cor 12:1-11) and prayer and intercession.

All of these weapons are to be harnessed by the believer in the battle against the flesh, evil and suffering. The battle of the mind is won primarily by fighting the devil's lie with the truth of God's Word. The truth of God's Word leads to faith. (Romans 10:17) Faith as it grows brings the empowerment of the Holy Spirit. (John 14:12) And as the believer grows in the empowerment of the Spirit they grow in their ability to fight for the freedom of others who are suffering the consequences of evil and darkness. (Matt 10:1; Acts 1:8) Even though lies lead to agreements, strongholds and death - truth is greater and leads to faith, power and freedom.

Truth leads to faith. Faith leads to power. Power leads to freedom.

We can see how this works from seeing how Jesus defeated Satan's temptations in the wilderness as He began His earthly ministry. (Luke 4:1-15) *First*, we must observe from this account is that it occurred almost entirely in the unseen spiritual realm. Luke tells us that Satan took Jesus somewhere where he could see "all the kingdoms of the world in a moment of time." (Luke 4:5) And that Satan took Jesus to the top of the temple in Jerusalem. (Luke 4:9). So, the warfare we are to fight is a war that primarily is occurring in the spiritual realm with consequences in the physical realm. This spiritual realm operates under laws that transcend our physical laws. This warfare cannot be fought with fleshly, material weapons. If we are going to be faithful laborers for our Lord we must learn how to wield spiritual weapons in this unseen realm so we can engage evil and suffering in this world.

Second, we cannot have victory over temptation unless we are filled with the Holy Spirit. If we live by the flesh we will fall to temptation and bondage to sin every time unless we are filled with the Spirit and learn to walk with the Spirit. Luke 4:1 tells us that Jesus was full of the Holy Spirit before He was led into the desert where He was tempted by the devil. Luke chapter three gives us the account of Jesus' baptism and the filling of the Holy Spirit. It is important to understand that it was Jesus' humanity that was baptized by the Holy Spirit. He had set aside His deity and "emptied himself by taking the form of a servant, being born in the likeness of men." (Phil 2:7) Everything Jesus did in the flesh was by His humanity empowered by the Spirit. Otherwise, if it was by His deity He had victory over the devil's temptation we would not be able to follow in His steps and live like He lived. Jesus had victory over Satan because He was "full" of the Holy Spirit. And likewise, we can have victory over any and every temptation of the enemy and his armies when we are filled with the Holy Spirit. This can be seen in 2 Corinthians 10:3-4, when Paul says, "For though we walk in the flesh, we are not waging war according to the flesh. For the weapons of our warfare are not of the flesh, but have divine power to destroy strongholds." Unfortunately, too much of our warfare today in the church is being waged with the flesh rather than by the Spirit.

Third, the devil will flee if we resist him by faith standing on the truth of the Word of God. This is a wonderful promise from the scriptures along with the truth that God will not allow us to be tempted beyond what we can handle. (1 Cor 10:13; James 4:7) Jesus was tempted beyond what any person will ever have to withstand.

Fourth, in this life the devil and his army will never stop tempting us. Luke 4:13 tells us that the devil left Jesus, but would come back again at "an opportune time." This is why it is so critical to stay sober and alert and not let our defenses down.

Finally, we gain power and authority by resisting the devil and his temptations. After Jesus' victory over the devil in the desert He returned "in the power of the Spirit." (Luke 4:14) When we fall to temptation and the devil's lies we give him access and control in our life and we quench the power of the Spirit in our life. It is when we stand on the Truth and fight temptation with all the spiritual weapons that we grow in the power and authority.

The devil offers a false vision of prosperity and his schemes are to corrupt God's beautiful vision of prosperity by selling us a lie so he gains control. But the Father has sent Jesus to rescue us and empower us by the Holy Spirit to experience abundant life and real prosperity and to fight for others freedom into this life of prosperity. The glorious promises of God cannot be experienced without learning to engage evil and suffering with the weapons of warfare that have divine power to destroy strongholds.

Here is a summary from this chapter of some key aspects to a biblical understanding of suffering and the spiritual realm:

1.) We must believe in the reality of the devil and his demons if we are going to understand evil and suffering.

2.) God created the angelic realm and humanity with "free-will" and the source of evil is the abuse of this gift.

3.) Lies lead to agreements. Agreements lead to strongholds. Strongholds lead to death.

4.) In Jesus' victory over Satan we are set free from the power of sin; free from guilt, shame and condemnation; free from the power of the law; and free from the power of death.

5.) Our weapons of spiritual warfare are the armor of our identity in Christ, the sword of the Spirit - the Word of God, the spiritual disciplines, the spiritual gifts and prayer and intercession.

6.) Truth leads to faith. Faith leads to power. Power leads to freedom.

CHAPTER SEVEN
Different Kinds of Suffering

One of the greatest causes of confusion in our lives is a lack of understanding the source of suffering and the purpose of suffering. This confusion inhibits our ability to grow close to God and discern His voice in our lives. Our ability to get clarity and freedom from this spiritual confusion comes when we start to understand there are different kinds of suffering and therefore different ways to respond to suffering.

One of the most misused New Testament passages in the midst of suffering is Matthew 16:24, "Then Jesus told his disciples, 'If anyone would come after me, let him deny himself and take up his cross and follow me.'" We have all heard people refer to some kind of suffering they were enduring as "the cross they were bearing." Most of the time this is a misuse of this passage and a misunderstanding of the source and cause of their suffering. It assumes that all suffering is the same and that God has brought it upon them to bear up under. Taking up our cross primarily refers to our identification with Christ and His mission. It refers to our calling and purpose in life as we submit our will to the Father's will. The cross of our Lord does not just represent the suffering of our Lord, but also the victory He won. Suffering is an unavoidable life experience, but Jesus has given us power and authority to battle it by faith. Our spiritual life will experience great confusion if we are not able to distinguish between the different kinds of suffering so we know what spiritual promises to harness as we engage the suffering.

The Bible distinguishes between different kinds of suffering. Often the tendency is to combine all suffering into one category, but this adversely affects how we respond to and understand suffering. If we do not understand the different kinds of suffering and the right biblical approach to deal with the suffering our relationship with God and understanding of His promises will be confused, and our understanding and experience of prosperity will be radically confused.

Ultimately, all suffering is a result of sin, but there are different kinds of suffering for different circumstances. There are seven main kinds of suffering revealed within the Bible that we will look at within this chapter. Many of these different forms of suffering can overlap with each other in certain life circumstances, but they can also stand alone.

The seven kinds of suffering we will look at are:

- Suffering as a result of sin
- Suffering as a result of the Father's discipline
- Suffering as a result of injustice
- Suffering as a result of demonic activity
- Suffering as a result of persecution
- Suffering as a result of divine judgment
- Suffering as a result of divine mystery

Suffering as a Result of Sin

We have already covered much of this in a previous chapter, but here is a quick summary. All suffering is ultimately a result of sin. And sin begins with believing a lie of the devil. When we come into agreement with a lie it puts us in bondage and can open us to a demonic stronghold. We live in a fallen world that is experiencing the destructive consequences of sin, which first took place in Satan's heart then in Adam and Eve's heart and now in every human heart.

We live in a culture today that is growing in its denial that there are consequences to our actions and responsibilities tied to our actions. This progressive agenda that is being taught in our education system and promoted in political arenas is counter to clear biblical teaching. This agenda is not primarily a political agenda but a demonic agenda that is destructively impacting the emotional and spiritual health of our society. Satan is the father of lies and the great deceiver who in this modern era has successfully cloaked his very existence from the secular mind and even some religious minds. He has also been successful in clouding the thinking of many believers and churches when it comes to understanding the role of sin our lives. God's Word is clear that there are consequences for our sin in this life as well as eternal consequences. The good news of the Gospel of Jesus Christ is that Jesus has paid the highest price to cover the eternal consequences of our sin so we can live forever with Him. However, this does not mean that we are saved from the consequences of our sins in our present life. For example, if a husband gives into the temptation of pornography, but confesses it and repents, God will forgive him. However, that husband will suffer the immediate consequences of his wife's broken heart and mistrust that he will have to earn back through vulnerability and faithfulness.

Proverbs 16:18 says, "Pride goes before destruction, and a haughty spirit before a fall." Pride is at the root of all sin. It is basically imposing one's will over God's will. It is at the root of Satan's fall and his attack on Adam and Eve in the garden. Pride puts us in opposition to God and God in opposition to us. 1 Peter 5:5 says, "…God opposes the proud, but gives grace to the humble." Pride manifests itself in many different forms of sin. Pride manifests itself in sexual immorality. Behind all the different aspects of sexual immorality is a prideful belief that we can do whatever we want with our body and that we are not accountable to the One who created our body. This reveals a great arrogance in the face of the facts that we had nothing to do with our existence, DNA or personality. All forms of sexual immorality can cause great suffering. Emotional despair, relational trauma, dysfunctional family life, devastated community and a host terrible sicknesses and diseases are just a few of the forms of suffering that result from the sin of sexual immorality.

Another way pride manifests itself is in how we view our time. Pride says, "I am going to do what I want with my time." This prideful attitude is revealed in primarily one of two ways. A person either gets caught up seeking the things of the world, "the desires of the flesh, and the desires of the eyes and pride of life," (1John 2:16) or they get consumed with laziness. Great suffering is inflicted upon society and the world when people love the world and pursue the things of the world. (1 John 2:15-17) Many forms of anxiety, worry and diseases go with those going strong after the world and what it has to offer. The fruit of the Spirit of love, joy and peace are not possible in a life caught up in pursing the prosperity offered by the world.

Laziness is a sin. It is one that is not talked about very much, but it creates all kinds of suffering in the individual, family and society. Laziness can bring a destructive spirit of poverty over whole generations and people groups. Poverty is not more holy than wealth as has been asserted at various times throughout Christian history. Laziness and the poverty that comes with it is not necessarily the result of injustice and oppression. Stephen Adei, an African biblical scholar, distinguishes between the poverty that emerges from a failure of hard work and the poverty that emerges from oppression:

> "Poverty is a recurring theme in the Bible. It is also the experience of many Africans, for half of those in sub-Saharan Africa live on less than US $1.00 a day. Many are poor because they live in a world where injustice and a skewed economic order mean they lack access to education, land and other

means of improving their material conditions (Jas 5:1-6). Nowhere do the Scriptures equate material poverty and piety, and Christians must work to remove the barriers that prevent people from escaping from poverty (Lev 25:38-55; Luke 3:10-14; 18:22; Col. 4:1)…The Bible does, however, speak harshly to those who are poor because they have not used their God-given mind, strength and resources. Laziness or slothfulness are condemned…Those who work hard, learn a trade, improve their knowledge and skills, are entrepreneurial, learn to save and invest small amounts, and who are faithful to God are often able to improve their material conditions (Prov 21:5).[xxvi]

African scholar Ogbu Kalu has written that although Pentecostals can fall prey to predatory forms of heath and wealth gospel, that their refusal of the "verdict of poverty" has by and large been beneficial to the African nations.

"Pentecostals conscientize the individual to fight back, to refuse to accept defeat, want, failure and pessimism or negativity. This would make the person in the image of the rulers and controllers of wealth. In the Bible, Jabez, among others, refused to accept defeat and cried to the Lord, worked hard to reverse the verdict of poverty. The contours of the prosperity genre do not bear much repetition; suffice it to say that it does not teach the individual that he should not apply managerial techniques or not to work hard; much to the contrary these self-help aids are taught at special seminars during outreaches…It is not a 'crossless' Christianity but refuses to idolize suffering. Quite often, the discussion on why certain prayers are not answered, leads back to sin and the patience taught by suffering. However, as the movement broadened, some preachers, in the heat of competition, have moved into positive thinking, urging members to repeat certain laws or principles and 'claim'".[xxvii]

Sin in our lives and in the world always brings about suffering in one form or another. It is a lie to believe that our sin only affects us. At the root of sin is a pride that basically believes that we can acquire a more prosperous life doing things our way rather than submitting to God's will and ways.

Suffering as a Result of the Father's Discipline

There is a suffering that is very personal for those who are followers of Jesus. This suffering results from sin, but is specifically brought on believers by our loving heavenly Father as discipline so that we will turn back to Him from our wicked ways. The writer of Hebrews quotes Proverbs 3:11-12 in Hebrews 12:5-10;

> "My son, do not regard lightly the discipline of the Lord, nor be weary when reproved by him. For the Lord disciplines the one he loves, and chastises every son whom he receives. It is for discipline that you have to endure. God is treating you as sons. For what son is there whom his father does not discipline? If you are left without discipline, in which all have participated, then you are illegitimate children and not sons. Besides this, we have had earthly fathers who disciplined us and we respected them. Shall we not much more be subject to the Father of spirits and live? For they disciplined us for a short time as it seemed best to them, but he disciplines us for our good, that we may share his holiness."

Our heavenly Father disciplines us because He loves us. A father who does not discipline his children does not love them. Discipline is a sign of love. Unfortunately, many Americans today believe that if you love you won't be corrective. The social progressive message today is that the opposite of love is correction, when in reality the opposite of love is indifference. Loving correction actually reveals the heart of the Father for the good of His children. Also, our heavenly Father disciplines us because He desires "that we may share his holiness." What an amazing truth about the heart of our heavenly Father, that He wants us to be like Him and to share His holiness. Sin is not compatible with holiness. The Father sent Jesus to take care of our sin problem so we could be like Him. This is why the writer of Hebrews exhorts us to,

> "Consider him who endured from sinners such hostility against himself, so that you may not grow weary or fainthearted. In your struggle against sin you have not yet resisted to the point of shedding your blood…Therefore lift your drooping hands and strengthen your weak knees, and make straight paths for your feet, so that what is lame may not be put out of joint but rather be healed." (Hebrews 12:3-4, 12-13)

Anytime a believer enters into a time of suffering and it is revealed to them by conviction that their suffering is a result of their sin they are to go to prayer and confess their sin. They are also to take action to end the sin immediately so that the healing process can begin and the suffering can end. James also exhorts believers who are sick and suffering and cannot get breakthrough to come to the elders of the church for prayer.

> "Is anyone among you suffering? Let him pray. Is anyone cheerful? Let him sing praise. Is anyone among you sick? Let him call the elders of the church, and let them pray over him, anointing him with oil in the name of the Lord. And the prayer

> of faith will save the one who is sick, and the Lord will raise him up. And if he has committed sins, he will be forgiven. Therefore, confess your sins to one another and pray for one another that you may be healed. The prayer of a righteous person has great power as it is working." (James 5:13-16)

Another place we can see the Father's discipline of His children is in how we partake of the Lord's Supper. As we said before sin is not compatible with holiness. And partaking of the Lord's Supper is far from just a symbolic Christian ritual. It is an active participation with Jesus and His Body the Church. It is not just a remembering of what Christ did for us, but it is a time of making sure that we are not participating in sin. This is proven by the severity of the consequences of not taking the Lord's Supper seriously. The exhortation to the Church in 1 Corinthians 11:27-32 has been overlooked by much of the church today.

> "Whoever, therefore, eats the bread or drinks the cup of the Lord in an unworthy manner will be guilty concerning the body and blood of the Lord. Let a person examine himself, then, and so eat of the bread and drink of the cup. For anyone who eats and drinks without discerning the body eats and drinks judgment on himself. That is why many of you are weak and ill, and some have died. But if we judged ourselves truly, we would not be judged. But when we are judged by the Lord, we are disciplined so that we may not be condemned along with the world."

So, we can see that the discipline of the Father here for His children who were not properly examining their lives is that some of them were experiencing weakness, illnesses and some even had died. But again, God's grace is available if His children will receive the conviction of the Holy Spirit and repent they will be forgiven their sins and experience healing. (Ja 5:13-16) It is important to understand that not all weakness and sickness that a believer experiences is the discipline of our Father for specific disobedience. All suffering that we experience in this life is used by the Father to refine us, strengthen us and in a general sense discipline us to share His holiness. Hebrews 12:11 is just as applicable for when we are suffering the consequences of discipline for specific sin as it is for when we are suffering for other reasons. Suffering in general is to be seen as a discipline.

> "For the moment, all discipline seems painful rather than pleasant, but later it yields the peaceful fruit of righteousness to those who have been trained by it."

Suffering as a Result of Injustice

Another form of suffering that is revealed in the scriptures is suffering as a result of oppression and injustice. This kind of suffering takes many different forms, but a common theme is that its various forms disproportionately affect the poor. The poor lack resources and education to be able to contend with corruption, oppression, and injustice. God has made all human beings in His image, therefore He is concerned with justice for those least likely to receive it; the poor, widows, orphans, and aliens. All through Deuteronomy (chapters 12-26) we can see a system designed to abolish every form of oppression. The phrase "remember that you were slaves in Egypt" recurs throughout the text as a reminder to keep God's commands. This is to remind the Israelites that since they were delivered from oppression they should not oppress others.

Another form of injustice that the Bible mentions is that of human trafficking. The scope and depravity of this tragedy are immense. Present day human trafficking is facilitated by criminal networks that are able to exercise tremendous coercive power over their victims. Louise Shelley who is an international expert on human trafficking writes,

> "The international links of the traffickers allow them to deploy violence at all stages of their network. Their ability to intimidate both the victim and the family at home differentiates contemporary trafficking from the slave trade of earlier centuries. Victim's compliance is achieved by threatening family members. The threats against loved ones are not idle but are often carried out, adding veracity to the traffickers' words 'If you do not do what we want, we will hurt your family.'"[xxviii]

Matthew K. Daniel draws attention to God's heart for the trafficked in Scripture and connects it to present efforts to liberate and give hope to victims of trafficking:

> "The Bible includes instances of slavery and trafficking. Joseph was sold as a slave to the Ishmaelites (Gen. 37:28). Naaman's servant girl was trafficked and worked as domestic help (2 Kgs 5:2). Daniel and his friends were also trafficked (Dan. 1:3-6). In each case, the context and purpose for the trafficking were different. The prevalence of slavery and such trafficking in biblical times necessitated laws that God's people should follow. The OT law commanded God's people to protect the widow and the fatherless – that is, the people who are vulnerable (Exod. 22:21-23). When Christ came, he said that he had been sent to free the captives (Luke 4:18). We are called to follow in his steps. We should be salt and light and should work to release the oppressed by delivering them from physical captivity, breaking their shackles of shame, and welcoming them with love. Our calling is to offer them physical, emotional, and spiritual freedom. We must reach out to them with the news that God can bless them with a new identity, a future of hope and eternal life'."[xxix]

Injustice is a consequence of our fallen world. It is the result of mankind taking justice into its own hands and thinking they can best determine what is right and wrong without God. Throughout history when authority and power have been misused great injustice has come to masses of people. And the suffering that results from that injustice is often hopeless poverty and radical oppression.

Social justice issues are very popular today. The millennial generation has been called the mercy generation and has taken up many social justice causes. This is a good thing, but the Church must be careful that it does not fade into a social gospel where social activism overrides gospel mission. Social justice should be a result of the Church's gospel mission in the world not the mission itself. We have to ask the question, "Did Jesus come to bring social justice or spiritual justice primarily? Where do we see Jesus or Paul work to combat and change the cultural structures that promoted injustice? They loved and transformed individual people and called them into a new community called the Church, which modeled social justice within the fellowship and outside into the community. The Church is to empower marketplace believers to bring social justice into the marketplace and to the ends of earth, but this should not be removed from the greater mission of spiritual justice. In some places in the world the social justice involvement is an inroad into the planting of churches that can carry on the gospel mission of spiritual justice. Real lasting transformation only occurs when the heart is genuinely transformed not just the physical circumstances.

Suffering as a Result of Demonic Activity

Most Christians in the world are much more in tune with the unseen realm in their interpretations of reality than western Christians. They are much closer to the world of the gospels than are most western Christians. Kwame Bediako recounts a story told by the theologian John Mbiti about an African scholar who spent ten years learning theology in the west and finally achieved his doctorate. In that time he learned ancient languages and carefully studied Bultmann and Tillich. When he returned to his village he found his older sister possessed by a demon, and the villagers were all looking to him for help. Mbiti recounts his experience:

> He looks around. Slowly he goes to get Bultmann (German liberal Theologian) and reads again about spirit possession in the New Testament. Of course he gets his answer: Bultmann has demythologized it (that is, according to Bultmann such things do not exist in reality). He insists that his sister is not possessed. The people shout, 'Help your sister; she is possessed!' He shouts back, 'But Bultmann has demythologized demon possession' (it does not exist)."[xxx]

Regardless of the West's primarily materialistic worldview and liberal theological interpretation, the primary worldview of the Bible is one of spiritual warfare. Much suffering in this world comes directly from demonic influence and attack. This was prophesied in the beginning when God decreed over the ancient serpent who deceived Adam and Eve, that from that time forward there would be war between the child of the devil and the children of God. In Genesis 3:15, God tells Satan, "I will put enmity between you and the woman, and between your offspring and her offspring; he shall bruise your head and you shall bruise his heel."

One of the most graphic examples of suffering due to demonic attack is the story of Job. In Job's life we can see that demonic activity was directly behind invading armies, loss of land, loss of material possessions, murder and the weather.

In the New Testament we can see many instances where suffering was caused directly by demonic activity. The suffering caused by demonic activity in the New Testament includes spiritual, emotional and physical suffering and adversely impacts individuals, families, communities and whole geographic regions.[xxxi] Jesus said in John 10:10 about the work of the devil, "The thief comes only to steal and kill and destroy."

Suffering as a Result of Persecution

Most of the suffering passages in the New Testament deal with suffering specifically as a result of being persecuted as a follower of Jesus Christ. It is misleading when these verses are applied to other areas of suffering. The New Testament speaks about a suffering that Christians are called to bear patiently and even consider it blessed to have suffered for the name of Jesus. Paul describes this kind of suffering as the gift of suffering for the sake of Christ (Phil 1:29-30) and Peter describes it as suffering for the name or suffering as a Christian (1 Peter 4:14, 16). This suffering comes because the world, which loves evil, despises Jesus and therefore also hates the bearers of the message of Christ. Jesus says in John 15:18, "If the world hates you, keep in mind that it hated me first." The suffering that is brought on by faithful witness to Christ and the modeling of Christian community to which the gospel gives birth is the kind of suffering that Christians should not only bear patiently and without complaint, but should also see as necessary to the Christian life.

One passage that is routinely cited in favor of the position that all suffering should be dealt with equally by Christians is Rom. 8:17, in which Paul says that it is necessary for heirs of Christ to "suffer with him in order that we also may be glorified with him." Douglas Moo has influentially argued that this passage should be understood comprehensively, as encompassing "the whole gamut of suffering, including things such as illness, bereavement, hunger, financial reverses, and death itself."[xxxii] Moo's interpretation of v. 17 downplays the fact that Paul provides the interpretation of the verse later in the same passage, in v. 35. In context, it is clear that in v. 17 Paul sees his own suffering for the name as a model of the way in which the Christian community must suffer for the name.

James D.G. Dunn has argued, the list in v. 35 "is not a mere literary form but is a firsthand expression of Paul's own experience…he naturally saw his experience as typical for all his fellow believers."[xxxiii] The Christian community in Rome should be prepared to suffer for the name of Christ, in other words, just as Paul has. It is in this way that Paul admonishes the Corinthians to imitate him as he imitates Christ (1 Cor. 4:16; 11:1).

This interpretation of the suffering in view in 8:17 is bolstered by its similarity to Phil. 1:29-30. He commends suffering for the name to the Philippians in v. 29, and then he makes clear that they are "engaged in the same conflict" that Paul himself continues to endure. It is clear in this passage that Paul does not mean that the Philippians should endure suffering in general for the sake of Christ, but only suffering that is due to their confession of Christ, just as Paul himself has.

Gordon Fee is helpful for understanding Paul's logic in this passage: "what Paul is not doing is offering encouragement to believers about suffering in general….here he is speaking specifically of their living for Christ in a world that is openly hostile to God and resistant to his love lavished on them in Christ."[xxxiv] The structural similarity between Phil. 1:29-30 and 8:17, coupled with the interpretation that Paul himself gives of v. 17 in v. 35, make it very likely that he is only referring to suffering on behalf of the Messiah in that passage.

So, suffering as a result of persecution is specifically suffering for Jesus and His mission. It is the suffering that comes with living on mission for Christ and a willingness to walk alongside people and bear their burdens that they may be set free from the bonds of the evil one.

Suffering as a Result of Divine Judgment

God is perfect therefore He is perfectly just. And to be just He must execute divine judgment. There are clear instances in the Bible where God declares for one reason or another that He is bringing divine judgment because of the sin of individuals or whole nations. The first great judgment we see within the scriptures is God's judgment upon the devil and Adam and Eve.

Then we see God's great judgment in the worldwide flood. (Genesis 6) Soon after the flood we can see God's divine judgment again when He scatters the nations and divides the languages at the tower of Babel. (Genesis 11) Throughout the rest of the Old Testament we can see God's divine judgment upon the nation Israel and upon other nations.

In chapter 18 of Jeremiah, verses 7-10, God states that He will bring divine judgment on any nation that continues to do evil in His sight, but will relent if that nation turns from its evil.

> If at any time I declare concerning a nation or a kingdom, that I will pluck up and break down and destroy it, and if that nation, concerning which I have spoken, turns from its evil, I will relent of the disaster that I intended to do to it. And if at any time I declare concerning a nation or a kingdom that I will build and plant it, and if it does evil in my sight, not listening to my voice, then I will relent of the good that I had intended to do to it.

Great care needs to be applied when we communicate the reality of divine judgment. It is clearer to state that God is working out His judgments in history rather than to try and identify when in fact such a judgment has occurred, unless it is specifically referred to within the scriptures. Attempts to identify certain historical events as divine judgment have to come with great care for they can ruin the Christian witness if they are misapplied.

The entire book of Revelation speaks of God's coming final judgment and wrath upon the world. There is clearly a difference between God's judgment upon believers and non-believers. 2 Corinthians 5:10 speaks of the judgment that all believers will experience, "For we must all appear before the judgment seat of Christ, so that each one may receive what is due for what he has done in the body, whether good or evil."

The judgment of believers is a judgment of our stewardship, which will result in different levels of reward and responsibility in the future kingdom. Many of Jesus' kingdom parables reveal this judgment. The parable of the talents is one example as recorded in Matthew 25:14-30. Also, the parable of the ten minas as recorded in Luke 19:11-27, reveals that authority and responsibility will be rewarded to those faithful servants of Christ at His coming. Each of these parables also reveals the wrath of God toward those who rejected the reign of His Son in their lives. Revelation 20:11-15 speaks about the Great White Throne judgment where believers are judged for their stewardship and unbelievers judged for their unbelief, which results in the second death and the lake of fire.

In practice it is nearly impossible to distinguish divine judgment from suffering as a result of divine mystery, which we will deal with next. Many who suffer when a divine judgment is executed are not directly involved in the sins that gave rise to the judgment but experience suffering as a result of Divine Mystery.

Suffering as Divine Mystery

The last kind of suffering we see within the Scriptures is suffering as a result of divine mystery. This is suffering that is humanly unexplainable and does not fall within one of the previous categories of suffering. This kind of suffering is not brought about by personal sin, though it is a consequence of sin in the world. One of its forms occurs when the righteous suffer unjustly while the wicked flourish. The Psalms in particular talk about this kind of suffering. They teach us that the proper response to this kind of suffering is the practice of patience while building our faith and expectation on the promises of God.

In the midst of unexplainable suffering we are to express our anger, confusion, and sadness to God, and to remind Him and ourselves of His promises to His people. The Psalms are full of complaints to the Lord and anguished confessions of His seeming absence. Psalm 22, which Jesus cried from the cross, and Psalm 88 offer some of the most dire outbursts of lament in the Psalms. The practice of lament, is something that needs to be recovered today among believers, but it also needs to be understood better. The biblical practice of lamenting is not an attitude of hopelessness or doubt. It is a place of faith that deals with the harsh realities in our lives when we are not experiencing the peace and promises of God. It is taking a stand on God's Word and Jesus' work on the cross in the midst of spiritual warfare and calling upon God to act on our behalf or others according to His promises.

These lament Psalms also teach us, as Augustine Pagolu says, "mere experience can lead to faulty perceptions of reality." When we live only according to what we see and experience, we come to doubt that the scriptural promises are trustworthy. It looks as though wickedness pays off. But the Psalms remind us that although God delays His justice, sometimes in order to allow the wicked time to repent (e.g. Ezekiel 18:23), but at other times for reasons that we frankly are not permitted to know (Isaiah 55:6-9), He will ultimately carry it out. Pagolu writes in response to Psalm 73 that,

> This lesson is particularly important for us in South Asia, where corruption flourishes and the righteous often struggle while those who lie, exploit and oppress seem to thrive....The psalmist had been feeling that he was weak and insecure, standing on slippery ground (73:1-3) whereas the wicked were strong and secure (73:4-12). But now he realizes that it is in fact the wicked who are on *slippery ground* (73:18). They are the ones who are weak and insecure while he is secure and strong with the Lord at his side. The psalmist recognizes that at any moment the wicked can be *cast* down *to ruin*. Their position is precarious as their power and prestige can disappear instantly in the face of *terrors*...We have all seen this happen! A politician or leader of industry may wield power one day, and on the next they are *destroyed* and are only

dimly remembered, rather like a bad *dream* (73:19-20). True, some may remain arrogantly self-satisfied throughout their lives, but when the Lord arises in judgment they will be despised and rejected, banned forever from his presence. They will have no more ultimate substance or power than a fantasy...When he sees the wicked from the Lord's perspective, the psalmist admits that his previous attitude was *senseless*. In his self-pity and bitterness, he had behaved like a *brute beast* towards God (73:21-2). He chooses strong words to describe himself to emphasize his stupidity. Yet, despite his previous attitude, he is sure of God's presence. God remains *always* at his side and holds him by the *right hand* (73:23; Ps. 23). Neither his difficulties nor his attitudes can separate him from God's care (Rom. 8:38-39).[xxxv]

According to Pagolu, the Psalms invite us in the midst of dark, mysterious suffering to practice patience and wait upon God and view the situation from God's perspective. God sees the suffering of the righteous and the flourishing of the wicked, and He knows when and how justice will be distributed.

A darker form of mysterious suffering, however, is an encounter with the power of death, which Paul describes in 1 Corinthians 15. This is the power that takes infants from their parents at a tender age and that allows entire villages to be demolished by tsunamis and earthquakes. Tom Long suggests that we distinguish between "small-d" death, our personal deaths, which are ultimately a consequence of sin, but which can be merciful when a believer is beset by sickness and advanced age, and "capital-D" death, which is a demonic force at work in the world. Long writes that

> Capital-D Death is a very different reality from small-*d* death. It comes toward us never as a friend but as an alien and destructive force. There is nothing natural about it. It is our enemy, and it is God's enemy; indeed, Paul calls it 'the last enemy'

(1 Cor. 15:26). Death in this form is out to steal life from human beings, but it does not stop with individuals. Death wants to capture territory, to possess principalities. It desires to dehumanize all institutions, poison all relationships, set people against people in warfare, replace all love with hate, transform all words of hope into blasphemy, to fuel the fires of distrust, to lead people to the depths of despair, to shatter all attempts to build community, and to make a mockery of God, faith, and the gift of life. It is 'the pestilence that stalks in darkness' and 'the destruction that wastes at noonday' (Psa. 91:6). [xxxvi]

We do not know the reasons why God allows this kind of suffering to occur in the world. What we can rest in is that God will make it all right in the end. Death and darkness will be excluded entirely from His kingdom (Isa. 9-11; Rev. 21-2). The consummation of the kingdom will mean that heaven has come to earth, and the will of God is done on earth as in heaven. God through Jesus has conquered the power of death, so mysterious suffering will be removed forever from the experience of the redeemed. In the interim, however, we are told that we must exercise patience and wait on the deliverance of the Lord. Patience, indeed, is central to the New Testament. It has been argued by Hans Urs von Balthasar that it is the most important virtue in Scripture:

> Hence the importance of patience in the New Testament, which becomes the basic constituent of Christianity, more central even than humility: the power to wait, to persevere, to hold out, to endure to the end, not to transcend one's own limitations, not to force issues by playing the hero or the titan, but to practice the virtue that lies beyond heroism, the meekness of the lamb which is led.[xxxvii]

Probably the greatest example of patience in the midst of mysterious suffering is Job. Even after the destruction of his property, children and his own health, we see the power of Job's patience and perseverance through the mystery. The New Testament in James 5:11, commends Job for his steadfastness in the midst of mysterious suffering. But it also reveals those who are patient and faithful will see the purposes of the Lord.

The word "mystery" in the Scriptures does not mean something that stays hidden from God's people. It represents God's divine plan that His children by faith can and should gain more revelation and understanding about. This is what Jesus meant in John 15 when He said to His disciples that He no longer calls them servants but friends so that they can know what the Father is doing. Jesus also promised in Matthew 7:7-8, "Ask, and it will be given to you; seek, and you will find; knock, and it will be opened to you. For everyone who asks receives, and the one who seeks finds, and to the one who knocks it will be opened."

John 9 records a story about a man born blind. Why he was born blind and suffered for many years remained a mystery until he encountered Jesus and the disciples asked Jesus why he was born blind. Jesus' answer in John 9:3 is very insightful for us as we encounter suffering as a result of divine mystery, "Jesus answered, 'It was not that this man sinned, or his parents, but that the works of God might be displayed in him.'"

The works of God that Jesus was talking about were first the man's physical healing and then the man's testimony of healing by Jesus.

Although we do not understand God's purposes and plans in the midst of mysterious suffering, we can by faith and patience seek understanding. Ultimately, we can take great comfort that nothing is a mystery to God and that He will remove all kinds of suffering from His kingdom He is preparing for those who know Him.

Here is a summary from this chapter of some key aspects to a biblical understanding of suffering and the spiritual realm:

1.) All suffering is ultimately a result of sin and its rebellion against God.

2.) Suffering as a result of the Father's discipline is unique for those who know Jesus and used to turn them from disobedience back to the Father's heart.

3.) Suffering as a result of injustice is caused by the fallen state of humanity that takes justice into its own hands disregarding God and His ways.

4.) Suffering as a result of demonic activity includes spiritual, emotional and physical suffering and adversely impacts individuals, families, communities and whole geographic regions.

5.) Suffering as a result of persecution is a unique form of suffering that only followers of Jesus experience because the world and the devil hate God's people.

6.) Suffering as a result of divine judgment is because God is perfect and will bring judgment on all sin and rebellion.

7.) Suffering as a result of divine mystery requires trust and patience in God's sovereignty and His willingness to give revelation and understanding to those who seek Him.

CHAPTER EIGHT
Big "S" and Little "s" Suffering

Life is full of seasons of suffering. They are unavoidable. How we handle them and what we do with them is critical. Seasons of suffering test our faith. They are the refining fire of our faith to test its genuineness and to strengthen it. Seasons of suffering often are intimately associated with the different seasons of our life. There are certain sufferings that are a part of specific seasons of our life and there are other sufferings that can come upon us in any season like sickness or financial struggles. There are different levels of suffering from trauma and grief to sickness and sadness. A season of suffering is not one traumatic event, though that event could lead us into a season of suffering. A season of suffering is an extended time in our life where we are specifically struggling with certain issues. It is how we apply our faith and walk through these different seasons, which help form the person we become.

My early childhood was fairly idyllic, as far as I can remember. My earliest season of suffering was a year and a half period of time in Middle School during the period of time when the government experimented with busing kids from one part of town to join kids from another part of town. It was a war zone of fighting and racism. I was jumped while walking home from school and pulverized several times. It was hard to make friends, but the Lord was gracious to me and provided two African American brothers Gerald and Darrell who befriended me, otherwise I am not sure I would have made it through that season. Most people have experienced a season of suffering of some kind in their adolescent years especially if there is the trauma of having to move to a different community or state during those years. Other seasons of suffering in my life included my mother's battle with cancer, romantic and emotional struggles, vocational restlessness, seasons of grief, loss and failure, seasons of marital and parenting struggles, seasons of questioning calling, seasons of spiritual dryness and loss of zeal. The list could go on and on. We all have our unique stories and our unique seasons of suffering which help form who we are becoming.

We cannot begin to understand suffering and the seasons of our suffering without understanding the difference between little "s" suffering and big "S" suffering. Possibly the greatest barrier to our proper understanding of suffering is our lack of understanding this important distinction.

> Big "S" suffering is the suffering believers are uniquely called to share in as followers of Christ. Little "s" suffering is the suffering shared by all mankind that believers are called to fight against by faith.

We must understand that to follow Jesus we are to share in His sufferings, which means we are to enter into a lifetime season of big "S" suffering where we are to take up our cross and follow Him (Matt 16:24) and by faith fight the world of little "s" suffering. We cannot truly "Count it all joy…when we meet trials of various kinds" (James 1:2) if we do not first understand what Jesus meant in Matthew 5:10-11, "Blessed are those who are persecuted for righteousness' sake, for theirs is the kingdom of heaven. Blessed are you when others revile you and persecute you and utter all kinds of evil against you falsely on my account." This by no means is a minimizing of the gravity and trauma of the little "s" suffering that people go through in the world. It is however, a magnifying of the big "S" suffering that Jesus went through because of His love for the world and His desire to end once and for all the source of suffering and bring freedom.

In this chapter, we will define what big "S" suffering and what little "s" suffering are and how they work together with faith to promote the mission of Christ in the world and bring the power of the Holy Spirit to fight suffering in the world.

The Sufferings of Christ We Are to Share In: Big "S" Suffering

Things radically change when we get more interested in God than self. Our life begins to be reoriented from the kingdom of this world to the kingdom of God. Our heart begins to enlarge for the things of God and our eyes begin to see beyond the material into the spiritual. It usually takes a lifetime of different seasons of suffering to help us in this glorious transformation. C.S. Lewis has said that suffering "plants the flag of truth within the fortress of a rebel soul."[xxxviii] Different seasons of suffering challenge our philosophical commitments and our worldview. We all have a fortress we have built around our rebel soul. This fortress consists of protective walls we have raised because of deep hurts, bad habits and lingering hang-ups. We all come into this world with a rebel soul. A soul that naturally is guided by its own desires over those of its Creator. Suffering will either result in the fortifying of our fortress or a surrendering to the flag of truth planted by the Gospel deep inside our soul. Suffering can help us surrender the priority of self-interest and embrace the priority of God-interest. Our rebel soul begins its journey of freedom as we become more interested in God than self. When the flag of truth takes root inside our soul the Holy Spirit takes over and our heart begins to transform as we get the heart of the Father for the lost and broken in the world.

The call to follow Jesus is a call to big "S" suffering. Big "S" suffering is being more interested in God than self. It is a surrender of self to the grand purpose and plan of God in this world. It is an embracing of the heart of the Father for the lost and broken-hearted in the world. Big "S" suffering is a denial of the idea that we can pick and choose our theology to fit our self-interests. Matthew 16:24-25 states, "Then Jesus told his disciples, 'If anyone would come after me, let him deny himself and take up his cross and follow me. For whoever would save his life will lose it, but whoever loses his life for my sake will find it."

Following Jesus was never to be just about saying a prayer or making a decision for Jesus. It was never to be just trying to do the right thing or sin-management. Following Jesus was never to be just about denominational affiliation or catechism or baptism. Following Jesus is about embracing the saving grace of Jesus and surrendering self to the cause of Christ in this world. It is about a willingness to share in the sufferings of Jesus so those in darkness can experience the eternal prosperity of the Father.

We can see from Paul's life what this denial of self and taking up our cross looks like. In Act 9:15-16 Jesus told the disciple Ananias to speak this prophecy over Paul: "Go, for he is a chosen instrument of mine to carry my name before the Gentiles and kings and the children of Israel. For I will show him how much he must suffer for the sake of my name."

Obviously, this is a personal calling over Paul's life and not every follower of Christ is called to the same level of suffering as Paul, but every believer is called to share in Christ's sufferings. Paul makes this very clear in Romans 8:16-17, "The Spirit himself bears witness with our spirit that we are children of God, and if children, then heirs – heirs of God and fellow heirs with Christ, provided *we suffer with him* in order that we may be glorified with him."

Paul is describing here big "S" suffering that any follower of Jesus must understand and be willing to share in. In several other verses Paul and Peter mention this sharing in the sufferings of Jesus.[xxxix] In Philippians chapter three Paul longs to "share his sufferings." And in Colossians 1:24-24 he states,

"Now I rejoice in my sufferings for your sake, and in my flesh I am filling up what is lacking in Christ's afflictions for the sake of his body, that is, the church, of which I became a minister according to the stewardship from God that was given to me for you, to make the word of God fully known."

These all refer to big "S" suffering that Jesus referred to in the sermon on the mount where the blessed are those who suffer for His name. We need to define clearly from Jesus' life what the sufferings of Christ are that we are to share in before we can effectively engage all other forms of suffering. Little "s" suffering consumes us when we are not more interested in God than self and clouds our ability to embrace big "S" suffering. So, what is big "S" suffering that we are to share with Christ? It is to embrace His heart and mission for the world and a willingness to share in everything that comes with that. He didn't call people into sharing disease, oppression and poverty. He called us to fight those things with the power of the Spirit as He did. In Acts 5:41, we see the apostles "rejoicing that they were counted worthy to suffer dishonor for the name." This is part of big "S" suffering. Here is a brief summary of some of the big "S" sufferings that Jesus calls us to share with Him as we join Him on His mission:

- Ridicule for preaching the gospel of the kingdom (Mt 5:10-12; 24:9-14)
- Compassion for the helpless and harassed (Mt 9:35-37)
- Anguish over the state of people's souls (Lk 19:41; Jn 11:35)
- Heal the sick, raise the dead, cleanse the lepers, cast out demons (Mt 10:8)
- Comfort the brokenhearted (Jn 11)
- Care for the affliction of the poor, orphan, widow and prisoner (Lk 4:18-19; Ja 1:27; Ps 68:5-6; Ps 102:20; Isa 61:1-2)
- Deliver the demonized (Mt 10:1; Mk 5:1-20; Lk 10:17-20)

- Bring wholeness to fragmented sexual lives (Jn 4:1-45; Jn 8:1-11)
- Make disciples and plant multiplying churches (Mt 16:18; 28:18-20; Mk 3:13-14)
- Prayer and vision for the local and global (Acts 1:8)
- Willingness to prioritize Christ's mission over building a home, portfolio or career (Mt 8:20; Lk 12:13-21)
- Willingness to sacrifice time, agenda and sleep to minister to people's needs (Mt 8:14-17)
- Disciplined time of prayer and fasting with the Father when the world is sleeping and feasting (Mk 1:35; Lk 6:12)
- Willingness to suffer physical persecution for His name (Matt 5:10-12)
- Willingness to glorify God even in death (Jn 17:1-5; Phil 1:20-21, 3:10)

This is not the Christianity that is being preached or taught primarily in America today, but it is the Christianity of the New Testament. This is what Jesus meant when He asked those who wanted to follow Him to count the cost before starting the journey. The chasm between this brief list and how most believers in America see the Christian life is alarmingly wide. I believe this chasm helps explain why so many believers are stuck in their walk with God because of some little "s" suffering. Without understanding Big "S" suffering we cannot have a proper understanding of little "s" suffering and we will tend to embrace little "s" suffering rather than fight it with the spiritual weapons God has given us. We will work out the practical workings of this in the next section of the book.

When we take an honest look at our lives and what consumes most of our time here in America we are often consumed with self and our little "s" sufferings rather than engaging the little "s" sufferings of the world with the power of the Holy Spirit. We will now look at just what little "s" sufferings are and how we can better approach them.

The Sufferings We Don't Have to Share In: Little "s" sufferings

Many Christians do not realize the spiritual resources available to them to fight off much of the suffering they experience in this world. Many believers approach life and suffering not with an "all things are possible" with God attitude, but with a passive acquiescence to the reality of suffering in their life. Suffering is inevitable in this life, but how we handle it is critical. Without first embracing the big "S" suffering that we are called to in following Jesus, we miss out on the full resources available to us to fight by faith much of the little "s" suffering we experience and others experience.

James 1:2-3 says, "Count it all joy, my brothers, when you meet trials of various kinds, for you know that the testing of your faith produces steadfastness." It is important to understand that all trials can be used to test and strengthen our faith. But all trials are not to be handled the same way. This is why in verse 5 we are told to ask for wisdom from God in how we are to handle different trials. So it is critical to understand the difference between big "S" suffering and little "s" suffering because we are to handle them differently.

James chapter five has some amazing promises and practices that the church should be fully engaged in. In these verses we can see how James makes a differentiation between big "S" suffering and little "s" suffering. James 5:13-18 states,

> [13]"Is anyone among you suffering? Let him pray. Is anyone cheerful? Let him sing praise. [14]Is anyone among you sick? Let him call the elders of the church and let them pray over him, anointing him with oil in the name of the Lord. [15]And the prayer of faith will save the one who is sick, and the Lord will raise him up. And if he has committed sins, he will be forgiven. [16]Therefore, confess your sins to one another and pray for one another, that you

may be healed. The prayer of a righteous person has great power as it is working. [17]Elijah was a man with a nature like ours, and he prayed fervently that it might not rain, and for three years and six months it did not rain on the earth. [18]Then he prayed again, and heaven gave rain, and the earth bore its fruit."

The word for suffering in James 5:13, is the same as in James 5:10 (noun form), "As an example of suffering and patience, brothers, take the prophets who spoke in the name of the Lord," and refers in all other usages in the New Testament to big "S" suffering.[xl] Then in James 5:14 he mentions, "Is anyone among you sick?" The word used here refers to any kind of weakness[xli] but in context here specifically sickness. So James is making a clear distinction here between big "S" suffering in 5:10, 13 and small "s" suffering in 5:14. And he is giving a different approach to the different kinds of suffering. In the midst of big "S" suffering we are to pray, and James here does not elaborate more. But in the midst of sickness, which is just one example of little "s" suffering, James gives clear direction on how we are to handle it within the church. The church and the elders are to harness the power of healing prayer and the forgiveness found in Christ. It is noteworthy to mention that James does not say that the "prayer of faith" might heal the sick person, but that the "prayer of faith will save the one who is sick." The word used here for "save" is the Greek word, "sozo" which is used for salvation and healing. Also, James points out the "great power" of the righteous person's prayer and equates our power in prayer to Elijah's!

The sufferings we do not have to share in are oppression, disease and poverty. That is a big statement so let me explain. Jesus did not suffer from oppression. He came to defeat the works of the devil (1 John 3:8) so we too can walk in emotional and spiritual freedom and battle for other's emotional and spiritual freedom through the power of the Holy Spirit. Jesus did not suffer poverty. He lived a simple life, but was supernaturally provided for (Matt 4:11) as well as supported by the other disciples. (Luke 8:1) He didn't have a home of His own, but was invited into many homes. He gave us an awesome promise in Matt 6:33, "But seek first the kingdom of God and his righteousness, and all these things will be added to you." "All these things" refers to the material provisions talked about in the previous verses of food and clothing. He came to bring this good news to the poor stuck in the bonds of poverty. And He calls His church to preach the good news to the poor and help them out of poverty of soul and body. As far as we know, Jesus never suffered from sickness or disease. This is an argument from silence, but if He did we know nothing about them. What we do know is that He came to take our sicknesses and heal us (Matt 8:17). He poured out His Holy Spirit upon us and commanded us to also heal the sick (Matt 10:7-8).

We live in a fallen world and people do get sick, get diseases, fall into poverty and get oppressed by demons. But Jesus has given us the power of the Holy Spirit and His gifts to battle these little "s" sufferings for the strengthening of faith and freedom. Many have tried to use Paul's thorn in 2 Corinthians 12 to support the idea we are to embrace our small "s" sufferings rather than fight them with faith. Paul was told by God after he repeatedly prayed for healing, "My grace is sufficient." If God similarly tells us in prayer that we will not be healed, then it is a sin for us to keep praying for healing. But Paul's statement is particular and focused on the specific thorn in his flesh. It is not to be turned into a general principle. We know this because the commission to the disciples included the charge to heal the sick (Matt. 10:7-8; Jas. 5:14-15). Some respond that heaven rather than healing is our hope. And if we are going to die of something why keep pressing in for healing? This just reveals a lack of faith and expectation while we are here on earth, and a missing of the sharing in the big "S" sufferings of Christ. We need to learn from Paul's faith and expectation in 2 Corinthians 1:8-11,

> "For we do not want you to be unaware, brothers, of the affliction we experienced in Asia. For we

were so utterly burdened beyond our strength that we despaired of life itself. Indeed, we felt that we had received the sentence of death. But that was to make us rely not on ourselves but on God who raises the dead. He delivered us from such a deadly peril, and he will deliver us. On him we have set our hope that he will deliver us again. You also must help us by prayer, so that many will give thanks on our behalf for the blessing granted us through the prayers of many."

In American Christianity we have not taught people how to die well. The topic of how to die is non-existent within most books on discipleship. American Christianity has adopted more of the American dream of retirement perspective than a biblical perspective on dying well. One of the main reasons for this is a lack of understanding big "S" and small "s" suffering. Part of big "S" suffering as we saw in the previous section is a willingness to glorify God even with our death. When we have this outlook that Jesus and the early church had it sheds a whole new light on how we see and deal with all the different little "s" sufferings that come our way in life. In 2 Corinthians chapter 1, Paul had come to the end of his rope. Death and despair were overshadowing him, but even in this dark state, Paul and his companions held onto their expectation, "that all things are possible with God." They believed that God would deliver them, even if He has to raise them from the dead. So, here is one great example of why we continue to pray for healing even when death is knocking at the door. It is important to understand that this kind of faith and expectation is not possible without first embracing big "S" suffering in our call to live for Christ and His mission. Sometimes we know death is near and it takes spiritual discernment to know how best to release someone in prayer to go home to Jesus. However, our consistent problem in American Christianity is that the physical consequences of aging are too often revealing a weak and inadequate faith, which cannot carry people boldly to finish well for Christ. We will look more at the practical aspects of this in the last section of this book.

Steadfastness in Suffering

Suffering and trials test our faith and produce either doubt or steadfastness. (James 1:2-8) Doubt divides the soul. Steadfastness unites the soul. No one has perfect faith for we are all in process of rooting out some level of doubt. Questioning God is a normal part of our relationship and faith journey, but doubt is dangerous because it doubts God's goodness and breaks trust. It is one thing to ask the "why" questions, but it is dangerous to doubt God's character. James describes the one who doubts as being double-minded. (James 1:5-8) The Greek word actually means a "two-souled" person. It describes a person who is not whole and whose soul is fractured and in desperate need of healing and deliverance. In the midst of suffering and trials, as our faith is being tested, the goal is steadfastness leading to further spiritual maturity. Steadfastness is a critical aspect of our faith and spiritual growth. It can only grow through the testing of our faith. So, suffering is necessary for our spiritual development. Someone can find God without suffering, but no one can continue to grow in their relationship with God without growing through suffering and trials. And that includes growing through both big "S" suffering and little "s" suffering. If we are to share in the sufferings of Christ, then suffering is necessary not only for our spiritual growth but also for the mission of Christ in the world. Malcolm Muggeridge shares his experience with this truth,

> "Contrary to what might be expected, I look back on experiences that at the time seemed especially desolating and painful with particular satisfaction. Indeed, I can say with complete truthfulness that everything I have learned in my seventy-five years in this world, everything that has truly enhanced and enlightened my existence, has been through affliction and not through happiness, whether pursued or attained. In other words, if it ever were to be possible to eliminate affliction from our earthly existence by means of some drug or other medical mumbo jumbo…the result would not be

to make life delectable, but to make it too banal and trivial to be endurable. This, of course, is what the Cross signifies. And it is the Cross, more than anything else, that has called me inexorably to Christ."[xlii]

And Tim Keller says of the importance of suffering,

"Over the years, I also came to realize that adversity did not merely lead people to believe in God's existence. It pulled those who already believed into a deeper experience of God's reality, love, and grace. One of the main ways we move from abstract knowledge about God to a personal encounter with him as a living reality is through the furnace of affliction…Believers understand many doctrinal truths in the mind, but those truths seldom make the journey down into the heart except through disappointment, failure, and loss."[xliii]

While trials test our faith and produce either doubt or steadfastness, testimonies build our faith and produce joy and life. Testimonies come as a result of our faith under trial producing steadfastness. Doubt actually cuts off fellowship with God and therefore works against testimony. A testimony is simply testifying about what God has wonderfully done in, through or to our life. James 5:11 speaks of the testimony produced by Job's steadfastness, "Behold, we consider those blessed who remained steadfast. You have heard of the steadfastness of Job, and you have seen the purpose of the Lord, how the Lord is compassionate and merciful." God honored Job's steadfastness not only by revealing Himself to Job, but also by restoring Job's health, doubling his fortune and blessing the latter years of his life more than the beginning. (Job 42:10-17) Don't you think Job looked at trials differently the rest of his life – with greater faith? At first it is hard to enter trials with joy because we have not experienced the effects of steadfastness or the joy of testimony.

(James 1:2) Proper perspective on suffering and trials for the believer is to look at it with joy. This joy is rooted in the fact of great expectation that God is going to intervene into the situation. Though the exterior situation might not change immediately, our interior is being transformed and faith is being strengthened by steadfastness. And steadfastness removes doubt and strengthens trust in God who will intervene at some point and make all things new.

Friday and Sunday Faith

It makes a world of difference if we look at suffering from God's perspective rather than man's perspective. It also makes a world of difference if we look at prosperity from God's perspective rather than man's perspective. Salvation is the liberating process whereby our eyes are opened to see God's perspective and freedom from man's myopic perspective. It is an awesome thing the first time we get a vision for what our Lord Jesus did for us on the cross on that history making Friday afternoon. It is an equally awesome thing to get a vision for what God has done for us on that history making Sunday morning when He defeated the power of death for us and opened new life to us through Jesus' resurrection. We get hung up in our faith when we cannot see from God's perspective. Proverbs 29:18 says, "Where there is no prophetic vision the people cast off restraint." So, where there is no fresh revelation of God's Word people get discouraged and their souls die because they are stuck with just man's perspective on things. If we are only able to look at the world with man's perspective our view of prosperity becomes banal and our view of suffering becomes burdensome.

As I write this chapter I am in India visiting some dear friends who were sent out from our church as church planters among the unreached. This is a vast nation with a very complex history of Hindu, Buddhist, Muslim and Christian faiths intertwined among 1.3 billion people speaking hundreds of different languages. Evidence of extreme suffering is everywhere and can be overwhelming for someone from the West where it is not so evident. In preparation for my trip I have been reading a book on the history of India. It was shocking to read the history of regular suffering experienced by the people of this land. Here is just one example of horrifying suffering during a famine in 1770:

> "…it is on record that the husbandmen sold their cattle, they sold their implements of agriculture; they sold their sons and daughters, till at length no buyer of children could be found; they ate the leaves of the trees and the grass of the field; and when the height of the summer was reached, the living were feeding on the dead. The streets of the cities were blocked up with promiscuous heaps of the dead and the dying; even the dogs and the jackals could not accomplish their revolting work…At length a gloomy calm succeeded. Death has ended the miseries of a great portion of the people; and when a new crop came forward in August, it had in some parts no one to gather it in. The number which fell in this period of horror has been variously estimated, and may, perhaps, be moderately taken as three million."[xliv]

How is one to process or make sense of such suffering strictly from man's perspective? A person's perspective or worldview radically impacts how they see suffering and prosperity. If man is left to his own perspective on suffering and death, he either will create a religion of works-based-salvation or a philosophy of absurdity. A religion of works, which defines most religions except Christianity, tries to overcome suffering and attain salvation by human effort. A philosophy of absurdity states that the reality of death makes everything in life "absurd" including all of man's philosophy and technology. But when our eyes are open to God's perspective, hope comes alive. Since God raised Jesus from the dead, God, not death has the final say about life and eternity. This means two things; man cannot save himself by works and that life has purpose and is not absurd. If God is ultimate reality, then we should seek and fear God and not fear death. If we have God's perspective, then the source of all suffering was defeated on Friday and death itself was defeated on Sunday.

Trials test our faith while testimonies build our faith. A testimony does not require a test or suffering. When we are serving God the miraculous can occur anytime. This is not just to be a believed possibility, but a pursued reality. We grow through suffering and trials and we grow through the power of testimony. We have focused on who Jesus is and what He has done for us but often failed to live in the reality of what Jesus has called us into and what He wants to do through us. We are called not just to be Friday Christians, but also Sunday Christians. We are called to "share his sufferings" and to know "the power of his resurrection."(Phil 3:10) Oswald Sanders put it this way, "The degree to which we allow the cross of Christ to work in us will be the measure in which the resurrection life of Christ can be manifested through us."

Some leaders throughout church history have contrasted a "theology of the cross" with a "theology of glory." They would go on to say that the greatest revelation of the character of God was in the suffering and death of the cross of Christ. This focus on the suffering of the cross somewhat removed from the victory of the resurrection has instilled an out of balance view of suffering and prosperity within the church. We get into trouble when we have a theology of the cross that excludes a healthy theology of glory. And we also get into trouble if we have a theology of glory, which excludes a healthy theology of the cross. Too often people have only viewed Job's story through the eyes of suffering and have missed the beginning and end of the story where God showers him with prosperity. One of the clearest examples of holding both a "theology of the cross" and a "theology of glory" is Paul's words in 2 Cor. 4:10-12,

> "...always carrying in the body the death of Jesus, so that the life of Jesus may also be manifested in

or bodies. For we who live are always being given over to death for Jesus' sake, so that the life of Jesus also may be manifested in our mortal flesh. So death is at work in us but, life in you."

Paul exhibited what it was to be a Friday and Sunday believer. Being both a Friday and Sunday Christian is where true prosperity is found. It is living by faith where we fight for prosperity and fight against suffering by the Word of God and the power of the Holy Spirit. It is very important to understand that to fight for prosperity it is imperative to embrace big 'S' suffering, which is to share in Christ's sufferings. If we do not understand and embrace big "S" suffering we will not be able to develop a Friday and Sunday faith. And we will not see the imperative to pursue the power and gifts of God and partner with Him in bringing His love and healing to a hurting and oppressed world.

It is a strange spiritual reality that many believers are more comfortable receiving suffering and trials than they are receiving spiritual gifts and answered prayer from God. This is because we feel guilt and shame and inside we feel like we deserve to suffer and that we are not worthy to receive of His goodness. Some have received Christ's work on Friday for the forgiveness of their sins, but do not feel like they can keep receiving the Spirit empowered life from Sunday. We need a Friday and Sunday faith if we are going to live in prosperity in a suffering world.

Here is a summary of a biblical understanding of suffering from this second section of the book that we will apply practically to real life issues along with the theology of prosperity from the first section:

1.) Suffering either moves us toward God or it moves us away from God.

2.) Only faith has the ability to put suffering into perspective for this life and eternity.

3.) We cannot understand nor learn the purposes of suffering until we settle the "goodness" of God question in our heart.

4.) We cannot understand nor learn the purposes of suffering until we get over the "why" questions and open our hearts to the "what for" questions.

5.) Suffering is used to strengthen our faith, build our character and equip us to minister in power like Jesus.

6.) We must believe in the reality of the devil and his demons if we are going to understand evil and suffering.

7.) God created the angelic realm and humanity with "free-will" and the source of evil is the abuse of this gift.

8.) Lies lead to agreements. Agreements lead to strongholds. Strongholds lead to death.

9.) In Jesus' victory over Satan we are set free from the power of sin; free from guilt, shame and condemnation; free from the power of the law; and free from the power of death.

10.) The weapons of spiritual warfare are the armor of our identity in Christ, the sword of the Spirit-the Word of God, the spiritual disciplines, the spiritual gifts and prayer and intercession.

11.) Truth leads to faith. Faith leads to power. Power leads to freedom.

12.) All suffering is ultimately a result of sin and its rebellion against God.

13.) Suffering as a result of the Father's discipline is unique for those who know Jesus and used to turn them from disobedience back to the Father's heart.

14.) Suffering as a result of injustice is caused by the fallen state of humanity that takes justice into its own hands disregarding God and His ways.

15.) Suffering as a result of demonic activity includes spiritual, emotional and physical suffering and adversely impacts individuals, families, communities and whole geographic regions.

16.) Suffering as a result of persecution is a unique form of suffering only followers of Jesus experience because the world and the devil hate God's people.

17.) Suffering as a result of divine judgment is because God is perfect and will bring judgment on all sin and rebellion.

18.) Suffering as a result of divine mystery requires trust and patience in God's sovereignty and His willingness to give revelation and understanding to those who seek Him.

19.) Big "S" suffering is the suffering believers are uniquely called to share in as followers of Christ. Little "s" suffering is the suffering shared by all mankind that believers are called to engage and battle by faith.

20.) The sufferings we do not have to share in are oppression, disease and poverty.

21.) Suffering and trials test our faith and produce either doubt or steadfastness. Doubt divides the soul. Steadfastness unites the soul.

22.) Trials test our faith while testimonies build our faith.

23.) We are called not just to be Friday Christians, but also Sunday Christians. We are called to "share his sufferings" and to know "the power of his resurrection."

Section Three: Prosperity through Suffering

"And the Lord blessed the latter days of Job more than his beginning. And he had 14,000 sheep, 6,000 camels, 1000 yoke of oxen, and 1,000 female donkeys. He had also seven sons and three daughters. And he called the name of the first daughter Jemimah, and the name of the second Keziah, and the name of the third Keren-happuch. And in all the land there were no women so beautiful as Job's daughters. And their father gave them an inheritance among their brothers. And after this Job lived 140 years, and saw his sons, and his sons' sons, four generations. And Job died, an old man, and full of days."

Job 42:12-17

"Since therefore the children share in flesh and blood, he himself likewise partook of the same things, that through death he might destroy the one who has the power of death, that is, the devil, and deliver all those who through fear of death were subject to lifelong slavery."

Hebrews 2:14-15

SECTION THREE: PROSPERITY THROUGH SUFFERING

CHAPTER NINE
Cultivating A Culture of Faith

True prosperity thrives in a culture of faith and deteriorates in its absence. Just because a crowd is gathered every Sunday, songs are sung, the offering is taken and even the Word preached does not necessarily mean there is a culture of faith present. Whether a church is small or large the importance of its faith culture is often overlooked. More talk and church conferences today seem to focus on corporate culture ideas rather than faith culture ideas.

The trend seems to be a loss of sensitivity to the spiritual realm and a heightened sensitivity to the material realm. Of course, we need to be aware of the material realm around us, but we are to be growing more in tune with the spiritual unseen realm as a Body of believers. We can see the importance of a culture of faith in Jesus' ministry. When there was a lack of faith present, it quenched His miracle-working ministry. This was especially evident in His hometown.

We can see the importance of a faith culture throughout the book of Acts, and it was Paul's motivation for writing his epistles. In 1 Thessalonians 5:19-22 Paul states, "Do not quench the Spirit. Do not despise prophecies, but test everything; hold fast what is good. Abstain from every form of evil." This is the environment, a culture of faith, where we can learn to fight for prosperity and fight against suffering.

Fighting for prosperity is pursuing the blessings of God's promises and commands for us as individuals and for the church body. The fullness of these blessings will not be experienced until after Jesus' return. God invites us to participate in these blessings now by fighting against suffering by exercising our faith. But the fact that we will not experience the fullness of these blessings until Jesus' return does not mean that we can't experience them at all now. We do this by applying God's promises to the suffering circumstances of our lives and the lives of others with the expectation that we will see those circumstances change by the power of the Holy Spirit. Fighting against suffering sounds counter to what some scripture says about rejoicing in our sufferings or counting our sufferings a blessing, but it is not. Fighting against suffering and rejoicing in suffering are two sides of the same coin. We rejoice when we are counted worthy to suffer for our Lord, but that does not mean we do not pray and have others pray for our deliverance from the suffering and persecution.

We cannot make sense of suffering without faith. And we cannot experience true prosperity without suffering. True prosperity comes through suffering. This is why it is so critical to develop a healthy theology of both suffering and prosperity. We cannot truly be rich toward God any other way. Job's prosperity after his suffering was deeper and better both materially and spiritually. Job 42:12 states, "And the Lord blessed the latter days of Job more than his beginning." We hear much about the suffering of Job, but we miss the reality of God's heart for His children, which is to bless them. For the majority of Job's life, he experienced the blessings of God, but for him to deepen in his experience of God and receive more of His blessing, he had to go through suffering.

Jesus' prosperity after His suffering was deeper and richer. I know that statement will raise eyebrows with some theologians. I am not saying that Jesus and God were lacking anything in the fullness of their Being. God never works against Himself but always for His glory. And by bringing children into eternal fellowship with Him, His glory was magnified. Jesus' glory was magnified in His suffering, because through it He saved us so we could share in His eternal glory – real prosperity. Hebrews 5:8-9 gives insight into this wonderful mystery. "Although he was a son, he learned obedience through what he suffered. And being made perfect, he became the source of eternal salvation to all who obey him."

Real prosperity is learning to live by faith in the tension between the victorious miracles of Hebrews 11:32-35a and the brutal sufferings of Hebrews 11:35b-38.

> [32] And what more shall I say? For time would fail me to tell of Gideon, Barak, Samson, Jephthah, of David and Samuel and the prophets— [33] who through faith conquered kingdoms, enforced justice, obtained promises, stopped the mouths of lions, [34] quenched the power of fire, escaped the edge of the sword, were made strong out of weakness, became mighty in war, put foreign armies to flight. [35] Women received back their dead by resurrection.
>
> (faith in tension)

Some were tortured, refusing to accept release, so that they might rise again to a better life. [36] Others suffered mocking and flogging, and even chains and imprisonment. [37] They were stoned, they were sawn in two, they were killed with the sword. They went about in skins of sheep and goats, destitute, afflicted, mistreated— [38] of whom the world was not worthy—wandering about in deserts and mountains, and in dens and caves of the earth.

To live in this tension we must learn to fight for prosperity and fight against suffering by the Word of God and the power of the Holy Spirit. It requires developing a healthy theology of prosperity and suffering as well as participating in a culture of faith where these theologies can be worked out in the details of life. Too much of church strategy has been on being culturally relevant rather than cultivating a faith culture, which is eternally relevant. Job's faith stands out because he held on to faith even in the midst of a lack of a faith culture. The community of friends that surrounded Job did not give counsel that helped Job increase in his faith. In the end God dealt with this lack of faith culture, "After the LORD had spoken these words to Job, the LORD said to Eliphaz the Temanite: 'My anger burns against you and against your two friends, for you have not spoken of me what is right, as my servant Job has.'" (Job 42:7)

In each of our church communities we have to ask if we are cultivating a faith culture where people are learning and growing in their ability to fight for and experience the prosperity that comes with the gospel of Jesus Christ. We also have to ask if we are cultivating a faith culture where people are learning how to grow in faith in the midst of suffering and learn how to fight suffering by the power of the Holy Spirit.

In this chapter we will examine four key aspects of a culture of faith before we apply these principles to the issues of wealth, health and deliverance in the final chapters. Four key aspects of a culture of faith are:

1.) A culture of faith is characterized by the experience of the assurance of salvation of each believer.
2.) A culture of faith is characterized by submission and accountability to the Word of God and empowerment and direction by the Holy Spirit.
3.) A culture of faith is characterized not by one member of the Godhead, but by a fully Trinitarian theology and experience.

4.) A culture of faith is characterized by bold faith language that speaks the truth in love.

Assurance of Salvation

A culture of faith is characterized by the experience of the assurance of salvation of each believer. The importance of living in the experience of the assurance of our salvation has been minimized in many Christian circles. It has just remained a theological truth for many and has not become a living experience. There are some denominations that do not believe in the assurance of salvation and teach that a believer can lose their salvation for several different reasons. This position that one can lose their salvation has held people in legalism, fear and bondage rather than liberate them.

The truth is if we can do something to lose our salvation, we can do something to get our salvation. This would violate the most beautiful and fundamental truth of the gospel, "For by grace you have been saved through faith. And this is not your own doing; it is the gift of God, not a result of works, so that no one may boast." (Ephesians 2:8-9) The grace of the gospel is a free gift, but one that when truly given gives rise to good works. If we are liberated by grace, that liberation is for something. It is to fight for the blessings of God in our lives and the lives of others, rather than the bondage of continuing to follow our fleshly desires. There is no greater prosperity message in the world than the gospel of Jesus Christ. And when we learn to live in the reality of the assurance of our salvation, we experience freedom from sin, shame, guilt, condemnation and the fear of death.

One of the most popular questions used during evangelism has been something like, "If you were to die tonight are you sure you would be with Jesus in heaven?" This is a critically important question, but it is one that believers should be processing more deeply and personally rather than using it as an evangelistic question. It seems that today there is a trend where doubt and skepticism is processed more than the experience of the assurance of salvation. In many circles it is even communicated that it is ok to doubt your salvation. Again, as we discussed earlier doubt is dangerous and the lack of the assurance of our salvation quenches faith and keeps the door open for bondage and strongholds in our life.

So, on a scale of 1 to 10 how sure are you that if you died right now you would be with Jesus in heaven? (Where would you put your circle on this scale?)

1..........10

It is a simple exercise and a simple graphic, but what it reveals about how we see ourselves, and how we understand the prosperity of the Gospel is profound. If we circle any number under 10, even 9.5, we leave space for doubt to grow and the door open for guilt, shame, condemnation and fear. It is critical to understand that our answer to this question is never to be based on our feelings alone. And our answer is never to be just an intellectual decision. Assurance that is merely cognitive will not produce faithful discipleship. But our assurance is to be rooted in the dynamic experience of personal relationship with God based on the truth of the Gospel.

Once we start to step out in faith and apply the overwhelming truth of the Gospel to our life then we will start to experience its power and our feelings will follow. The harsh reality is, if any believer circles anything below a 10, they are basically saying that Christ's death, burial and resurrection is not sufficient nor powerful enough to secure their salvation. The truth is that even right in the midst of our sin we have the assurance of salvation, because we did nothing to secure it. Christ did for us that which we could not do for ourselves. Right after we have sinned, whatever the sin is, if we by faith apply the Gospel we will walk in freedom and sin, shame, guilt and condemnation will not overwhelm us. It is a faith step, to apply the Gospel and stand on the assurance it has for us.

For faith to continue to grow there must be a growing experience of the assurance of our salvation. The assurance of our salvation is not a static possession. It is a positional truth about a believer's life that must be applied in our life and grown into. If it is not attended to, our assurance can decline and shame and fear can take over. So, whenever we doubt or sin we must apply the truth of the assurance of our salvation for faith to grow. It is amazing how much time we spend consumed with thinking about ourselves. This will only lead to more doubt and bondage. Active faith is intentionally thinking about God and what He has done for us and applying that truth to the circumstances of our lives. Here is a simple illustration of how to apply this to our lives.

Suppose we are overwhelmed with bad thoughts or we have just sinned (we can all insert our own experiences here). This is a critical moment, a crisis of faith. We can either give into our bad thoughts, the shame, the guilt, the condemnation or we can by faith apply the Gospel. In that moment if we pull out our journal, piece of paper or even a napkin and write on it 1....10 and circle 10 saying, "My salvation is secure because of what Jesus has done for me, and it is sufficient to forgive me and deliver me from any and all sin and doubt," then faith is cultivated in our heart. 1 John 1:9 states, "If we confess our sins he is faithful and just to forgive us our sins and cleanse us from all unrighteousness." The more this step of faith is taken in our lives the more our feelings and thoughts are transformed. Obedience to God's Word is very difficult if not impossible if we are led by our feelings. We must be led by faith and the power of the Holy Spirit. We are to live in the assurance of our salvation at all times, even in the midst of our sin. The radical liberating truth is that if we know Jesus we are always a "10," even when we sin.

1.........⑩

"My sheep hear my voice, and I know them, and they follow me. I give them eternal life, and they will never perish, and no one will snatch them out of my hand. My Father, who has given them to me, is greater than all, and no one is able to snatch them out of the Father's hand. I and the Father are one."
John 10:27-30

"Epaphras, who is one of you, a servant of Christ Jesus, greets you, always struggling on your behalf in his prayers, that you may stand mature and fully assured in all the will of God."
Colossians 4:12

"And we desire each one of you to show the same earnestness to have the full assurance of hope until the end."
Hebrews 6:11

"let us draw near with a true heart in full assurance of faith, with our hearts sprinkled clean from an evil conscience and our bodies washed with pure water."
Hebrews 10:22

"Now faith is the assurance of things hoped for, the conviction of things not seen."
Hebrews 11:1

"I write these things to you who believe in the name of the Son of God that you may know that you have eternal life."
1 John 5:13

A false sense of over-confidence and an under-confidence in the assurance of our salvation are dangerous. This false over-confidence is a confidence that is strictly rooted in the cognitive, and missing the relational aspect of faith. We need to be growing toward confidence in the assurance of our salvation. Being over-confident with this truth would be a similar false confidence that the Pharisees held onto because of their heritage, education and position. This over-confidence masks spiritual pride and legalism, which is really putting confidence in our works rather than in Christ's works. Over-confidence focuses more on one's works and accomplishments than on Christ's works and accomplishments.

Being under-confident with this truth reveals another aspect of pride, which is self-loathing that deep inside is saying that Christ's grace is not sufficient to love us and save us. Under-confidence focuses more on one's inadequacies and problems than on Christ's adequacies and solutions. A faith confidence confesses any over-confidence and looks to root out any under-confidence while trusting completely in the grace of Jesus. Faith confidence does not hesitate to circle 10 in relation to our assurance of salvation.

A culture of faith cannot be cultivated if believers and the church community are not growing in the assurance of salvation. This is a critical experience in our ability to fight for prosperity and to fight against suffering. The core of real prosperity is the assurance of who we are and the security that our life and destiny are in God's hands. Much of suffering is due to core issues related to sin, shame, guilt and condemnation. Without the assurance of salvation it is hard if not impossible to get freedom from the bondage of these things. Remember, in Jesus we are always a 10, even when we sin.

Word and Spirit

A culture of faith is characterized by submission and accountability to the Word of God and empowerment and direction by the Holy Spirit. An understanding and experience of Word and Spirit is necessary for the cultivation of a culture of faith where we can learn to fight for prosperity and fight against suffering. In the following graph we can see the road to true prosperity is a healthy Word/Spirit journey toward becoming a follower of Jesus Christ. We can also see the danger of not cultivating a healthy Word/Spirit culture by the other three quadrants of Fan, Fundamentalist and Feeler. The graph portrays the definition of true prosperity as living in faith-in-tension where we fight for prosperity and fight against suffering by the truth of God's Word and the power of the Holy Spirit.

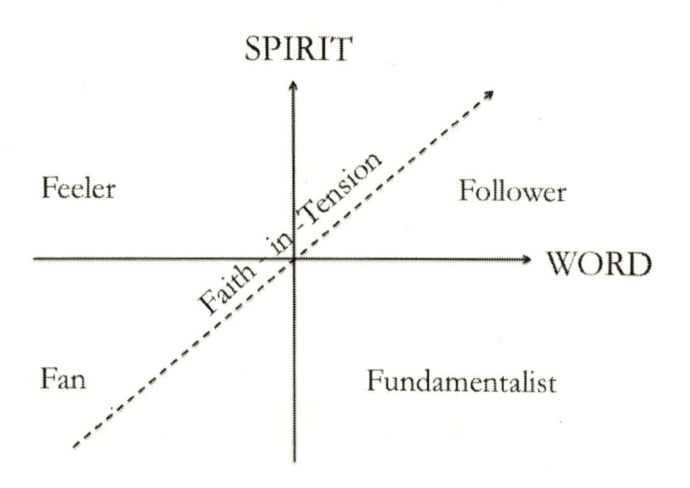

```
                        SPIRIT
                          ↑
                          |        ↗
            Feeler        |  ⟋  Follower
                          | ⟋
                          |⟋
        ──────────────────+──────────────→ WORD
                       ⟋  |
                    ⟋     |
            Fan  ⟋        |  Fundamentalist
              ⟋           |
```
(Faith-in-Tension diagonal)

Who is a "Fan?" We all come into this world looking for heroes and followers. We are all looking for someone to look up to who is worthy to follow and who will never let us down. We all have heroes and idols. Fans are fickle and want to be able to follow God on their own agenda and are in bondage to idolatry. This is a universal experience. We all enter the world in this spiritual state. There are three people in the New Testament that represent well a "Fan", Judas (Matthew 26-27), King Herod (Luke 23:6-16) and Pontius Pilate (John 18-19).

Judas had every opportunity that the other disciples had, but he never could submit to Jesus' agenda. He wanted it his way. Both King Herod and Pontius Pilate were the classic skeptics. They were curious about Jesus, but not curious enough to continue the discussion with Him. They were actually looking for fans themselves. They were both people pleasers not God pleasers. Fans are people pleasers. They are fickle, which means they easily discard one hero for another or one idol for another if it does not satisfy them or meet their perceived need. This is where we all began. We are Fans – born self-absorbed and alienated from God by sin. We are prone to be spectators, insecure in our role in life.

One big proof of this is the power of pornography. Someone has rightly noticed that how we engage our sexual life is how we engage life itself. It is much easier to just spectate sex (pornography) rather than do the hard work of developing our soul to approach someone in healthy intimacy. It is much easier to sit and watch sports and play video games than it is to do something hard and good.

How does a "Fan" process prosperity and suffering? They are completely susceptible to the world's ways: 1 John 2:15-16 states, "Do not love the world or the things in the world. If anyone loves the world, the love of the Father is not in him. For all that is in the world – the desires of the flesh (Hedonism) and the desires of the eyes (Materialism) and pride of life (Egotism) – is not from the Father but is from the world." Fans are lost in the sea of relativism, not being able to stand upon the firm ground of biblical truth. They are alone with their emotions, mind and will and only can harness the power of man separated from the power of the Holy Spirit. They are susceptible to the oppression of the devil and all his minions. For the devil has blinded their eyes from believing and put them in bondage to all kinds of idolatry. They are incapable of making sense of suffering and seeing its eternal significance in their life and in the world. We are only set free from this bondage as we encounter and receive the love of the Father through Jesus Christ and become a "Follower".

Who is a "Fundamentalist"? No one today wants to be known as a fundamentalist, especially a religious fundamentalist. It used to have a positive meaning in some circles, but today it mostly is perceived as negative. But for many of us, because of our church environment and spiritual growth experience, we have fallen prey to spiritual fundamentalism. The Scribes and Pharisees best represent the Fundamentalist position in scripture (Matthew 26:57-68). The Fundamentalist represents someone who has grown in Bible knowledge but has not grown in the ways of the Holy Spirit, as portrayed in the graph.

A Fundamentalist is about keeping the law and making himself feel better by judging others. This person would also be the dutiful Christian who serves the Lord out of duty and not delight. These are the kind of people who can do great harm to people on their spiritual journey. Many of us have encountered them in our church experience. And many have been deeply wounded and de-churched because of fundamentalism and its lack of active fellowship with the Holy Spirit. Rules without relationship birth rebellion. This adequately describes the Fundamentalist position.

How does a "Fundamentalist" process prosperity and suffering? Typically, someone who is Word focused but has a deficit in fellowship with the Holy Spirit will struggle with the idea of fighting for prosperity. They are adverse to the idea of earthly prosperity, even though they often embrace it themselves like the Pharisees and Scribes in the New Testament. Many evangelical leaders have publically condemned health and wealth pastors for their opulence, while they themselves live with material prosperity far above the average churchgoer.

In general, they will be more consumed with "sin-management" and performance based spirituality than pursuing spiritual gifts and increasing one's faith. They are more comfortable and spend more time talking and teaching about the importance of suffering than pursuing by faith the spiritual resources to defeat suffering. Within this camp are those who have embraced a theology that denies the present power of the Holy Spirit working through signs, wonders and miracles in the church today. Typically, they have a more established theology of suffering than they do a theology of prosperity. They are more focused on the "Kingdom not yet" than the "Kingdom now".

Who is a "Feeler"? They are typically the folks who are in search of the goose bumps. They would be those who tend toward letting their personal experience dictate truth in their lives. They are led more by their feelings and beliefs of culture than by the Word of God. They are led by their emotions. Feelers are also in pursuit of a spiritual experience and often at the expense of the truth. Some of these folks can be represented in the scripture by Simon the magician, (Acts 8:9-24) who longed for the power of the Holy Spirit, but not necessarily the truth. We are to experience God for sure, but our pursuit is not to be the experience itself or even the manifestation. It is to be for God Himself.

How does a "Feeler" process prosperity and suffering? Typically, a feeler will embrace the blessings of God for them personally, but will be at a deficit in dealing with suffering. In general, feelers are led by their emotions and swing from spiritual highs to lows. They see suffering as something to avoid completely and have little room for the use of suffering. Often there is an unbalanced use of victorious language that is removed from the reality of life. They are more comfortable with a theology of prosperity than a theology of suffering. And typically, they are more focused on pursuing the manifestations of the "Kingdom now" rather than issues of the "Kingdom not yet."

Who is a "Follower"? Jesus asks us to follow Him. And this relationship is a Word and Spirit relationship. Jesus is the Word. John 1:1-2 states, "In the beginning was the Word, and the Word was with God, and the Word was God. He was in the beginning with God." Jesus is the truth. In John 14:6 Jesus states, "I am the way, and the truth, and the life. No one comes to the Father except through me." God called a few of His servants to write down the record of scripture (Old and New Testaments) by the inspiration of the Holy Spirit. The Father and the Son have sent forth the Holy Spirit in our hearts to aid us in living this Word-Spirit new life. Jesus states in John 16:13, "When the Spirit of truth comes, he will guide you into all truth." As we have illustrated in the above graph, it is detrimental to our spiritual growth to be at a deficit in either the Word or Spirit. To follow Jesus these must go together. A healthy representation of this Word-Spirit life would be the early church as found in the book of Acts (Acts 2:42-47; 4:27-37).

We can see Jesus bring Word (Truth) and Spirit together in John 4:23-24, "But the hour is coming, and is now here, when the true worshipers will worship the Father in spirit and truth, for the Father is seeking such people to worship him. God is spirit, and those who worship him must worship in Spirit and truth." James Dunn sheds great light on the meaning and importance of these verses:

> "As most commentators agree, the talk here (in v.24b) is not of man's spirit, nor is there any suggestion that worship must be a purely interior affair. Rather the worship looked for is worship in the Spirit, the Holy Spirit, the Spirit of truth…In other words, Spirit is God's mode of communication with men. Consequently he looks for men to respond in the same manner – to worship in Spirit and truth…'In Spirit' must imply 'by inspiration of Spirit' – that is, charismatic worship – for in the immediate context worship in Spirit is set in pointed contrast to worship through temple and sacred place. The worship that God seeks is a worship not frozen to a sacred building or by loyalty to a particular tradition, but a worship which is living, the ever new response to God who is Spirit as prompted and enabled by the Spirit of God."[xlv]

Worship is to characterize the posture of the entire life of the follower, not just when they attend church. Charismatic worship as defined here is not necessarily endorsing a certain denomination or stream of spirituality. It is defining life and worship that is open to the gifts and movement of the Holy Spirit along with the truth of God's Word.

How does a "Follower" process prosperity and suffering? A follower lives fighting for prosperity and fighting against suffering by the truth of God's Word and the power of the Holy Spirit. The follower is in pursuit of the best theology of prosperity and suffering so as to synergize them beautifully together. The follower is concerned about both the "Kingdom now" and the "Kingdom not yet". To foster a culture of faith there must be a healthy Word-Spirit journey.

A Fully Trinitarian Experience

A culture of faith is characterized not by devotion to one person of the Godhead, but by a fully Trinitarian theology and experience. Our God is amazing and there is none like Him. He is worthy of all our praise and glory. Healthy culture and community is not possible without the reality of the Trinity. Only the triune Father, Son and Holy Spirit, who is one God who is three persons in perfect unity and diversity, can explain the universal experience and desire for love and community. A "solitary god" knows nothing about relationship.

A healthy culture of faith that is characterized by a fully Trinitarian theology and experience will be multiplying the "good works" and "greater works" of the eternal and abundant life Jesus gives us. All Christians are familiar with the term "eternal life." But when asked what it actually "is" not much is given beyond the answer that when we die we will be with God forever. This of course is true, but it misses the important reality that "eternal life" is not just an experience for the future when we die, but entails a radical reframing of our present reality.

"Eternal life" as it is communicated in the New Testament is first about a radical relational transformation and secondly, about living in and experiencing this life now. John 17:3 describes this relational shift, "And this is eternal life, that they know you the only true God, and Jesus Christ whom you have sent." John 5:24, describes "eternal life" as an experience to be lived in now, "Truly, truly, I say to you, whoever hears my word and believes him who sent me has eternal life. He does not come into judgment, but has passed from death to life."

So, just what kind of life is this "eternal life" that we are to live in once we come to Jesus? Ephesians 2:10 gives us some insight into what we are to expect by faith in living this new life. "For we are his workmanship, created in Christ Jesus for good works, which God prepared beforehand, that we should walk in them." What are these "good works" that we were created by God to walk in? Jesus is our example and we are to look to Him to find insight into what these good works are and how to walk in them.

In John 5 Jesus visited the pool of Bethesda where there was a multitude of sick and lame people. On this visit He only healed one man, and it happened to be on the Sabbath. This raises all kinds of questions. Why did Jesus only heal one person among a multitude? Jesus answers this question in verses 19-20; "So Jesus said to them, 'Truly truly, I say to you, the Son can do nothing of his own accord, but only what he sees the Father doing. For whatever the Father does, that the Son does likewise. For the Father loves the Son and shows him all that he himself is doing. And greater works than these will he show him, so that you may marvel.'" The religious leaders were more concerned about it being the Sabbath than they were in the healing testimony of the lame man. Jesus healed the man on the Sabbath to also reveal that He was the Lord of even the Sabbath. In the rest of John chapter 5, Jesus speaks of His intimate relationship with the Father and how He seeks to do the will of the Father. Jesus shows us that the key to walking in "good works" and the key to ministry is hearing the voice of the Father.

Jesus in John 15:15 makes this statement, "No longer do I call you servants, for the servant does not know what his master is doing: but I have called you friends, for all that I have heard from my Father I have made known to you." When we come to Jesus He leads us to the Father and as children of God we are privy to the will and works of the Father. He desires to speak His works – good works – into our hearts that we may walk in them.

Walking in the good works of God is a supernatural dynamic experience with the triune Father, Son and Holy Spirit. Jesus says in Matthew 5:16, "In the same way, let your light shine before others, so that they may see your good works and give glory to your Father who is in heaven." Good works as Jesus describes them are not just any good deed, but works in partnership with the Trinity, which accomplish the will of the Father and lead others to God. And finally, Jesus says in John 14:12, "Truly, truly I say to you, whoever believes in me will also do the works that I do; and greater works than these will he do, because I am going to the Father." A culture of faith nurtures the supernatural work of the Spirit in the life of believers and rejoices in the testimonies of what God is powerfully doing through the ministry of the church body. A culture of faith fosters the "good works" and "greater works" that God has created for His children to walk in.

How does a fully Trinitarian theology and experience help us process prosperity and suffering in a healthy way? It allows us to break out of a limited idea of what "good works" or "greater works" can be. Our spiritual growth is limited if we are not growing in our experience with each Person of the Trinity and growing in our understanding of their role in our spiritual development. For example, we can know about the grace of Jesus and the power of the Holy Spirit, but if we have not experienced the lavish love of the Father we will struggle to be secure in our identity. We may know the love of the Father and the power of the Spirit, but if we do not know the grace of Jesus, we can be held captive to a spirit of bitterness, judgment or religion. Or we may know the love of the Father and the grace of Jesus, but if we are not pursuing the empowerment of the Holy Spirit we will have a hard time breaking bondage and addiction in our lives. These are not heretical ideas, but actually guard against falling into either tritheism (three separate Gods) or modalism (just one God with three different forms it can be represented in). When we pursue intimate relationship with the one God by developing relationship with the Father, Jesus and Holy Spirit we uphold the relational dynamics seen in scripture between the three persons of the Godhead and between them and people. Practically, this growth begins in our lives when we begin to relate to each Person of the Godhead as we see them represented in scripture.

A fully Trinitarian theology and experience will equip us to fight for prosperity and the great testimonies we can see in Hebrews 11:33-35a. And it will also equip us to fight against suffering and faithfully endure suffering, even the kinds we can see in Hebrews 11:35b-38. A culture of faith is characterized by a fully Trinitarian theology and experience.

A Renewed Faith Language

How we communicate our faith is important. A culture of faith is characterized by bold faith language that speaks the truth in love. (Eph. 4:15) We need a renewed language of faith, one that is more biblically accurate and speaks the truth in love and does not water down our responsibility in our partnership of faith with God.

Often we have shied away from asking people directly about their faith in fear that they may feel judged or condemned. We have treated faith more as a static thing than as a dynamic thing to be exercised and strengthened. I grew up in a tradition that emphasized "making a decision for Jesus", but after that decision was made there was not much talk about increasing faith and taking steps in faith. The Gospels are full of accounts where Jesus calls His followers to examine their faith and to grow in it. One of these better known accounts is found in Matthew 17:14-21 as well as Mark 9:14-29, where a desperate father had brought his epileptic son to Jesus' disciples for healing, but they could not heal him. Jesus rebukes the crowd as being a "faithless generation." And He rebukes His disciples for having "little faith." In Mark 9:22b-24 we can see Jesus' response to what would appear as a faith statement, but was actually revealing a lack of faith.

> "'But if you can do anything, have compassion on us and help us.' And Jesus said to him, 'If you can'! All things are possible for one who believes.' Immediately the father of the child cried out and said, 'I believe, help my unbelief!'"

The father's request models the "faithless" attitude that has unfortunately permeated many believers and many church cultures. It is a sobering thing to think about how Jesus would respond to our church culture today? He says in Luke 18:8, "…when the Son of Man comes, will he find faith on earth?" Jesus made this comment right after He finished telling the parable about the persistent widow and how important it is to keep praying with faith. But after Jesus rebukes the father, the father responds with a renewed faith language, "Immediately the father of the child cried out and said, 'I believe; help my unbelief!'"

We need a renewed faith language and a culture of faith where we are encouraged to both speak the truth in love to one another and be open and honest with our lack of faith individually and corporately. We must recover a culture of faith even though there have been abuses. In some church traditions faith language has been used inappropriately, and it has brought condemnation upon those who were suffering. This just raises the importance of developing as a transparent and loving community along with cultivating a faith community. Paul makes this same point in 1 Corinthians when he inserted chapter 13, an extended meditation on love that occurs in the midst of his discussion of how the spiritual gifts are to be used within the Body of Christ.

We also have to learn to admit that we lose some faith battles. The reason this is such a struggle within much of the church is that there is a deficit in understanding and living within the biblical worldview, which is a worldview of spiritual warfare. Too often the evangelical copout is used: "Well, it must be God's will." Yes, God is sovereign, but not everything that happens is God's desired will. He created angels and humans with "free-will." There are other wills at work in this world that oppose the will of God. God has given us the gift of faith and it is to be used to overcome mountains and push back darkness. This can clearly be seen in Matthew 6:9-10, 13, but often is overlooked. "Our Father in heaven, hallowed be your name. Your kingdom come, your will be done, on earth as it is in heaven…And lead us not into temptation, but deliver us from evil."

Jesus taught us to pray and work for the will of the Father to be done. And He taught us to pray that we would be delivered from evil. The word for "evil" here can also mean, "evil one." What Jesus wants us to know is that we are in a spiritual battle, a clash of wills. We are to work toward living in and from God's will, just like Jesus did. But what this means is that there have been battles lost throughout history. And for one reason or another, battles with sickness and disease are lost, battles for relationships and families are lost, battles for churches and nations are lost. We must develop a renewed faith language that is adequate for these battles whether won or lost. The good news is that though we will lose some battles in this life, the war has been won by Jesus, and God's will shall prevail when heaven comes to earth.

How does a renewed faith language help us process prosperity and suffering? We need a language that is spiritually sensitive to those we are ministering to and that is led by the Spirit into speaking the truth about prosperity and suffering. This renewed faith language will be spiritually sensitive and adjust its language in specific situations according to the faith atmosphere. For example, our language should be different when dealing with an unbeliever than with a believer. Good questions should be asked before entering into a time of ministry. This renewed faith language will keep taking steps of faith to press into situations with the great promises of God and it will endure patiently the learning process of suffering.

For example, if a person is struggling with disease, faith would be modeled by pressing into healing with all of God's resources, and at the same time, learn and grow from the process. And if the disease takes the person's life, faith does not stop there, it asks the Father if He would raise the person to life. We have not taken seriously Jesus' command, "and proclaim as you go, saying, 'The Kingdom of heaven is at hand. Heal the sick, raise the dead, cleanse lepers, cast out demons.'" (Matt. 10:7-8) Some will say that this does not apply for us today, but in the Great Commission (Matt. 28:18-20) Jesus commanded the disciples and church, "teaching them to observe *all* that I have commanded you" (italics mine). A healthy faith community will pursue and embrace the spiritual gifts. Jack Deere states,

> "Each of the miraculous gifts, as well as the other spiritual gifts that are not normally classified as miraculous, have valuable contributions to make to Christ's body. But these contributions will never be made, and the growth that could have come to the body will be lost, unless the leadership of the church learns how to cultivate these gifts within the body."[xlvi]

Another example of the application of a renewed faith language would be for the church to take seriously James 5:13-18. Here, James commands the church to pray with those who are suffering in general, to praise with those who are cheerful and to pray for healing for those who are sick. He says in verse 16-17, "The prayer of a righteous person has great power as it is working. Elijah was a man with a nature like ours, and he prayed fervently that it might not rain, and for three years and six months it did not rain on earth. Then he prayed again, and heaven gave rain, and the earth bore its fruit." James uses Elijah's prayer of faith to encourage us to grow in this prayer to see great testimonies with the church and to hold up hope at all times.

Cultivating a culture of faith is critical if we are going to fight for prosperity and fight against suffering by the Word of God and the power of the Holy Spirit. A healthy culture of faith is defined by the growing experience of the assurance of salvation, a healthy Word and Spirit journey, a fully Trinitarian theology and experience and a renewed faith language.

We are now ready to take our theology of prosperity and suffering and our healthy culture of faith and apply them to the specific situations of poverty and wealth, sickness and health, and oppression and deliverance in the remaining chapters.

CHAPTER TEN
A Faith in Tension Approach to Poverty and Wealth

I'd like to begin this chapter by returning to our original question, "What makes you feel prosperous?" I once was invited to an exclusive monthly gathering. Each person there had been extremely successful according to the world's standards. They would invite different speakers in on occasion that had a particular expertise in finance, technology or politics to have an open discussion. I am the friend of one of them so he invited me to come and present about the state of religion in the world. I am far from an expert, but we did have a lively respectful conversation.

What became clear very quickly was that none of them had any interest in spiritual things or God. Several of them believed that religion was the main problem in the world and that any real solution to the world's problems was not going to come from religion. They started their meetings by reviewing the progress of their recent stock picks and their new business ventures. For them, "feeling prosperous" was staying healthy into the later years of life, making more money than other rich people and being able to hopefully leave their children in a more successful place than themselves. The issue of faith was not even considered as a factor in their prosperity, it actually was seen as a threat to it.

The problem here is not that they are rich and successful according to the world's standards. The problem is not that they enjoy investing and making a profit. And it is good to want to leave the world a better place and to leave an inheritance to your children. The problem is that their idea of "feeling prosperous" does not address the most important aspects of life – the questions of the heart. Feelings flow from the heart. Feelings are rooted in something much deeper than statistics, numbers and possessions. The old saying, "Money can't buy love," is true. To ignore the deeper aspects of the soul is to harden one's heart to the spiritual world and eternity. Jesus has some clear teaching on this and I believe most people when they think about Jesus' words will agree with Him. However, for one reason or another some are not willing to explore a different path for prosperity. Nor are they willing to be honest with the true state of their soul.

Jesus told the following parable about the economics of God in response to a man who was trying to draw Him into a discussion about the economics of the world. The economics of God consist of more than just physical resources. *The economics of the world are at war with the economics of God.* Luke 12:15-21 states,

> "And he said to them, 'Take care, and be on your guard against all covetousness, for one's life does not consist in the abundance of his possessions.' And he told them a parable, saying, 'The land of a rich man produced plentifully, and he thought to himself, 'What shall I do, for I have nowhere to store my crops?' And he said, 'I will do this: I will tear down my barns and build larger ones, and there I will store all my grain and my goods. And I will say to my soul, 'Soul, you have ample goods laid up for many years; relax, eat, drink, be merry.' But God said to him, 'Fool! This night your soul is required of you, and the things you have prepared, whose will they be?' So is the one who lays up treasure for himself and is not rich toward God."

Jesus tells this parable to shed light on the tenth commandment and the dangers of coveting. Coveting is the key disposition stimulated by the economics of the world. Contentment is the key disposition stimulated by the economics of God. *Contentment is necessary to live in true prosperity.* Coveting and the economics of the world blind the soul from seeing there is much more to life than the abundance of one's possessions. *Money can be a detriment to our relationship with God and is limited in its possibilities.* But we are called to live in the economics of the world and steward worldly possessions for God's kingdom and glory. So, how do we live in the world and steward worldly possessions and at the same time be "rich toward God?"

Being "rich toward God" is true prosperity. Being "rich toward God" transcends one's socio-economic status. It is ultimately not about what we physically possess, but how we steward it. True prosperity challenges the wealthy in their stewardship but also fights against the bondage and circumstances of poverty. *Poverty in all of its forms is bondage and to be battled against by the promises of God and the power of the Holy Spirit.* True prosperity also fights for the blessings of God. *God is a good God who desires good things for His children, even material things.* The material blessings of God must be stewarded well so we don't fall prey to covetousness but grow in being "rich toward God."

In this chapter we are going to look at how to practically deal with poverty and wealth so we can learn to live in prosperity in a suffering world. We will first look at the proper way to view money. It should never be viewed in isolation, but always as part of the 3M's: Motive, Mission and Money. Then we will look at the importance of understanding our Stewardship Calling. There are three primary stewardship callings: Standard, Minimalist and Capacity. And finally we will look at the importance of a healthy faith culture to fight against poverty and to fight for true prosperity.

Motive, Mission and Money

The two most powerful questions that can be asked about any decision pertaining to money are: What is my motive and what is my mission? We are susceptible to the bondage of the economics of the world if we talk about the stewardship of money outside the context of motive and mission. This is what God warned the Israelites of in Deuteronomy 8:17-18, "Beware lest you say in your heart, 'My power and the might of my hand have gotten me this wealth.' You shall remember the Lord your God, for it is he who gives you power to get wealth..."

God does not need our money. His kingdom does not run like the kingdoms of the world. When motive and mission are removed from the discussion the economics of the world take over rather than the economics of God. One main principle of the economics of God is that if the motive and mission do not line up with God's heart and mission it doesn't matter how much money is given or ministry done it will bear no eternal lasting fruit. Jesus states in John 15:5, "I am the vine; you are the branches. Whoever abides in me and I in him, he it is that bears much fruit, for apart from me you can do nothing." Jesus makes this point even stronger in Matthew 7:21-23,

> "Not everyone who says to me, 'Lord, Lord,' will enter the kingdom of heaven, but the one who does the will of my Father who is in heaven. On that day many will say to me, 'Lord, Lord, did we not prophesy in your name, and cast out demons in your name, and do many mighty works in your name?' And then will I declare to them, 'I never knew you; depart from me, you workers of lawlessness.'"

Plenty of people can give a lot of money, but if the motive and mission are misdirected it has no eternal benefit to them. 1 Corinthians 13:3 says, "If I give away all I have, and if I deliver up my body to be burned, but have not love, I gain nothing." Love here is referring to one's heart that is motivated by the love of God, not just by any arbitrary definition of love. In God's economy He will redirect funds that are wrongly used and move them toward His larger purposes. He is most concerned with the state of our hearts.

Matthew 7:21-23 is a sobering passage. It reveals that powerful ministry can occur even when the hearts of the ministers are far from the will of the Father. Paul touches on this when he speaks of people preaching from envy and rivalry. (Phil. 1:15-18) The answers to the world's problems are never going to be answered or solved only by throwing money at them. This is not the way of the kingdom of God. Jesus modeled this for us when He first sent out the disciples to preach the good news of the gospel and minister the power of the Kingdom of God. He told them not to take any provisions or do any fund raising, but to trust the Lord to provide. (Matthew 10:7-10) This I believe was primarily to make the important point that the economics of God are radically different than the economics of the world. And He did it to put a priority on motive and mission rather than physical provision.

Faith, which flows from a God honoring motive, and mission is never limited by lack of money. Luke chapter 8 reveals that there were many from all different socio-economic positions that financially supported Jesus's and the disciples' itinerant ministry, but it was a natural result of those who got caught up with Jesus' heart and mission. Encouraging followers of Jesus to be willing to give more and even give sacrificially is important since it is one sign or possibly the main sign that they are living under the economics of God. We are commanded in 2 Corinthians 9:7, "Each one must give as he has decided in his heart, not reluctantly or under compulsion, for God loves a cheerful giver." So, any discussions about our money and resources should not be removed from a larger and deeper discussion about our motive and mission.

God is not against prosperity. He is for prosperity with purpose. But purpose has to be divine purpose, which is in line with God's will. Prosperity untethered from God's purposes results in bondage to the economics of the world and the deadly C's of coveting, comparing, competing and consuming. We need purpose to prosper. We need God's purpose if we are going to eternally prosper and be "rich toward God." Many people live today with margin-less lives with their head down just being busy and every now and then look up for a brief moment to get a view of where they are going in life. It is one thing to not be sure where we are going when we are 7 years old, but quite another when we are 37 or 67. Peter Kreeft has said,

> "…what is the point and purpose of life? Why was I born? Why am I living? What's it all about? Most people in our modern Western society do not have any clear or solid answer to that question. Most of us live without knowing what we live for. Surely this is life's greatest tragedy, far worse than death. Living for no reason is not living but mere existing, mere surviving…We need a meaning to life more than we need life itself."[xlvii]

I once received a letter from some friends that I will never forget. It finished with; *"We are getting older but still playing golf and a little tennis and working in the garden."* As I read this last sentence of the letter something deep inside of me flared up. God touched my heart. Is that all there is to live for? There has got to be more – *I want more!* I want to live for more! My heart will not be satisfied with the American dream of retirement. That exhausting, rat race pursuit of accumulating "enough" wealth to someday be able to stop working and live the remainder of my days on earth in reasonable comfort and security while pursuing recreational and social pleasures.

But then why are so many people in bondage to the American dream of retirement? It would appear they are without the ability to be set free to something bigger which will engage their hearts and dreams? There has been a lot of writing lately about this issue of purpose and meaning. We are all driven by a purpose, but not all purposes are equal. Many live their lives never being clear on their purpose. People are hungry for anything, which will help them grapple with this issue in their lives. But it would appear that within our society the pursuit of affluence is winning out over all other options, which have been presented. And the bondage to the American dream of retirement continues to our personal and national detriment.

    Our modern society has been described as the "modern fragmented social world." Within this fragmented social structure there is a growing and even paralyzing experience of loneliness and isolation where there is a void of lasting intimate relationships, family heritage and any deep connections with the larger community. Postmodernity has brought us the belief that "meaning" has died because post-moderns claim there is no objective realm to find what is genuinely true. This leaves individuals and the larger society even more alone in this fragmented world with a nagging restlessness and the natural default of finding meaning and purpose within the American dream of retirement. Purpose is ultimately meaningless and incapable of bringing ultimate satisfaction without having a transcendent personal mission behind it. Lesslie Newbigin has said,

> "Purpose is a personal word. People entertain purposes and seek to realize them; things, inanimate objects, do not have purposes of their own. An inanimate object, such as a machine, may embody purpose, but it is the purpose of the designer, not its own. If I come across a piece of machinery or equipment and have no idea of its purpose, I can of course take it to pieces and discover exactly how it works. But that will not explain what it is for. Either the designer, or someone who knows how to use it successfully for the purpose for which it was designed, will have to

tell me. There will have to be personal communication."[xlviii]

Mission drift is something that plagues us all and has been the plight of much of church history. Mission drift is what occurs when the supernatural powers behind the economics of the world and the American dream of retirement slowly and subtly erode clarity of purpose and mission from believer's lives and the life of the Church. We are currently in an unprecedented time in world history where there is more personal wealth accumulation among a greater number of people than in any other time in history. However, this wealth accumulation has not in and of itself equated to making people happier and healthier. Philosopher William Barrett has stated,

> "Modern civilization has raised the material level of millions of people beyond the expectations of the past, but has it succeeded in making people happier? To judge by the bulk of modern literature, we would have to answer 'no'; and in some respects we might even have to say it has accomplished the reverse."[xlix]

There is today an exciting momentum behind generous giving toward eradicating some of the world's problems related to health and economics. Many of these great endeavors the Church can join in and help lead with other organizations to accomplish some wonderful things. But the more exciting and fruitful thing that is occurring today is the result of wealth creation in many areas of the world.

> "It is a fact that aid – wealth distribution - does not lift people and nations out of poverty. Wealth creation does. The biggest lift out of poverty in the history of mankind has happened in our generation. This has been achieved not through aid but by trade; wealth creation through business. As is demonstrated by the escape of hundreds of

millions from dire poverty in both India and China since the 1980s, one cannot tackle poverty without a determined pursuit of wealth creation."[1]

It is important that the Church today equips and empowers its marketplace people with a vision of wealth creation toward economic blessing to all people. However, there is a great danger in the process of mission drift. Christ followers are called first and foremost to the main problems of the world, which are sin and death. Jesus came to eradicate this big problem and call His Church into His mission of bringing this good news to the hearts of all people. Motive, Mission and Money are practically lived out by Growing, Going and Giving.

The 3M's should be expressed in our lives by the 3 G's. Our giving should be a by-product of our growing in the Lord and our going on daily mission with the Lord. The 3 G's are a result of the transforming work of the Gospel within our soul. After we come into a relationship with Jesus everything should change. We start the process of growing into the person God created us to be. We start laying hold of God's purpose for our life, which changes how we approach every day. And we begin to see and handle our money and resources in light of His kingdom rather than the kingdom of the world. This is what it means to be "rich toward God." Jesus said in Matthew 6:19-21,

> "Do not lay up for yourselves treasures on earth, where moth and rust destroy and where thieves break in and steal, but lay up for yourselves treasures in heaven, where neither moth nor rust destroys and where thieves do not break in and steal. For where your treasure is, there your heart will be also."

Our true treasure is uncovered not necessarily by what we have accumulated, but by determining our motive and mission behind how we have used our resources. It is only when our motive is revealed that we can determine whether we are storing up treasures on earth or in heaven. If we are followers of Jesus we should be growing in our ability and desire to live for the will and works of our heavenly Father rather than our own will. The process of spiritual growth is the process of learning to live by the Holy Spirit's power, which transforms the motives of our heart. This process will radically affect how we view the purpose and mission of our life. As our motive and mission are being transformed by the Holy Spirit's power we will become greater and more cheerful givers of our resources for furthering God's work in the world.

Our Stewardship Calling

Stewardship is a major theme from the beginning of the Bible when God gave Adam and Eve the command to take dominion over the earth to the New Testament commands and parables. *God is a good God who desires good things for His children, even material things.* For most of our western church history, wealth and affluence have been looked at with suspicion and wealthy Christians have been made to feel less holy and guilty because of their wealth. This message contradicts God's heart and desire for his people. John Schneider puts it like this,

> "The ancient monastic vow presumes that life with a minimum of possessions (poverty), and certainly without luxuries, is spiritually better than life with abundance. Even among Protestants, certain elements of this tradition are making a strong comeback in our day. Their main form is not rigorous asceticism, but a gospel of simpler living, which extols the virtue of radically reducing one's consumption for spiritual as well as moral reasons. This is in response to a growing awareness that something is badly wrong – spiritually wrong – with the way the economic culture is affecting the spiritual character of the church. The trouble with these approaches is that they cannot very well

integrate the strong biblical theme – and it is a very strong theme from beginning to end – of physical delight as God's ultimate vision for human beings."[li]

The fact is that we all struggle to be at peace with how to handle wealth and affluence. One reaction to this negative view of wealth has been the growing health and wealth movement. Some of this shift has been good in that it has awakened the church to God's heart and desire to bless his children even with material blessings. Unfortunately, some of this movement has moved into the dangerous waters of a name-it-claim it superficial faith that fleeces the masses and lines the pockets of charismatic spiritual leaders. There is a better way that stays away from a negative view of wealth and stays away from making wealth the priority. Schneider sheds more light on this,

> "However, it also seems clear in the Bible, from beginning to end, that there is a way to be affluent that is good. In fact, as I will seek to show, it is a fundamental biblical theme that material prosperity (rightly understood) is the condition that God envisions for all human beings. It describes the condition that God desired for human beings when he created the world. It describes the condition that God has in view for human beings for eternity."[lii]

We all have a stewardship calling. This calling transcends what job we hold or how much money we make. To live at peace and to live in the spiritual blessing of contentment we must know what our stewardship calling is. There are three main stewardship callings we can find in the bible:

The Standard Calling: steward what money/possessions come to us for the Kingdom; stay in our place and be faithful unless we are called into a minimalist or capacity calling.

The Minimalist Calling: steward as little money/possessions as possible for the Kingdom; this can be just for a season or for a lifetime.

The Capacity Calling: steward as much money/possessions as possible for the Kingdom; these people have the gift of making money and maximizing resources as well as stewarding worldly power for the Kingdom of God.

    Most of us begin and stay within the Standard Calling. You might think that since most of the world lives in poverty that most of the world would be living in the Minimalist Calling. But that is not true, because as we will see, the Minimalist Calling is a very specific calling and it can be given to a "rich young ruler" or it can be given to middle class "fisherman" or it can be given to the "poor." One's socio-economic state does not determine one's stewardship calling. Just because someone is wealthy and knows how to make money does not mean they are living out of a Capacity Calling for the Kingdom of God. And just because a Christian divests of their wealth and gives 90% of their income away does not mean they are living out the Minimalist Calling for the Kingdom of God.

    The problem today is that some Christians are pushing the minimalist calling as the best and most spiritual calling, which puts undo guilt and legalism on believers and robs them of the joy of the Father in blessing them. As we will see there is nothing more holy or acceptable about the minimalist calling. The other problem today is that some Christian leaders are pushing the capacity calling as the best calling and that all believers are to lay hold of it. This unhealthy health and wealth message also puts people under guilt and reorients their affections from God and His mission to God and His handouts.

    Someone who is living in poverty does not need to be told that wealth is evil for they are lacking the basics and at the same time they don't need to be told a name-it-claim-it get rich formula. They need to be led into a faith where God works on them from the inside out and delivers them from the bondage of poverty. Poverty is bondage imposed upon a person and sometimes even embraced by the person as their identity. Just because the bondage of poverty is thrust upon a person or group of people through injustice does not mean they have to live with a spirit of poverty. The bondage of poverty is not the same as the minimalist calling, which is a willful divestment and choosing of a simpler life. It is not an embracing of a poverty mentality. *Poverty in all its forms is bondage and to be battled against with the promises of God and the power of the Holy Spirit.* One of the most overlooked promises is Matthew 6:33, "But seek first the kingdom of God and his righteousness, and all these things will be added to you." We in the west have often watered down this promise to a form of simple anxiety relief and therapy rather than the radical promise it is for provision for the poor and a base line of contentment for the wealthy.

Some people have taken Proverbs 30:7-9 as their standard by which Christians should judge their stewardship. It states, "Two things I ask you; deny them not to me before I die: Remove far from me falsehood and lying: give me neither poverty nor riches; feed me with the food that is needful for me, lest I be full and deny you and say, 'Who is the Lord?' or lest I be poor and steal and profane the name of my God." Again, Schneider gives us insight,

> "This prayer is rich in wisdom. But it is in my view mistaken, in the larger context of Proverbs (and of the Old Testament as a whole), to make this wise saying into a standard for measuring the morality of a person's lifestyle, as some do…As Jesus indicated in the Gospels, the right frame of mind is to presume to receive no more than "our daily bread" and if that is all we get, let us be grateful and satisfied…But neither this proverb nor the Lord's Prayer gives grounds for the inference that God will not bless us, or others, with considerable fortune – much less that considerable fortune is in

and of itself an evil…Nowhere in the book of Job does the main character plead to God for material wealth, but only for restoration of his integrity. God restores his riches anyway. In none of these instances is the modesty of desire anything like a teaching that condemns the condition of affluence in the extreme."[liii]

If this proverb is the standard then it will create an unhealthy view of affluence and wealth and blessings from God. Yes, there can be great dangers to receiving wealth and being affluent. The scriptures are full of warnings about the possible dangers associated with riches. This proverb points out the main danger that riches can draw our hearts away from the Father. They can lead us into comfort and isolation. Wealth has a way of isolating people from community. They can also rob us from growing in our longing for Christ's return because we have settled for the good life here. And riches can subtly make us "lukewarm" in the eyes of our Lord.

We have to deal with the complexities of the minimalist or capacity callings versus the standard calling, which is less complex. Our current calling does not mean we will stay there. We must be willing and open to move into either the minimalist or the capacity position no matter what our socio economic position is. What is important is to live in a place of peace with our wealth, giving and sharing and be clear of our calling. This will maximize our spiritual growth. None of these positions reflect a more spiritually mature position. When we are clear on our calling we can be at peace with our finances and grow in faithfulness.

Soon after I graduated from seminary, I was out to lunch with a single friend of mine who had recently graduated from Law School. During our lunch as we were talking about our futures, he said to me, "I really respect the path you have taken, it is a higher calling." Throughout church history the idea that fulltime vocational ministry is somehow a higher more important calling than other vocational paths has been encouraged. This has had a detrimental impact upon people's understanding of vocation and mission. What is most important is not the specific vocation but clarity of our stewardship calling whether it is the standard, minimalist or capacity calling.

It is critical that the 3 M's of motive, mission and money are applied to each of these perspectives. If I am living under the standard calling I must live in that calling unless I am called to pursue the minimalist or capacity calling. What is my motive? Is it minimalist out of guilt or calling? Is it minimalist because of mission or misery (the belief that poor is better and more holy)? Is the calling we are moving toward a capacity position? Do we desire power and money or do we desire to maximize our resources and worldly power for God's kingdom?

We need to learn to nurture each of these callings within our churches and reinforce that we should be willing to transition from one to the other if we are called to. Again, most people will fall into the standard calling unless they are uniquely called into the minimalist or capacity calling. Stewardship is easiest and simplest with the standard calling, but gets more complex when we move into the minimalist and capacity callings. We must beware of ranking these perspectives in any order of holiness and spiritual maturity. The issues must always be personal calling.

A crisis of faith occurs when we are called to transition from one calling to another. Sometimes a change in vocation will bring this about and at other times the Lord just leads and calls us there. The big question is what stewardship calling was Jesus living by? Jesus was clearly a minimalist during His active ministry years. Jesus said in Luke 9:58, "Foxes have holes, and birds of the air have nests, but the Son of Man has nowhere to lay his head." Most likely Jesus transitioned into the minimalist calling from the standard calling that He grew up in. We cannot be sure what calling Jesus grew up under. We do know that He did not grow up in poverty as many have promoted. Martin Hengel shows us,

"We should note first that Jesus himself, did not come from the proletariat of day-laborers and landless tenants, but from the middle class of Galilee, the skilled workers. Like his father, he was an artisan, a *tekton*, a Greek word which, means mason, carpenter, cartwright and joiner all rolled up into one (Mark 6:3)."[liv]

Most likely the disciples started out in the standard calling like most people do as we have seen. We do know that they did not come out of poverty but were middle class fisherman. When they encountered Jesus, He called them to a minimalist calling to leave everything and follow Him. Paul most likely transitioned to the minimalist calling when Jesus called him on the Damascus road. But Jesus did not call all of his followers to the minimalist calling. Many that were part of his larger disciples outside of the twelve were not called to a minimalist calling. In fact, many of them supported Jesus and the twelve. (Luke 8:3)

The minimalist calling does not necessarily mean experiencing a minimalist life all the time. We need to heed Jesus' incredible promise to Peter after he pointed out to Jesus that he and the other disciples had left everything to follow Him. Mark 10:29-31 says,

"Jesus said, 'Truly, I say to you, there is no one who has left house or brothers or sisters or mother or father or children or lands, for my sake and for the gospel, who will not receive a hundred fold now in this time, houses and brothers and sisters and mothers and children and lands, with persecutions, and in the age to come eternal life.'"

One of Jesus' points is that for those who are called to the minimalist calling they won't necessarily experience a minimalist life all the time. Jesus and His disciples were well cared for by many other disciples who supported them with food and nice houses to meet in as they traveled.

In Jesus' encounter with the "rich young ruler" He calls this man into the minimalist calling because Jesus knew it was the only way for this man to break free from the unhealthy bonds of class, power and wealth. This account is found in all three of the synoptic gospels (Matthew, Mark and Luke). Luke is the only one who specifically identifies this young man as a ruler, which means he was part of the ruling religious class. This account reveals the spiritual clash between Jesus and the economics of God with a rich person of the ruling class that was abusing the people and embracing a system of values that contradicted the heart of the Mosaic Law while appearing to uphold the law. Jesus' words to this "rich young ruler" are some of the most severe and radical we find in the scripture. After Jesus questioned the "rich young ruler" about keeping the Law He said these striking words:

> "When Jesus heard this, he said to him, 'One thing you still lack. Sell all that you have and distribute to the poor, and you will have treasure in heaven, and come, follow me.' But when he heard these things, he became very sad, for he was extremely rich. Jesus, seeing that he had become sad, said, 'How difficult it is for those who have wealth to enter the kingdom of God! For it is easier for a camel to go through the eye of a needle than for a rich person to enter the kingdom of God.' Those who heard it said, 'Then who can be saved?' But he said, 'What is impossible with man is possible with God.'" (Luke 18:22-27)

The disciples were obviously shocked by Jesus' words. Believers throughout church history have remained confused about what Jesus is saying here and questioning whether it is possible to come to Jesus without a minimalist calling. Is there a way into His kingdom as a wealthy person without getting rid of one's wealth? Yes, Jesus' encounter with Zacchaeus (Luke 19:1-9) reveals not only a very wealthy person coming to faith in Jesus without being called to a minimalist calling, but someone who came to Jesus and remained in his wealth creating job. Zacchaeus embraced a capacity calling for his life. He first made retribution to all that he robbed and then gave to the poor, which reveals he had embraced the gospel message in his heart. And as far as we know he remained a chief tax collector, but now used his power and money for the kingdom of God. Both the parable of the talents (Matthew 25:14-30) and the parable of the minas (Luke 19:11-27) reveal the importance of stewardship of all God gives us. John Schneider gives great insight into the parable of the minas when he says,

> "There is not much in Christian theology today that honors God as a warrior-king, or that honors the courage of godly people in the marketplace. But this is a parable of power and the enlargement of dominion through wealth. It is a parable that honors the fearsome courage and strength of a warrior and king, who will not stop until his realm is enlarged over all the earth. It is a parable that honors the strength and courage of his servants who are fruitful in the worldly realms of power. It is a parable that honors the enlargement of people who would become stronger, and would make their master stronger, through the creation of wealth. And it is also a parable of dire warning against a spirit of timidity and fruitlessness in our response to the world. It takes us back, through Christ, into something more profound…the creation itself, and the existence of dominion and delight that God envisioned for human beings."[lv]

One of many challenges of the capacity calling is the constant evaluation of whether one is enjoying what God has given verses indulging in material affluence and power. Things are more complex today with the spread of affluence. A capacity calling needs to be defined by "affluence without attachment." *The gospel frees us from bondage to consumerism and makes possible living in "abundance without attachment."*

Everyone, regardless of which stewardship calling they are living under need to apply the 3M's of Motive, Mission and Money in their lives by learning the 3 G's of Growing, Going and Giving. Those called to the standard and capacity callings need to heed the sharp warnings found in scripture of the dangers of wealth and apply the 3 M's so they are remaining connected to the church community learning to share, give and support. They need to watch that they do not create "silos" of just wealthy friends and wealthy lifestyles. Charles Murray writes about the development of 'superzips' where the top 1-5% wage earners cluster around each other in exclusive zip codes whereby eliminating their contact with the poor. In full disclosure, I live and minister within one of these "silos" in Aspen, Colorado. There are virtually no poor people within our community except for the occasional homeless person that drifts through.

It is especially critical for us to get involved in God's global mission and get our feet on the ground in the tough places of the world. I am writing this while on the plane with my son to go to India where we have some gospel partners. Don't misunderstand this is not to appease some form of guilt or to make ourselves feel good. It is because of Acts 1:8 mission. These "superzips" might not have any physical signs of poverty but they are stricken with a poverty of soul, which creates a hardness of soul that is tough to break. It is also critical that we model a church community that is willing to break down the "silos" and develop intimate fellowship across socio-economic lines.

Those called to the capacity calling need to learn to partner with the church and leverage their wealth creation for God's kingdom in their sphere's of influence such as the marketplace, geo-politics, education, philanthropy, technology, entertainment, etc. Those called to the minimalist calling need to watch for self-righteousness and pride that sees their dedication and calling as more worthy or holy. They need to honor the other callings and not forget that much of their financial support will be coming from their brothers and sisters in the standard and capacity callings. Again, no matter which calling we are living under the important thing is that the 3 M's are being applied through the 3G's and that an open heart is maintained that is willing to transition to a different calling when the Lord calls. It might be for just a season or it might be for a lifetime. Peace and maximum fruitfulness and fulfillment is attained when we operate in the zone of our stewardship calling. True prosperity, "being rich toward God" is found when we are obedient and at peace with our stewardship calling.

Poverty and Wealth in a Faith Culture

A healthy faith culture nurtures healthy stewardship discussions. There is a special trust and intimacy that takes place when people can share openly about their financial issues. This stewardship discussion should have as the ultimate goal that people become "rich toward God," which is true prosperity. Being "rich toward God" is being Godward in all our pursuits. We are either moving toward God and His economics or away from God and in bondage to the economics of the world. *The economics of the world are at war with the economics of God.* Jesus said in Matthew 6:24, "You cannot serve God and money." He also says in Matthew 12:30, "Whoever is not with me is against me, and whoever does not gather with me scatters." A healthy faith culture is going to be alert to this struggle and provide avenues for gospel transformation through discussion, prayer and ministry.

How is poverty and wealth handled within the church community? This is a big question that each faith community should wrestle with and pray through. The idea of "moral proximity" as it is applied to Acts 1:8 is a great guide. In Acts 1:8 Jesus says, "But you will receive power when the Holy Spirit has come upon you, and you will be my witnesses in Jerusalem and in all Judea and Samaria, and to the end of the earth." The first place that poverty should be eradicated should be within the church family, then moving out from there to the city, the region, then the nations. *Poverty in all its forms is bondage and to be battled against with promises of God and the power of the Holy Spirit.* Wealth is much harder to handle within the church, because the issues are more complex and often hidden or not acknowledged. Paul's words to Timothy in 1 Timothy 6:9-10, 17-19 are a great guide to the church to help it deal with the wealthy:

> "But those who desire to be rich fall into temptation, into a snare, into many senseless and harmful desires that plunge people into ruin and destruction. For the love of money is a root of all kinds of evils. It is through this craving that some have wandered away from the faith and pierced themselves with many pangs…As for the rich in this present age, charge them not to be haughty, nor to set their hopes on the uncertainty of riches, but on God, who richly provides us with everything to enjoy. They are to do good, to be rich in good works, to be generous and ready to share, thus storing up treasure for themselves as a good foundation for the future, so that they may take hold of that which is truly life."

These words of caution are not just for the rich, but for anyone who "desires to be rich." Paul is harsh toward those who desire riches and who are susceptible to cultivating a love of money. He does not say there is anything wrong with being rich, but encourages them to watch their attitude toward riches and to leverage their riches to become "rich toward God."

True prosperity is living in the tension between evil and suffering and the goodness of God by the power and promises of the Gospel. We should be seeing people set free from all the forms of bondage associated with poverty and its mindset and people coming into greater experiences of spiritual and material prosperity. *God desires to be sought for who He is not just what He gives.* These expressions of prosperity all need to have at the center a heart that ultimately desires to be "rich toward God." His gifts and blessings are to be seen as the overflow of the heart of our heavenly Father to bless His children.

A healthy faith culture is one where all three stewardship callings: the standard calling, minimalist calling and capacity calling are valued and nurtured within the church community. Often these different callings do not get along well together, so we must nurture them and come to see that they actually work beautifully together to allow us to live in prosperity in a world of suffering. To cultivate a healthy faith culture we must nurture all three of these callings and they must all be able to exist in unity and support each other.

The standard calling is the calling that the vast majority of believers live under. This would include the majority of people who are working in the marketplace and it would include the majority of people who serve in full-time ministry today. This group would include people in all the different socio-economic categories. People in this calling do not necessarily have the gift of making money or have a powerful or public sphere of influence. They are busy working, providing for their families, serving in the local church and being good citizens. The goal within the faith community is to help them grow in their stewardship through the 3M's of Motive, Mission and Money through Growing, Going and Giving. As they grow spiritually and learn to be a part of local and global missions their giving will follow their heart's purpose. James addresses business people directly in James 4:13-16,

> "Come now, you who say, 'Today or tomorrow we will go into such and such a town and spend a year there and trade and make a profit – yet you do not know what tomorrow will bring. What is life? For you are a mist that appears for a little time and then vanishes. Instead you ought to say, 'If the Lord wills, we will live and do this or that.'" As it is, you boast in your arrogance. All such boasting is evil."

James shows that most important for our stewardship is learning to evaluate our motive and see if we are surrendered to the "Lord's will." When the Lord is allowed to lead and be involved in our decisions then we begin to learn what it is to be on mission with Him. When these two things come into alignment we begin to have a healthy perspective and stewardship of our resources. A healthy faith culture cultivates the alignment of our priorities and spending with the will and work of the Father. It values those in the marketplace and works to equip them to maximize their power, wealth and influence to bring light to the darkness in the world. We can change our vocation and our location but nothing will change until our heart gets aligned through the 3M's and 3G's.

A healthy faith culture should also be upholding the minimalist calling as a reality for those in the standard or capacity calling. It is not just missionaries and full time vocational workers who get this calling, it should be anyone at anytime for many reason. Jesus can call anyone to embrace this calling at anytime. A healthy faith community should uphold this calling to be able to simplify for a season or for a lifetime.

The reality is that we have more time to focus on kingdom work under the minimalist calling. This is why Jesus and the disciples were called to it. Also, for a season or for a lifetime it can be what it takes to sever the bondage of earthly riches and their attachment to the economics of the world. This is why Jesus called the rich young ruler to it. There are some ministries and some missions to the unreached people groups in the world that will require this kind of calling. But one does not have to move to a different country to be called to live this calling.

Just like the standard calling, those called to the minimalist calling will grow in their stewardship through the 3M's and 3 G's. The goal of this calling is to minimize material things and money in our lives so we can be more focused on Christ's mission. Those living within this calling must be careful they do not become prideful thinking their calling is more holy or that every believer should move into this calling. We all need to be at peace with our calling and place and encourage others and be open to our Lord's calling to transition to a new calling if led.

People called to the capacity calling are people who have first been faithful serving in the standard or minimalist calling. It is a dangerous lie to say, "I am going to work hard and make a bunch of money so that I can retire and do missions." It is very hard for someone who has become very wealthy without growing in the 3M's and 3 G's to transition from the bondage of riches into the capacity calling.

Jesus' encounter with the rich young ruler illustrates this point and this is why Jesus called him to leave everything and follow Him. It very well might have been that if the rich young ruler did abandon his riches to follow Jesus, at some point he would gain them back again if he had the gift of making money and did not stay in the minimalist calling. I have some friends who are incredibly gifted and influential people and have the capacity to be very rich, but are called to a standard and minimalist calling. I also have friends who are incredibly gifted with the gift of making money and have transitioned from the standard calling to the capacity calling.

Capacity people need to watch that they do not create their own mission projects in isolation from the local church. This is dangerous and there is no precedent for it within the New Testament. When mission gets untethered from the local church and local elders and commissioned leaders it can easily experience mission drift and fade into just humanitarian efforts. That is a strong statement, but we must fight against independent efforts because of the difficulties of sometimes working within the church community. This is part of the process Jesus has called us into, which is to be a growing community of standard, minimalist and capacity stewards who work together for the Kingdom of God. Here are a few key things I have learned from some high capacity people who are serving the Kingdom well:

- Press into the community of the local church and do not silo.
- Get your hands dirty, don't just write the checks, but be involved.

- Network with others from different stewardship callings and help launch people.
- Open your home(s) and be hospitable to all people not just the wealthy.

A healthy faith culture helps stimulate "social capital" within the church community and for believers to take out into the marketplace. This is one reason why people want to invest in America because there is still some social capital left –trust. When corruption takes over in the marketplace and government a city, state, and nation lose social capital and lose global trust. This is one of the many blessings marketplace believers can bring to corporate life, government, politics, education, etc. When the 3M's and 3 G's all work together in a faith community it creates "social capital." And this "social capital" brings a huge blessing to the marketplace. Steven Pearlstein says,

> "In the current, cramped model of American capitalism, with its focus on maximizing output growth and shareholder value, there is ample recognition of the importance of financial capital, human capital and physical capital, but no consideration of social capital. Social capital is the trust we have in one another, and the sense of mutual responsibility for one another, that gives us the comfort to take risks, make long-term investments, and accept the inevitable dislocations caused by the economic gales of creative destruction. Social capital provides the necessary grease for increasingly complex machinery of capitalism, and for the increasingly contentious machinery of democracy. Without it, democratic capitalism cannot survive."[lvi]

"Social capital" is lost when we get consumed with achieving results and thinking big and are willing to compromise our stewardship calling and character to gain so-called success. We pursue what we see is success. For many of us the definition of success that has been pushed on us is "what we produce." If producing is driving us then failure will derail us into deep shame. True success, true prosperity is not what we produce, but the depth and health of our relationships along with faithfulness to our stewardship calling for the Kingdom.

All things are bigger with God. However, He might want us to become smaller so He can make us bigger. "If we are too big for a small thing, we are too small for a big thing." 1 Peter 5:5-7 says, "God opposes the proud but gives grace to the humble. Humble yourselves therefore under the mighty hand of God so that at the proper time he may exalt you, casting all your anxieties on him, because he cares for you." God will "exalt you," meaning He will prosper you and He will maximize your fruitfulness and fulfillment when we humbly learn to walk in our stewardship calling.

So, what makes you feel prosperous? I hope the 3M's of Motive, Mission and Money and the 3 G's of Growing, Going and Giving will be helpful to you in this critically important quest for true prosperity. I also hope the three categories of stewardship calling; Standard, Minimalist and Capacity callings, will help bring you to a place of powerful peace as you learn to live in prosperity in a suffering world.

CHAPTER ELEVEN
A Faith in Tension Approach to Sickness and Health

Just now in the process of writing this chapter, a friend stopped by for prayer. He was just diagnosed with cancer. Nothing so abruptly interrupts and shocks our lives like sickness, disease and the reality of death. Until we are hit with a serious illness or confronted with death, we often overlook just how important our health is to our definition of prosperity. What does embracing prosperity and engaging suffering look like in this situation? And how should believers and the Church minister to those who are sick, diseased and facing death? As a pastor I have the privilege to be invited into peoples' lives in the midst of their battle with all kinds of health issues. These times are trying and can even be traumatic but sometimes triumphant when healing comes. Over the years I have observed that the main factors that determine how people view sickness and health are how they view the origin and eternal state of the human body. Or another way of putting it would be how they view prosperity and suffering.

The eastern worldviews see no eternal value in the physical body or in our unique personal identities. Suffering is seen as illusion and an expected result of bad karma. There is no guarantee of freedom from suffering or sickness. Islam sees the body as strictly an instrument to submit to Allah in the chance that he may accept you. There is no personal relationship between the individual soul and God within Islam. The Judeo-Christian worldview begins in Genesis chapter one by affirming the goodness of all creation. All through the Bible the value of the entire being of mind, body, and spirit is upheld along with the promise of restoring and resurrecting the physical body as well as being transformed into a new creation that will exist for all eternity in fellowship with God. This is the framework we are to use to build a healthy view of sickness and healing from.

In western culture we have for the most part been content with technological advancements to try and solve the practical problems of sickness. Very little time is spent in pursing root causes, the philosophical and theological ramifications of sickness. Sadly, much of the western church has taken a similar approach and left the solutions to sickness to the medical field rather than bringing the power of the Gospel to bear alongside medical technology. Science and technology are a gift from God who has given mankind the ability to do amazing things. It is important to understand that whether it is medicine or strictly supernatural it is all God's gift of healing. Later in this chapter we will discuss better how to integrate the spiritual and medical means of healing.

Biblical Principles for Sickness and Health

The faith in tension approach to sickness and health we have been building within this book attempts to stay away from over spiritualization and spiritual abuse on one hand and away from a strictly intellectual and medical approach on the other. This approach is built upon the following biblical principles we have looked at in the previous chapters.

God's heart is to save, heal and deliver – always.

The sufferings we do not have to share in are oppression, disease and poverty.

God does not guarantee healing or spiritual maturity in this life, but has made provision for both to be pursued by faith.

God has given spiritual gifts to be pursued so we can set the harassed and helpless free.

God expects us to engage suffering the way Jesus and the early church did.

Saying that God's heart is to save, heal and deliver always does not mean that He will save, heal or deliver every time, but that it is His desire, it is His heart. Everything we believe about God needs to be built upon His ultimate goodness, that He loves us and has good things for us and is working toward completing that good work. When God created mankind in the beginning it was good. It was healthy not sick. But with the fall of mankind all creation has been susceptible to sickness, decay and death. His heart for His people in the Old Testament was that they would be free from sickness and disease (Deut. 7:15). Though He allows sickness and disease He does not afflict from His heart. (Lam. 3:33) And His desire for all to be saved and healthy is expressed in many different ways within the New Testament (1 Tim. 2:3, 3 John 2). There is no guarantee of our experience of health in this world, but there is provision made by Christ for us to pursue not just spiritual maturity but physical health as well. We do not have to share in spiritual oppression, disease or poverty for we can fight them with the weapons of faith. Sam Storms says,

> "Jesus promised that all who follow Him would suffer persecution, slander, rejection and oppression. But He never said that about sickness. Nowhere in the Bible are obedient children of God told to expect sickness and disease as part of their calling in life. Sickness is not a part of the cross we are called to bear."[lvii]

The weapons of faith are the spiritual gifts given to the Church to build each other up and fight poverty and sickness of all kinds. God expects His Church to fight sickness of all kinds the way Jesus and His early followers did. The scriptures say in Acts 10:38, "…God anointed Jesus of Nazareth with the Holy Spirit and with power. He went about doing good and healing all who were oppressed by the devil for God was with him." When Jesus was asked by His disciples about a man born blind He stated, "It was not that this man sinned, or his parents, but that the works of God might be displayed in him." God's people are to engage and fight against sickness and disease and the dark consequences of a fallen world. When Jesus heard the report of His friend Lazarus' bad health, He stated, "This illness does not lead to death. It is for the glory of God, so that the Son of God may be glorified." This is the longest recorded healing story and reveals the three primary reasons why God heals: 1) for the glory of God 2) because of God's love for us 3) and to build our faith. God's people are to fight for freedom from sicknesses because it is a way to reveal God's love, built up faith and magnify the testimony of His goodness and glory. Jesus makes it explicitly clear that we are to follow in His ministry to the sick in John 14:12, "Truly, truly, I say to you, whoever believes in me will also do the works that I do; and greater works than these will he do, because I am going to the Father."

In the rest of this chapter we will look at how to practically work these biblical principles out in the midst of fighting against sickness.

Getting Perspective on Sickness

There are some friendships in life that seem to just drop from the sky at a divinely appointed time. I will never forget the day that Bob (not his real name) walked into our church while he was on vacation. We immediately became friends in our first conversation where he invited me into his spiritual journey and his battle with advanced cancer.

Some relationships take awhile before they go deep. This one with Bob went deep immediately, maybe it was because I was a pastor and he was in the middle of stage four cancer. In our first conversation he shared with me his struggle and even anger with certain flippant comments made on social media about healing.

Things like, "I really get ticked off when I read on social media, 'God is so good…I prayed that my test results would come back negative – they did – God is so good!" To some, this communicates a "gum ball theology". If we just put a quarter in the machine, then we will certainly receive a gumball. Others call it a name-it-claim-it theology for healing. My friend went on to share that when he first was diagnosed that they prayed as well as many others that his surgery would eliminate the cancer and that he would be healed.

His surgery went well, but some time afterwards the results showed that the cancer had actually become more aggressive. "So, what happened to the gumball," he said, "Why didn't we get our prayers answered?" He went on to share that prayer after prayer for healing didn't get answered. It was in the mist of some of our following conversations that he emphatically said to me, "I do not believe I am going to be healed." And he added to that statement that he felt his faith was stronger than ever and that he was better off for being sick. This is when I asked him if I could question his perspective on his sickness and the issue of healing. I told him that his statements seemed to embrace sickness and missed the faith opportunity to continue to press in for healing.

Now, many people would have hammered me for being insensitive to a person about to die from cancer. But not Bob - he engaged and our conversation went into the depths of fighting sickness and at the same time learning from the sickness. He shared about the lessons he was learning from being sick with cancer. How it had caused him to slow down and appreciate the important things and rest in grace and not performance based religious ritual and that these things were sanctifying him. I rejoiced with him on that spiritual insight and growth, but also shared that there was more.

In James chapter one trials are seen as opportunities for growth and the strengthening of our faith. God does not intend for us to embrace the status of being poor or sick. These are inconsistent with God's design for shalom and flourishing. The trial or sickness was to be fought by faith. I went on to share that the only kind of suffering that we are called to rejoice in are persecutions for suffering for His name. All other forms of suffering we are called to fight with faith, unless, like Paul, we are told by God that we are not going to be healed. (2 Corinthians 12:9) It would be sin to continue to pray for healing when God told us we are not going to be healed, but we find that a rare case within scripture and in life. Bob said to me several times, "I desire to be healed, and I know God can heal me, but I do not believe I am going to be healed." My friend didn't have a clear word from God that he wasn't going to be healed. He just felt that he wasn't going to be healed – big difference. In James 5, general suffering (5:13) is separated from the specific suffering of sickness (5:14). He gives clear commands to those who are sick not to embrace their sickness but to fight it with the help of the prayer of faith and the anointing of oil by the elders of the church. It is sad today, that many churches do not have elders. Even if they do, they are not taking seriously the ministry of healing, which according to James 5 is a responsibility of the elders of the local church.

In my discussion with Bob he would focus on the blessing of his sickness to sanctify him and spent much time getting inspired by stories of other believers who experienced spiritual growth in the midst of their sickness. In response to this I affirmed the truth that suffering is used by God to sanctify us, but emphasized that it is also used to increase our faith and the empowerment of the Holy Spirit. Yes, sickness is used to lead us to greater intimacy with Jesus, but it is also to make us more like Jesus. And when Jesus was alive He healed people of sickness by the power of the Holy Spirit. (John 3:34) This is a faith in tension approach to sickness, both holiness through sickness and increased faith to fight sickness. It is a convergence of biblical prosperity and suffering. Many people use the story of Job to focus on the purposes of suffering, but forget the end of the story where God heals Job and restores his fortune.

Some believers focus on the idea that a Christian is a "spectacle of glory" when they continue trusting God even in the midst of suffering. But wouldn't the sick person who was healed of their sickness be a "spectacle of glory" also? Of course they would. All of the healings we find in Scripture brought glory to God. Sam Storms sheds light on this, "…contrary to popular thought, sickness and disease, in and of themselves, do not glorify God. Our unwavering faith and loyalty and love for God in spite of sickness and disease do glorify God."[lviii] In the midst of the trial of sickness many have taken comfort and understanding in Hebrews 12:11, "For the moment all discipline seems painful rather than pleasant, but later it yields the peaceful fruit of righteousness to those who have been trained by it." But many miss the next two verses vs. 12-13, "Therefore lift your drooping hands and strengthen your weak knees, and make straight paths for your feet, so that what is lame may not be put out of joint but rather be healed." Again, this is a faith in tension approach to sickness. We bring glory to God when we trust Him in the midst of sickness and we bring Him glory when we can testify of His healing power in our lives.

During the many conversations I had with Bob, he shared with me at different times the statements said to him and over him about his sickness. One of the statements Bob shared with me was from one of his doctors. He told Bob, "You will always be on medicine." We cannot forget the power of our words and the impact they have to either instill faith or fear. Well-meaning people in the health care business are often unaware of the careless statements they say to their patients. The reality is that no doctor knows absolutely if their patient will have to be on medication the rest of their life. Their data and history might lead them there, but to be presumptuous can actually curse rather than bless. It would be much more appropriate to state just the facts rather than a statement of certainty about their future condition. If someone can easily recall one of these statements, it probably reveals that it had a major impact on their thinking.

In ministering to sick people, well-meaning Christians are sometimes guilty of saying positive statements of healing over a person, when they didn't have clear confirmation. They were trying to bless, but their faith claim actually built a false hope within the person they were ministering to. In ministering to people, when they bring up one of these statements it is important to pray against any curses or statements that instilled fear and replace them with the promises of God's word. If someone has made emphatic statements claiming healing over a person, that person should be the one to intercede and fight for the healing and not stop until they are healed.

In western Christianity today there is often a lack of recognizing and understanding the role of spiritual warfare in dealing with sickness. Later in our relationship, during a time when Bob was really struggling for his life he said, "I can't be taken out until God is done with me." I believe that statement is true and can be supported by many passages. However, we cannot forget that we are at war with the powers of darkness. (Eph. 6:10-12) There are other wills exerted in this world than God's will and that is why we live in a fallen world. It is why Jesus commands us to pray, "Our Father in heaven, hallowed be your name. Your kingdom come, your will be done, on earth as it is in heaven…And lead us not into temptation, but deliver us from evil." (Matt. 6:9-10, 13)

The reason we are called to pray this is because people are exerting their fleshly wills everyday wreaking havoc all over the world and in the spiritual realm there are evil forces exerting their wills and bringing about evil of all kinds including sickness. We need to realize that sometimes we lose battles in this life. When someone gets sick or even dies we cannot say emphatically that it was God's will for there is an enemy at work. Why is this important? Because we are to continue to engage the spiritual battle fighting against suffering of all kinds and not fall prey to the apathetic prayer of just praying, "God's will be done." Yes, in the big picture God's will will be done "on earth as it is in heaven." But He has given us responsibility and authority and power to play a role in His will being done. Faith is a bigger factor than we have realized in this fight. We must always hold the two biblical truths of God's sovereignty and our free will together as true. They are never to be pitted against each other for they are both clearly supported in scripture. And this is especially important to remember in ministering to the sick.

It was a privilege to journey with Bob through his struggle with cancer. It was a mutually edifying relationship where there was freedom to wrestle out loud with each other's struggles and big questions. My struggles were from the pastoral side and his from the side of needing healing. We both we able to unify in our desperate cry to our loving heavenly Father the same cry of a father desperate for the healing of his son, "…I believe; help my unbelief!" (Mark 9:24) The last words I heard from my friend were, "Whether He heals me or not, my hope is in Jesus alone." Bob is perfectly healed and will be for all eternity and so will all who know the healer of our souls – Jesus Christ!

A big question that is often raised is the fact that we are going to die at some point so when do we stop praying for healing and start helping the person prepare for death. This takes great pastoral care and sensitivity to the Spirit. I would suggest that the primary answer to this question is the desire of the patient. Are they continuing to ask us to pray for healing or are they at peace in going to the Lord? I do not believe we have done a good job preparing people to die well. Our goal should be to end like Paul saying, "For I am already being poured out as a drink offering, and the time of my departure has come. I have fought the good fight, I have finished the race, I have kept the faith." (2 Timothy 4:6-7) And we must live and minister with Paul's perspective, "For to me to live is Christ, and to die is gain."

Getting Perspective on Healing

More insightful than how we respond to sickness that has not been healed is how we respond when God does heal. When healing occurs it often brings about a crisis of faith. And it is often surprising how believers sometimes respond and struggle with what actually happened. Healing can take people into a crisis of faith exposing a deficit in their beliefs. Dallas Willard in his book *Hearing God* shares a very insightful story,

> "Agnes Sanford relates how, as the young wife of an Episcopal minister, her child came down with a serious ear infection. It lasted for six weeks while she prayed fearfully and fruitlessly. Then a neighboring minister called to see her husband and learned that the child was sick. Quite casually, though intently and in a businesslike child manner, he prayed for the little boy, who immediately shut his eyes, lost his fever flush and went to sleep. When the boy awoke, his fever was gone and his ears were well. Sanford remarks, "The strange thing is that this did not immediately show me a new world. Instead, it perplexed me greatly. Why did God answer the minister's prayers when He had not answered mine? I did not know that I myself blocked my own prayers, because of my lack of faith. Nor did I know that this [successful] prayer could not come from resentment and darkness and unhappiness, as a pipeline can be clogged with roots and dirt. This doubt and confusion remained in my mind, even though the child himself, whenever he subsequently had a bit of an earache, demanded that I pray for."[lix]

What do we do with these experiences? We can probably all relate to this doubt and confusion that Agnes shared. However, if we are not careful we can get lost in the analysis of healing and miss the acknowledgement of healing. Healing is a blessing from God, but it is also a mystery. When healing comes it can uncover many realities of the state of our faith. We are to take a childlike approach to healing otherwise we will get caught up in an intellectual battle with healing. This approach is seen in the childlike response of Agnes' son. He didn't get caught up in how he was healed. He received and rejoiced in his healing and he let it build his faith so that his first response when faced with sickness was to ask for healing prayer. Agnes had a different response that allowed for doubt and confusion to enter. Doubt and confusion as stated earlier in this book are enemies to faith, especially healing faith.

We should expect healing from our heavenly Father. We should rejoice and give thanks when healing occurs and we should take our healing questions to God and ask Him to increase our faith response the next time we are faced with a healing opportunity. Doubt and confusion will rob us of faith if they are not taken to God. They can lead to wrong thinking about God if they are not submitted to the promises of God's Word and they will keep us from stepping out in the ministry of healing. God is the One who heals. We cannot get too bogged down in why our healing prayers were not answered. We are called to keep stepping into the ministry of healing regardless of our results. Sam Storms sheds light on this when he says,

> "…God is far more pleased with our obedience than he is with our success. Success is not something we ultimately control. I can't guarantee that my prayers for the sick will result in healing. I can't promise that my word to you will be spot-on accurate. But I can control whether or not I am willing to step out and take a risk. And the risk is worth it…We please him not by always producing results but by always practicing obedience. So get rid of the idea that God is offended by your failure or that he will bench you for the rest of the game because you missed it."[lx]

When my sister was 11 years old she was diagnosed with scoliosis, which is curvature of the spine. My parents took her to the doctor where it was confirmed. The diagnosis for her future health was not very bright. At the time we were living in Tulsa,

Oklahoma and were part of a dynamic church and faith community. Friends and the church family rallied in prayer for Shelley's back. One of my parent's friends who was part of this faith community, was a successful businessman who also had a healing ministry that took him all around the world. It was during one of his healing services that Shelley's back was completely healed of scoliosis. My mother had taken her there, believing that God was going to heal her. In the weeks that followed the x-rays confirmed her miraculous healing. And to this day Shelley's back is healthy.

Fast-forward several decades. Our mother had just died from a lengthy battle with cancer. Shelley was very close with Mom and in the midst of her grieving she internalized the pain. It was about this same time that she was encouraged to undergo a preventative mastectomy, since our mother and grandmother both died of breast cancer. It was a long hard surgery and it was not long afterwards that she was diagnosed with the autoimmune disease called lupus. The lupus started wreaking havoc on her body and eventually attacked her kidneys. Her kidneys started to degenerate. In this time she called upon people to pray for her healing from lupus and the restoration of her kidneys. Many prayed. The elders of my church even stopped by Houston to pray for her, but the kidneys did not heal.

We were full of faith because we had just come back from praying for one of our ex-elders who was about to die and he miraculously recovered! But the kidneys still were degenerating to the point that she had to go on dialysis. We stood on the testimony of her back being healed and even visited our friend who prayed for her back to be healed. But the kidneys still were not healed. She got put on the kidney transplant list because you cannot survive too long on dialysis and your health can quickly fade away. Because of the unique nature of her condition, trying to get a good match for her kidney was going to be very difficult. My wife, Meshell and I, got tested as donors only to find out late into the process we weren't going to be a match. Over 50 people got tested and no kidneys were coming available that would work.

We were not getting our healing prayers for a restored kidney answered.

But the Lord was sustaining her health through many years on dialysis. She was known as the amazing patient. If you knew Shelley or saw her, you would never know that every night she had to plug into a machine that circulated fluid throughout her body to keep her alive. Still our prayers for a restored kidney were not answered. If we were all honest, our faith struggled to continue to pray for a miracle. There were repeated calls from the donor hospitals of hope for a possible kidney match, but repeated discouragement came when they failed to match. Shelley's faith was amazing through all of this. She held onto God as her healer and provider knowing in one-way or another He was going to heal her. Then the call came. A tragic accident occurred when a 12-year-old boy lost his life, but his parents made the decision to make his kidneys available. The initial tests looked more hopeful than any before. It was a miraculous match. Shelley has a new kidney today and it is working perfectly with no signs of her body rejecting it.

Some people will have a tendency to get hung up in the analysis of healing and say it was modern medicine that provided a kidney for Shelley and not God's miraculous healing. True, but who has provided the know-how so we can develop medicine? As people of faith, we give credit to God first no matter how the healing comes. We cannot forget that all medicine is a partnership with the Creator, even if the practitioners deny there is a God. In all medicine there is no guarantee of a positive outcome. There is always faith that what procedure was done will bring healing. This is true whether one believes in God or not.

Shelley actually has three kidneys now. We are still praying that her original two kidneys will be completely healed and that there will not be a need for another kidney in the future.

Using All Weapons Against Sickness

I have been advocating a faith in tension approach to sickness and healing in this book, which is an embracing of God's promises for health and at the same time fighting the suffering of sickness by the power of the Spirit. It is very sad that so many Christians are not experientially aware of the vast spiritual weapons that are available to them in the fight against sickness. A few of the most important weapons God has given us for the battle against sickness can be found in five different faith categories:

>Word and Spirit Faith
>Personal Faith
>Community Faith
>Charismatic Faith
>Waiting Faith

Word and Spirit faith is faith in tension faith. It is faith that both embraces the Word of God and at the same time embraces the Spirit-empowered life. As mentioned in a previous chapter it is easy to become either a Christian Fundamentalist who is all about the Word or become a Charismania Christian who is all about the Spirit. We cannot forget that Jesus did not begin His formal ministry until after His humanity was empowered by the Holy Spirit. (Luke 3-4) This was to be the model for the early church as well. Jesus commanded them not to leave Jerusalem until they were empowered for life and ministry.

The greatest weapon we have against sickness is Word and Spirit prayer. This is prayer that is based on the great promises of God's Word and is dependent upon the leading and empowering of the Holy Spirit. We are commanded to pray "in the Spirit" and to "pray without ceasing". Word and Spirit prayer stands on God's truth and harnesses all of the gifts of the Holy Spirit in its battle against sickness. If there is ignorance or worse if there is a rejection of the gifts of the Holy Spirit there will be a quenching of the Holy Spirit in our battle against sickness.

Personal Faith is another key weapon we have to harness in the fight against sickness. Hebrews 11:6 tells us, "And without faith it is impossible to please him, for whoever would draw near to God must believe that he exists and that he rewards those who seek him." The "radical middle" approach to personal faith is to stay away from a name-it-claim-it formula faith at one extreme and to also stay away from the other extreme which downplays the role of personal faith and just emphasizes God's sovereignty.

James Dunn in his book, *Jesus and the Spirit* has pointed out that nearly 2/3 of the references to faith in the Synoptic Gospels occur in relation to miracles. He points out three primary ways Jesus addressed the importance of personal faith for healing. Jesus often encouraged and exhorted people to have faith so they would see healing. (Mark 5:36, 9:23f, 11:22ff, Matt 9:28, Lk 17:6) After someone was healed He commended that person for their faith. (Mk 5:34, 10:52, Matt 8:10, Lk 7:9, Matt 8:13, 15:28, Lk 7:50, 17:19) And Jesus also rebuked people for a lack of faith. (Mark 4:40, 9:19, Matt 6:30, 14:31, 16:8 17:20) It was characteristic of Jesus to look for personal faith in those He was ministering to. And when there was a lack of faith there was a quenching of miracles. The greatest example of this was when Jesus visited His hometown of Nazareth where He found very little faith and hence was able to heal only a few people. (Mark 6:5-6, Matt 13:58)

But this idea of faith leaves us with some big questions. How do we get this kind of personal faith? It is not about acquiring it, but it is about receiving it. There is a deep connection between faith, vulnerability and surrender. It is staggering to realize that Jesus never had a checklist that He put before someone before they were healed. It was a state of the soul where faith manifested in deep vulnerability with a willingness to receive and to be touched that He was looking for. It was a complete surrender to His question: Do you want to be healed? Vulnerability and surrender are not things that are nurtured within our culture today. They are actually seen as weakness rather than essential elements in faith that moves mountains of sickness. C.S.

Lewis in his book, *The Great Divorce*, has the soul shouting from hell, "I don't want help. I want to be left alone." This sentiment lurks deep within every soul and is what tempts us to isolate from God and God's people where our help comes from. Faith is rejecting the idea we can handle it and we don't need any help. It is an opening of our heart to receive what we do not deserve from a gracious lovely God.

Spiritual disciplines are good weapons that should be harnessed to strengthen our personal faith in the battle against sickness as well. Especially the disciplines of prayer and fasting together. We see the power of these disciplines all through the scriptures. Another powerful spiritual discipline that enhances our faith and vulnerability is the practice of confession. James 5:16 states, "Therefore, confess your sins to one another and pray for one another, that you may be healed."

Community Faith is another critically important weapon in the warfare against sickness. As we have already seen, because of a lack of community faith in Jesus' hometown of Nazareth He was limited in the miracles He performed. There is power in the unity of faith and prayer of God's people. Jesus says these amazing words in Matthew 18:19-20, "Again I say to you, if two of you agree on earth about anything they ask, it will be done for them by my Father in heaven. For where two or three are gathered in my name, there am I among them." The power of community faith is seen all through the Bible. In Mark chapter two we have the beautiful story of the four friends who lowered their paralytic friend through a hole in the ceiling to get him close to Jesus. And Jesus commends the faith of the man's friends and as a result heals the man so he could walk. Western Christianity and its tendency toward an individualistic faith often minimize the importance of the corporate faith atmosphere of the church body. This faith atmosphere is critically important to be able to nurture the healing gifts.

Charismatic Faith is another important weapon in the war against sickness. I am defining charismatic faith as rooted in the pursuit and exercise of the 9 spiritual gifts found in 1 Corinthians chapter 12 verses 7-11. This is not an exhaustive list of spiritual gifts, but it is an important one that Paul was led to emphasize in his letter to the Corinthians. Each of these gifts can be used in the war against sickness and disease. I have seen time and time again the gifts of a word of wisdom or a word of knowledge used to not just encourage someone, but to give insight into a person's situation and healing.

Recently in one of our Sunday services one of our elders got a word that there was a woman present who had a debilitating issue with her hands. He asked her to come forward for prayer. She did and she was healed from a twelve-year battle! I know that this testimony raises many questions for those reading this, but would this healing take place if people were not willing to step out and embrace the gifts of the Spirit? Maybe or maybe not. There is a gift of faith available that enables people to trust God for greater things. People who grow in the gift of faith raise the expectation level for the whole church community that God desires to heal people today just like He did in the New Testament era. In verse nine Paul says that there are "gifts of healing" available within the Body of Christ. So, there are various types of the gift of healing available to be used in the fight against sickness and disease.

Then comes the "working of miracles." Miracles are to be part of the life of the Christian Church today. Prophecy and distinguishing of spirits are to be pursued and implemented within the church community for the "upbuiding and encouragement and consolation" of the church family. And finally, the spiritual gift of tongues and the gift of interpreting tongues are available to build up the body. Paul testifies to the power of his private use of tongues to strengthen himself. The gift of tongues when properly used can be a powerful weapon to utilize in personal battles against sickness and in intercession for others.

Unfortunately, within the American church today, we hear more about the abuses and dangers of these gifts than we do their power and blessing when embraced and used for God's glory. The nine spiritual gifts of 1 Corinthians 12 are most effective and healthy when they are pursued and practiced along with the pursuit of the nine fruit of the Spirit found in Galatians chapter five. To have a healthy faith in tension approach to the spiritual gifts means to never separate their practice from the pursuit of the fruit of the Spirit.

Finally, Waiting Faith is a critical weapon used in the battle against sickness and disease. Perseverance and endurance are critical characteristics in the development of a genuine and deep faith. They are a part of every major faith story in the Bible. And they are an essential part of every genuine faith story. In our pursuit of true prosperity waiting on God is essential in refining our identity and destiny. Our tendency is to come to God only in time of need and for help with our felt needs. But *God desires to be sought for who He is not just what He gives*. This is the essence of all true relationship and intimacy.

Experiencing lasting prosperity is not possible without freedom from co-dependent and performance based relationships. The goal of the spiritual life is union and communion with God and this is not possible without the testing of our faith by having to wait on God. We do not know how long Job had to wait on his healing, but his waiting was necessary to test and develop his faith. Without this process his soul would not be sufficiently ready to receive God's healing or His physical blessing. Without Job having to wait on God he would not have been ready to hear what God had to say to him. He would not be able to cry from his soul,

> "Then Job answered the Lord and said: I know that you can do all things, and that no purpose of yours can be thwarted. Who is this that hides counsel without knowledge? Therefore I have uttered what I did not understand, things too wonderful for me, which I did not know. Hear, and I will speak; I will question you, and you make it known to me. I had heard of you by the hearing of the ear, but now my eye sees you; therefore I

despise myself, and repent in dust and ashes." (Job 42:1-6)

Nothing fleshes out pride and self-sufficiency like having to wait on God in the midst of suffering. We are impatient characters. We live in an on-demand society. Our culture does not value waiting, perseverance or endurance. It values immediate results. It is in the midst of waiting on healing from sickness and disease that our faith is tested. Part of this waiting process is learning to fight off the temptation to believe a lie about God or a lie about ourselves. This is how the enemy undercuts our perseverance and endurance and keeps our faith from strengthening. It is very difficult to keep faith alive in the midst of intense long lasting sickness and disease. We inevitably wrestle with the "why me" questions and "why are others healed" and "why am I not experiencing healing"? There is a parable Jesus tells in Luke chapter 11 that can give us insight and encouragement in the midst of our waiting on God.

In response to the disciples asking Jesus about prayer, He gives them the Lord's Prayer and then tells them this parable,

> "And he said to them, 'Which of you who has a friend will go to him at midnight and say to him, 'Friend, lend me three loaves, for a friend of mine has arrived on a journey, and I have nothing to set before him; and he will answer from within, 'Do not bother me; the door is now shut, and my children are with me in bed. I cannot get up and give you anything'? I tell you though he will not get up and give him anything because he is his friend, yet because of his impudence (persistence) he will rise and give him whatever he needs. And I tell you, ask, and it will be given to you; seek, and you will find; knock, and it will be opened to you. For everyone who asks receives, and the one who seeks finds, and to the one who knocks it will be opened." (Luke 11:5-10)

Persistence in asking, seeking and knocking in prayer is critical for the strengthening of our faith in the midst of waiting on God. Each of these terms is an increasing intensity of intimate pleading to God to answer our prayers. For many of us the longer we wait, the more cynical we get and there is a loss in intensity of our prayers. Unless God gives us clear revelation like He did with Paul's thorn that we will not be healed, we are to continue asking, seeking and knocking for understanding and healing. It is in times like these that we need faith friends who will encourage us and exhort us to keep pressing in for healing.

The greatest temptation we will all face in the midst of waiting on healing will be to question God's heart and goodness for us. And this is why Jesus continues after the parable in stating,

> "What father among you, if his son asks for a fish, will instead of a fish give him a serpent; or if he asks for an egg, will give him a scorpion? If you then, who are evil, know how to give good gifts to your children, how much more will the heavenly Father give the Holy Spirit to those who ask him!" (Luke 11:11-13)

The greatest gift God can give us is Himself. Not only has He given us Jesus, He will continue to give us of Himself for all eternity through the gift of the Holy Spirit. Jesus purchased our healing when He purchased our redemption. He is in the process of healing our entire being; mind, body and spirit. Healing is available by faith. Healing is coming! Some of us have to wait longer than others. Only God knows why. *God's heart is to save, heal and deliver – always.* Lets keep fighting for it until it comes in this life or when we enter eternity. Jesus says in Luke 18:8, "…Nevertheless, when the Son of Man comes, will he find faith on earth?"

Our health is a critical element in our experiencing true prosperity. God's desire is that His children would be physically, emotionally and spiritually healthy. This is at the center of His redemptive work throughout history. We have been investigating a faith in tension approach to sickness and healing in this chapter. This requires us to get God's perspective on sickness and healing and to embrace all the weapons of warfare He has given us to fight sickness. In the next and last chapter we will look at a faith in tension approach to oppression and deliverance.

CHAPTER TWELVE

A Faith in Tension Approach to Oppression and Deliverance

We can be happy and joyful with a broken physical body, but we cannot be happy and joyful with broken unhealthy emotions. We are complex creatures with physical, emotional and spiritual components that are mysteriously intertwined. Emotional health and stability are an essential part of our spiritual growth and for experiencing true prosperity. I am currently journeying with two friends whose spouses are both struggling with Alzheimer's disease. It is a terrible disease that destroys memory and other mental functions. I have been told that it is like someone came and stole the person they loved and knew right out of their body. The trauma of this disease and other mental health diseases upon family and caregivers is often times extreme and can affect many generations. The good news is, Jesus offers spiritual transformation to everyone plus the awesome possibility of physical and emotional healing and health through faith in His name.

We are experiencing an explosion in emotional instability and mental disease in America today. And with it has come the emergence of a therapeutic culture where there is a growing need and dependence upon therapists and medications to be able to carry on somewhat of a normal life. The reasons for this are vast and complex. However, some research is starting to reveal that our highly individualized lives and radical individualistic culture are main sources of this growing epidemic. Joseph Hellerman has stated,

> "It might surprise you to learn that our therapeutic culture is a relatively recent phenomenon in world history. As Bellah (sociologist) and others have observed the origin and popularity of clinical psychology can be directly traced to the increasingly individualistic slant of Western relational values. In other words, the great majority of people in this planet never needed therapy until society began to dump the responsibility for making life's major decisions squarely upon the lonely shoulders of the individual. Our freedoms, as intoxicating and exhilarating as they often are have pushed us over the edge emotionally. We are reaping the consequences of decisions that were never meant to be made – and lives that were never meant to be lived – in isolation."[lxi]

Along with our radical individualistic culture is the relatively new phenomena of Social Media. People who have worked from inside this industry are now starting to sound the alarm about its detrimental consequences upon our emotional health as a society.

> "Chamath Palihapitiya, who joined Facebook in 2007 and became its vice president for user growth, said he feels 'tremendous guilt' about the company he helped make. 'I think we have created tools that are ripping apart the social fabric of how society works, he told an audience at Stanford Graduate School of Business, before recommending people take a 'hard break' from social media…Palihapitiya's criticisms were aimed not only at Facebook, but the wider online

ecosystem. 'The short-term, dopamine-driven feedback loops we've created are destroying how society works,' he said, referring to online interactions driven by 'hearts, likes, thumbs-up.' 'No civil discourse, no cooperation; misinformation, mistrust."[lxii]

Though these may be relatively new dynamics that are adversely affecting our society, the problems of emotional and mental health are nothing new "under the sun." The line between dealing with normative emotional struggles we all experience in life and mental disease and spiritual oppression and even the combination of these is a very mysterious line. To properly diagnose the true source of one's oppression is absolutely critical for healing to take place and to make sure that further trauma is not inflicted. Therapists, counselors and pastors all play a vital role in this process, and should work together for the proper diagnosis and healing process. In this chapter we are proposing a faith-in-tension approach to oppression and deliverance that stays away from seeing emotional and mental disorder only as physical disease on one side and away from seeing them primarily as demonic attack on the other. Ultimately, it is impossible to truly live in prosperity if the mind is not at peace with God and oneself.

Jesus articulated clearly in Luke 4 verses 18-19 what some of His ministry in bringing salvation to us would look like.

> "The Spirit of the Lord is upon me, because he has anointed me to proclaim good news to the poor. He has sent me to proclaim liberty to the captives and recovering of sight to the blind, to set at liberty those who are oppressed, to proclaim the year of the Lord's favor."

As we read the Gospels we can see that Jesus did just that. He healed people physically and mentally and He delivered them from the oppression of demonic forces. Jesus healed the physical mental disorders of things like epilepsy and He delivered those who were oppressed by demons and those whom it seemed were experiencing both. The message of Good News that we read about in the New Testament brings healing not just for our soul and body but for our minds as well. It is salvation for our whole being that makes possible physical and mental healing. The normative emotional state that is held up for all believers is summed up in Galatians 5:22, "But the fruit of the Spirit is love, joy, peace, patience, kindness, goodness, faithfulness, gentleness, self-control." Just because someone has brain damage or another form of mental disorder does not mean that they cannot experience some level of the fruit of the Spirit in their lives and grow in them like all believers should.

You might be reading this now and feel some sense of condemnation or shame because you are a professing Christian, but you have been struggling to experience the fruit of the Spirit as the primary emotional state of your soul. First, let me clarify that condemnation and shame are from the enemy who desires to rob us of the fruit of the Spirit. Second, Jesus' desire for us is freedom and regardless of our physical circumstances He has provided a way we can live in the joy of a life that understands and experiences true prosperity. Thirdly, in this chapter I hope to bring some very practical hope in how to lay hold of the fruit of the Spirit and the joy of a life captivated by God rather than held captive by lies, agreements and strongholds.

Biblical Principles for Oppression and Deliverance

The faith in tension approach to oppression and deliverance we have been building within this book attempts to stay away from seeing emotional and mental disorder only as physical disease on one side and away from seeing them primarily as demonic attack on the other. This approach is built upon the following biblical principles we have looked at in the previous chapters.

God's heart is to save, heal and deliver – always.

The sufferings we do not have to share in are oppression, disease and poverty.

God does not guarantee healing or spiritual maturity in this life, but has made provision for both to be pursued by faith.

Lies lead to agreements. Agreements lead to strongholds. Strongholds lead to death.

In Jesus' victory over Satan we are set free from the power of sin; free from guilt, shame and condemnation; free from the power of the law; and free from the power of death.

The weapons of spiritual warfare are the armor of our identity in Christ, the sword of the Spirit-the Word of God, the spiritual disciplines, the spiritual gifts and prayer and intercession.

Truth leads to faith. Faith leads to power. Power leads to freedom.

    We live in a physical and spiritual world. Mental disease can be strictly a physical disease, strictly a spiritual disease or a combination of both. Jesus healed both physical and mental diseases and made provision by His death and resurrection for the ongoing ministry of healing both physical and mental diseases. According to the scriptures sometimes there is something more sinister going on in our physical body and within our mind and emotions. The Bible teaches that the enemy of our soul, Satan, and other evil spirits "come to steal, kill and destroy." (John 10:10) The Bible never uses the language that a person is possessed by an evil spirit, but simply says that a person can be "demonized" or "oppressed" or "harassed".

    And yes, even a professing Christian can be attacked or even oppressed if they experience certain trauma or open a door to their soul. One of the greatest examples of this in the New Testament is the demonic attack upon Peter, the leader of the disciples. It is possible that Peter's pride reflected in Matthew 16 was the open door for Satan to influence him. Jesus' blunt rebuke was not even made to Peter, but to Satan who had influenced Peter. Matthew 16:23-24 states, "And Peter took him aside and began to rebuke him, saying, 'Far be it from you, Lord! This shall never happen to you.' But he turned and said to Peter, 'Get behind me, Satan! You are a hindrance to me. For you are not setting your mind on the things of God, but on the things of man.'" Later, toward the end of Jesus' earthly ministry He told Peter that Satan had asked to "sift him like wheat," but that He had prayed for him. It is no wonder that Peter later wrote in 1 Peter 5:6-8, "Humble yourselves, therefore, under the mighty hand of God so that at the proper time he may exalt you, casting all your anxieties on him, because he cares for you. Be sober-minded; be watchful. Your adversary the devil prowls around like a roaring lion, seeking someone to devour." Peter is writing this admonition to believers to beware of evil forces working against them and also to be alert and not give an open door to lies, agreements and strongholds.

In this chapter we will primarily be dealing with the spiritual side of mental and emotional oppression. The psychological and medical aspects we will only briefly mention, but it is important in the development of a faith in tension approach that we recognize there is an important place for all of these disciplines and they should work together for healing. This approach also recognizes that God has given all kinds of gifts to us to utilize in the healing process. One important caveat we need to mention is that Satan and demons also have a form of healing power and it is possible to experience a certain level of healing but also become more spiritually oppressed. The scriptures describe Satan as an angel of light (2 Cor. 11:14) and he sometimes uses cultic healing as an avenue to bring about further oppression. So, in all of our searching for healing it is critical to the state of our soul to know "Who" the source of our healing is, otherwise, we are possibly exposed to lies, agreements and strongholds that bring about further oppression in the long run.

Within the Church there has been basically two different approaches to deliverance ministry. On one side would be those who are on the Word side of the Word-Spirit graph from chapter nine. They traditionally minimize spiritual warfare and for them deliverance is primarily discipleship and medical help. On the other side would be the charismatics who are on the Spirit side of the Word-Spirit graph. Traditionally, they have taken a bold spiritual warfare approach to deliverance and sometimes shy away from clinical or medical help. Now, these are generalizations, and we want to build a healthy faith in tension approach that embraces some aspects from both these approaches, which we believe will represent the most biblical approach to deliverance ministry.

In this faith in tension approach to oppression and deliverance I am advocating that the vast majority of emotional and mental disorder issues have a spiritual root problem behind them. What I mean by spiritual root problem does not necessarily mean that there is demonic activity, it can simply be an issue of not caring for one's spirit. If someone does not care for their physical body it will become weak and susceptible to disease. The same is true for one's soul and spirit if it is not cared for. Jesus' message and ministry reveal that ultimately God has given us, "all things that pertain to life and godliness, through the knowledge of him who called us to his glory and excellence, by which he has granted to us his precious and very great promises, so that through them you may become partakers of the divine nature, having escaped from the corruption that is in the world because of sinful desires." (2 Peter 1:3-4) God's heart for us is that we would prosper in every aspect of our life and eternal life. Though the realities of living in a fallen world often do not feel like prosperity our heavenly Father is a good God and made provision for our deliverance from all forms of oppression. True prosperity is learning to become, "partakers of the divine nature." The rest of this chapter will layout a faith in tension approach to deliverance from oppression.

Getting Perspective on Oppression

Satan's desire is that our past is our future. He wants to keep us backward focused without hope for the future. From the beginning he has been a liar and set on bringing chaos and strife into all of God's good creation. He and his minions are especially at war with humans because we are created in the image of God and are heirs of our heavenly Father's promised eternal life. Satan's destiny has been cemented from the time he rebelled against heaven and ever since then he has been on the warpath to kill, steal and destroy all of creation. From the beginning his plan has been to corrupt and stamp out the seeds of faith and replace them with fears, doubts and lies. Once he gets a foothold here he can erode any remnant of hope. Once hope is eroded love starts to be corrupted. This is the destructive path of spiritual oppression. Doubt replaces faith. Fear replaces hope. Lies replace love. Oppression's goal is the fracturing of our soul and ultimately the fracturing of our relationship with God and others. As stated above, it is critical to understand that oppression does not necessarily need to be the result of demonic activity, it can simply be the result of not caring for one's soul and spirit. A simple illustration of this can be busyness. If we get caught up in busyness and a margin-less life we will be susceptible to stress. If stress is sustained long enough it will have an adverse affect upon our physical body as well as our emotional health.

If we are not willing to engage our past, it can be used by the evil one to destroy us. My wife, Meshell, remembers feeling unloved even at the early age of 4. Her perception and experience at this early age was that no one gave her attention or were willing to listen or talk with her. She felt unloved and uncared for. I am sure that her family would disagree and say that they loved her and cared for her, but her reality and experience was that no one actually did. And actually she cannot remember ever being told when she was young that she was loved or that she was ever shown any tender affection. So through her childhood and adolescent years her experience led her to come into agreement with the lie that she was unlovable. Believing that lie led her to step out to find love and affirmation in unhealthy ways and to other destructive patterns. All of this just led to more oppression and destructive thoughts. It led to a spiritual stronghold in her emotional and spiritual life that continued to wreak havoc. Through these years she was unaware of anything that could help her in this fight for her emotional health. However, when she was 18 something wonderful happened. A friend of hers that knew a little bit about her struggles invited her to a youth rally. It was on that night that she heard for the first time about Jesus and His desire to have a relationship with her. She had grown up going to church, but never heard the simple but powerful Gospel of Jesus Christ. That night she began walking with Jesus and began the process of learning to get freedom through His Word and the community of His people. Freedom from this lie and stronghold of not being lovable did not come immediately. It came over a period of time as she leaned upon God's Word, His Church and some powerfully gifted Christian counselors. No one can truly experience prosperity if they are not clear on what love is and how to experience it. She did not ignore or embrace her past, but she learned to appropriately apply the power of the Gospel of Jesus to her past, so she could gain perspective and freedom to move forward walking into God's destiny for her life. Without perspective and freedom from our past hurts we cannot live in true prosperity.

    My experience was quite different. I grew up knowing Jesus at a young age and knowing I was loved by Him and by my family. My first experience with spiritual oppression came in my High School years when I worked pulling cable for a telecommunications company. The men I worked with were very different than the people I grew up around or socialized with. First of all, they were much older than I was and many of them lived rough and hard lives. Their language and habits were raw to put it nicely. All day and every day they would look at women and talk about women in very disrespectful and vulgar ways. Month after month of this environment began to have an impact on me and to subtly and destructively corrupt the way I looked at women and thought about them. This lie led to an agreement in my mind that led to some destructive patterns in my youth. Though I was active in my church and youth group, this lie lingered until after college when I was convicted and willing to deal with it. The first big breakthrough for me was in the midst of a men's bible study where I heard other men confess their similar struggles and battles and see other men step in and fight for their freedom. It was in this environment that I was convicted about my past and the lies I had allowed to corrupt my thinking. After the men prayed for me, the man who led our study shared Matthew 5:8, "Blessed are the pure in heart, for they shall see God." It was like a ray of light that awakened and seared my heart to begin the healing process. It is not that I do not struggle anymore, but I have like Meshell learned to lean into God's Word and His Church to walk in more and more freedom as the lies have been replaced by the Truth. Satan desires our past to be our future. Thankfully, Jesus came to heal our past so we could live forward focused on the abundant and prosperous life God has for us.

How we view our body has a critical impact upon our present and future emotional and spiritual health. Not long ago I was out to dinner with some friends and noticed a chalkboard in the restaurant, which had this quote written on it: "Your body is not a temple, it's an amusement park. Enjoy the ride!" This quote summarizes the post-modern view of how we should view and treat our bodies. It is revealed in our culture's view of sexuality, diet, tattoos, fashion, extreme sports, etc. It should not be difficult to see that this view of one's body is selfish, narcissistic, and downright dangerous as it exposes our physical body and spirit to many destructive influences. It is amazing that anyone could hold this view of one's body since we had nothing to do with being born and existing in the first place. We had no say in our DNA and our personality, and we had no say in who our family would be. This arrogance when it comes to how we view our body and life is a big source of emotional and spiritual oppression.

The Bible is very clear about how we should view our bodies. The scriptures begin in Genesis stating that all humankind is made in the image of God. (Gen 1:26) The New Testament goes deeper into this idea and states that our bodies are to not just be viewed as temples, but are to be treated as they are actual temples for the presence of God. 1 Corinthians 6:19-20 states, "Or do you not know that your body is a temple of the Holy Spirit within you, whom you have from God? You are not your own, for you were bought with a price. So glorify God in your body." This is one of the most profound realities of what happens when the Gospel of Jesus transforms a person's heart. It is a sad reality today that so many Christians do not live knowing and experiencing this radical truth and growing in it. So, one of the most important and probing questions that can be asked is, "How do we view our body?" The answer to this question will open a window into the state of our spiritual and emotional health. Deliverance ministry was at the heart of Jesus' mission and one of the primary ways He practically and powerfully ministered to people. The transforming work of the Gospel is a full renovation of the heart. Jesus came to liberate our lives and clean out our "house" and come dwell through the Holy Spirit. Speaking about the importance of watching over our "house" Jesus stated in Matthew 12:43-45,

> "When the unclean spirit has gone out of a person, it passes through waterless places seeking rest, but finds none. Then it says, 'I will return to my house from which I came.' And when it comes, it finds the house empty, swept, and put in order. Then it goes and brings with it seven other spirits more evil than itself, and they enter and dwell there, and the last state of that person is worse than the first. So also will it be with this evil generation."

With this teaching and strong warning, Jesus is making the point that our "house" our "soul" is connected to the spiritual realm and it is critical to know Who the master of the "house" is.

These spiritual forces are much more powerful than we are, so we need a stronger Master to dwell and watch over the house. Salvation is all about God restoring His presence in our hearts and souls so we can experience the abundant and eternally prosperous life Jesus came to give us. True prosperity has Jesus as the Master of the "house." This is what John was talking about in 1 John 4:4 when he encouraged believers, "...for he who is in you is greater than he who is in the world."

There are many ways our "house" can get afflicted and even sometimes invaded. All of these experiences can devastate a person and rob them of any true experience of prosperity and instill serious emotional and mental health disorder. Jesus came to defeat all darkness and disorder and bring the peace of God upon our souls. Because of the deliverance work of Jesus we do not have to suffer the effects of oppression.

Getting Perspective on Deliverance

God's heart is to save, heal and deliver – always. It is one thing to write this statement and believe it and another thing altogether to apply it in ministry to someone who claims to have faith in Jesus, but is horrifically tormented in their soul. I know a couple whose child was traumatized at a young age. It was almost a decade before the gruesome truth came out. There are seasons where the torment and depression and self-hatred subside, but as time goes on it seems like the darkness is taking over, even in the midst of faithful prayer and ministry. This couple loves their child deeply and would do anything to get their child deliverance and relief – anything!

So, if it is God's heart to deliver and set free always, how do we apply that truth to situations like this that are so desperate? Some of the biggest tests of our faith occur when we or someone close to us are traumatized. Why would God allow this to happen? Where was Jesus? The enemy of our souls would have us question and doubt God's care and protection over us. Sadly, there has been much teaching within the church that has caused confusion and played into Satan's hand. The old hymn says, "Trust and obey for there's no other way to be happy in Jesus but to trust and obey." This is truth, but what has often been misrepresented is that if we just trust Jesus He will protect us and protect our children from the evil in the world. This is not how life works in this fallen world.

Yes, we can and should pray for protection and a healthy blessed life for our children and yes our heavenly Father desires that for us, but for now we live in a fallen evil world where bad things also happen to followers of Christ. This wrong view of how faith and life works was seen by the response of Eliphaz, one of Job's friends who was trying to make sense of Job's afflictions when he said in Job 4:7, "Remember, who that was innocent ever perished? Or where were the upright cut off?" Eliphaz was promoting a false view of life and how faith worked. Obviously, if anyone takes an honest look at the world, they can see that innocent and upright people have been afflicted throughout all of history – it started with Cain killing his brother Abel? It was this view that Satan took advantage of when he first asked God to tempt Job in Job 1:9-11,

> "Then Satan answered the LORD and said, 'Does Job fear God for no reason? Have you not put a hedge around him and his house and all that he has, on every side? You have blessed the work of his hands, and his possessions have increased in the land. But stretch out your hand and touch all that he has, and he will curse you to your face."

It is Satan's main goal to bring havoc into this world and into our lives and for us to blame God for it and to ultimately reject God. So, the bedrock of our faith must be to hold onto the goodness and faithfulness of God even in the midst of horrific trials realizing we are at war in this fallen world. But that is not all, for true prosperity is living by faith where there is a convergence of biblical prosperity and suffering. We have also been given faith resources to fight against these afflictions and Jesus came as our Deliverer showing us the way.

The sufferings we do not have to share in are oppression, disease and poverty. Jesus came in the power of the Holy Spirit setting people free from torment and oppression. (Matt. 9:35-10:1) The scriptures say, "When he saw the crowds, he had compassion for them, because they were harassed and helpless, like sheep without a shepherd." (Matt. 9:36) All through the Bible we are described as sheep. Sheep are defenseless animals. Without a shepherd they are exposed to attack without any way to protect themselves. The sheep are described as being "harassed and helpless" which is like saying they were mangled and cast down to the ground. Not only was it a major part of Jesus' ministry to set people free from this oppression, but He anointed and sent out His disciples to do the same. (Matt. 10:1) And not only did He send out His disciples to minister deliverance, but He asked them to pray that God would send more laborers to help with the ministry. (Matt. 10:38) It is sad that so much of the church has limited the scope of these laborers to just evangelists and not healers and delivers as well.

Ultimately, deliverance is a truth battle where lies, agreements and strongholds are overcome in a person's life by the power of the Holy Spirit. The seeds of truth birth faith in a person's heart. (Romans 10:17) When faith becomes active in a person's life it brings about the power of the Holy Spirit to overcome oppression of all kinds. When the power of the Spirit starts moving in a person's soul freedom is birthed. My friend Isabella's story illustrates how deliverance from oppression leads to flourishing.

> I grew up in a "disfunctional home". My parents did all they could in their own strength to give my sisters and me the best, even though at times their best was tinted with evil. I truly honor their genuine effort to be the parents we needed them to be, but the enemy found a way to bring chaos

through addiction and violence. My dad found his sense of security and identity in drugs and alcohol at a young age. I remember many times where I witnessed him being taken over by this furious rage and mom and I ending up being the victims of this evil monster that stole my dad's fragile heart. The thing is that when you are a child this kind of violence has a way of making you believe you deserve it and it deceives you into thinking you are disposable. "You have no value" was the lie that formed me throughout my childhood and adolescence.

The first time I thought about terminating this horrible night terror of life was at 8 years old. I was hiding behind the doors witnessing live a rated R extreme violent movie in my own house. The thought of having to keep going through life hiding behind doors, never having the confidence to walk through them, felt so hopeless. I was gripped by loneliness in my heart that I couldn't bear. I tried to find a sense of connection to others through false appearance but I always ended up feeling unworthy. Who would want to be my friend? Who would be interested in hearing my stories? And if they did, would I want them to discover how disgusting I was on the inside?

I hated myself. So much so that I would spend hours locked in the bathroom beating myself up. I really couldn't control the anger that aroused inside of me every time I looked myself in the mirror. All I saw was big bold letters on my front head that read "DISGUSTING". The first thing that came out of my mouth when I woke up in the morning to go to school was "I hate ... school, people, life, hot weather, math, exercising, teachers, dad... I hated everything. But I still cried out to God, deep in my heart.

My depression and suicidal thinking grew stronger and stronger. It was empowered by my obsession to hide and keep everything secret. I eventually tried to take my own life by grabbing the medicine basket in my house and taking every pill there was in it. To my own surprise, nothing really happened other than me passing out at school the next day. I was really hoping that this would spark an emergency signal in my mom's heart. But all I got was her cold distant look.

Two more years went by and I was on my last year of high school. I don't know how to describe what happened during this time other than I was being harassed by the devil at night, when I went to bed. These were not just nightmares. And they happened every night. One night I was falling in a dark tunnel, and the enemy's voice was like a presence on top of me, and with an evil laugh he was telling me how me and my sisters and my mom and dad were all going to burn in hell for eternity, and how I belonged to him. I woke up in complete shock, screaming and crying inconsolably. My mom suggested that I should maybe start seeing a therapist, which I agreed with all hopes that this would finally fix what was so wrong with me. Little did I know that through therapy I was going to discover yet another buried memory of being sexually abused when I was a child.

At this point my dad had stopped drinking and doing drugs, but that was just the external symptoms of a much deeper brokenness that took hold of all of us. Because of his abuse, he had suffered 7 heart attacks up until then. I had kept an eye on his unopened package of nitroglycerin for the last month or so. And this one afternoon the devil found the perfect opportunity of a confrontation with my dad to put me into robotic mode and have me take all twenty pills of nitroglycerin at once. I will never forget the feeling I had when I swallowed the pills. It was as if life was leaving my body and a dark thing was getting closer and closer to me. I believe that when we are on the verge of death, we cry out to God. And that's what I did. I kneeled down on the floor of my room and started asking God to forgive me, not just for taking those pills but to forgive me for everything! I didn't really have a relationship with the Lord at that moment, but I knew somehow that He was real. Next thing I know I woke up in the hospital three days later. The first person I saw when I opened my eyes the doctor was in utmost confusion. After she calmed me down, she explained to me what happened. And she said something I will never forget; " if you would've arrived just 5 minutes later it was going to be too late for you"... I have to be honest with you and tell you that right after she said that I wasn't that excited to be alive again.

The first morning I woke up at home after the hospital, before even getting out of my bed I challenged God in the most genuine way possible (if that even makes sense) and said to Him: "I'm tired of everybody telling me who you are! No more! If you are real then You need to show me because I can't live like this anymore, I don't want to. If You are real then show me that You love me!" ... that was my prayer. I started reading the Bible that was forgotten in the dust of the bookshelf in my house. Every time I opened it I asked God to help me see Him in His word. After a while of reading His word every morning, nothing extraordinary really happened. To be honest, it was kind of boring. I didn't understand half of the things I was reading. Until I read the story of the woman at the well and something happened to me. I started crying so hard, because I wanted that water! I didn't really know Jesus or understand who He was or what He did for me at the cross, but the one thing I knew was that I was thirsty and I wanted that water more than anything else!

One Sunday morning my dad invited me to go with him to this new church he started going to, the church where according to me at that time "a bunch of fanatics and lunatics go to!" I asked why would he ever go to "that" church and he didn't really answer. So I went. At the end of the service they invited people who had never received Jesus in their hearts before to pray and ask Jesus to come into their hearts. The whole thing sounded very strange to me but I didn't care. Seeing people lifting up their hands in worship was as weird to me as seeing cows flying in the skies. That's how unfamiliar I was with it. The first impression I had when I saw all these weird people dancing and lifting up their hands in the air was "these people are putting up a show!" But something touched my heart. All of a sudden I started desiring to have whatever it is they had that made them look so ridiculous and not care only because whatever it was they were feeling was so real in their hearts! Oh my God I wanted that! So when they invited people to ask this Jesus into their hearts I went all for it! I prayed that prayer like a little child. My heart was so empty and void of life that only this so called Jesus could change it! I invited Jesus in my heart, not really understanding what was happening but I just believed. A peace that I have never felt before came over me. I couldn't stop crying. I didn't quite know if I was crying because of repenting for my sins, or because of the brokenness I had in me, or because of these immense peace that was overtaking me, or because I invited Jesus into my heart or because of all of it at once! I cried all the tears I hadn't allowed myself to cry in the past. My eyes were closed in complete abandonment to the love of the Father. I can't really explain to you what I felt that moment. It was as if all this darkness that had wrapped me around its fingers for all these years, all of sudden disappeared. I didn't even realize it wasn't there anymore until I realized how the desire to not live wasn't there anymore! When I opened my eyes I realized that the service was finished, my dad was waiting for me in an almost empty room and my arms were lifted up high the entire time!

You know what was the most amazing thing, that next morning when I woke up - I HAD JOY! It was the first morning since I could remember at the time that I actually was happy to be alive! Jesus was the love of my life!

Now, many years since Isabella had this experience, she is still one of the most joyful people I know. This does not mean that she does not struggle at times, but that Jesus is her strength and the fruit of the Spirit are growing in her life.

Using all Weapons Against Oppression

Oppression destroys people's ability to live a prosperous life. It is the result of many factors that work together to rob us of the life God intends us to live. Five primary factors that contribute to oppression are 1.) Believing and embracing a lie 2.)

Experiencing generational oppression that has been passed down 3.) Developing sinful habits 4.) Experiencing abuse or trauma 5.) Experiencing demonic attack.

We have been given spiritual weapons to fight off oppression. There are five primary weapons that God has given His church to utilize in fighting all forms of oppression, 1.) The armor of our identity in Christ found in Ephesians chapter 6 2.) The sword of the Spirit, which is the Word of God 3.) The spiritual disciplines like fasting and scripture memory 4.) The spiritual gifts found in 1 Corinthians chapter 12 5.) Prayer and learning to intercede for one another. The detail working out of these weapons to fight oppression goes beyond the scope of this book, but should be fleshed out within the local body of believers.

We will focus here on "believing a lie" because it is behind every form of oppression. It goes back to the very beginning when Satan tempted Eve with the lie that God could not be trusted and that she could be like God. Once Eve came into agreement with the lie and ate the apple along with Adam they were in bondage to the stronghold of sin. Lies lead to agreements and agreements lead to strongholds. Behind every bit of oppression is sin and lies. Deliverance and freedom from oppression are ultimately about a truth battle inside the soul. If we suppress the truth in life we will only give strength to the lies and increase our bondage to oppression.

The greatest weapon against oppression is the Gospel of Jesus Christ. It is because of the Gospel that all of the weapons mentioned above are available in the fight for the freedom of the soul. *There is no greater prosperity message in the world than the Gospel of Jesus Christ.*

This is because only the Gospel can make us right with God by establishing a faith foundation for us to stand upon. This faith foundation is a whole new way of seeing and living; to "walk by faith, not by sight." (2 Cor. 5:7) This faith foundation consists of the truths about God that we have put our trust in for this life and eternity.

It is critical that our faith foundation is built upon the truth and not lies, for eternity is in the balance. When we embrace lies about God and about ourselves we expose our soul to oppression. It is impossible to truly live a prosperous life if we have come into agreement with lies about God and about ourselves. It is also impossible to experience truly satisfying relationships if we have embraced lies about God and about ourselves. So if there are lies residing in the faith foundation of our life no amount of counsel, therapy or ministry is going to be able to bring freedom or true prosperity until those lies are exposed and overcome by the truth. This is why Paul proclaimed in Romans 1:16-17, "For I am not ashamed of the gospel, for it is the power of God for salvation to everyone who believes, to the Jew first and also to the Greek. For in it the righteousness of God is revealed from faith for faith, as it is written, 'The righteous shall live by faith.'" The Gospel is the most prosperous message in the world because it is the power of God to save us by overcoming the lies and establishing a firm foundation of faith on God's promises. How does this work? Romans 10:9-10 says, "if you confess with your mouth that Jesus is Lord and believe in your heart that God raised him from the dead, you will be saved. For with the heart one believes and is justified, and with the mouth one confesses and is saved." And Romans 10:17 says, "So faith comes by hearing, and hearing through the word of Christ." So, *truth leads to faith.*

Once we put our faith in Jesus the power of God goes to work within our soul and saves us! So *faith leads to power.* We are declared righteous by God because of our faith and trust in Him to do it. Most all lies that keep us oppressed are either lies about God or lies about ourselves. It is critical to understand that it is not by our ability or will that we can replace the lies with the truth – it is only by the "power of God." It is not by just walking the aisle at church or saying a certain prayer or going through a certain class. We are saved when we surrender our heart and soul to Jesus. When we do this we enter into a relationship with God, which is based not on our works but on God's faithfulness to His promises. This is not a contractual relationship, which is based upon our efforts. So, our faith foundation gets established firmly upon God's faithfulness and promises. This is where the real war takes place at the foundation of our soul where we are either bound by lies or liberated by faith in the truth of the Gospel.

What does this look like? *Power leads to freedom.* This new life of faith stands upon the firm foundation of what God's power has done for us and sets us free from the lies of oppression. It is this new place we take our stand trusting God and fighting off any doubt about God's love for us or His goodness. This faith foundation is the rock of our salvation. It is the basis of our new identity in Jesus. It is the foundation we build a life of faith upon. If there are doubts at this foundation level we are not free to walk in faith and build a life of faith. If there are doubts about the goodness of God and His faithfulness to His promises we expose ourselves to a host of spiritual depression and oppression.

Some today try and say that doubting is good and that it helps refine our faith. Any doubting at the foundation level of faith about the goodness and character of God is always dangerous! That kind of doubting is radically different than the questioning of God's will and ways that goes along with walking in relationship with God. True saving faith that awakens true prosperity begins by us surrendering our heart to Jesus and trusting God by His power to establish a faith foundation in our life that we can build a life of faith upon.

Is it possible for a true believer to have their faith foundation fractured? Yes. If a believer opens their heart to start doubting God's goodness and character their foundation can be cracked and they can expose themselves to spiritual depression and all forms of oppression. Satan's ultimate strategy is to keep people blinded to the truth of the Gospel of Jesus Christ. He is in the business of persuading people to embrace one of the world's many prosperity messages. Satan's attack strategy with a believer is first to get them overcome with sin, shame and guilt and away from the foundation of the Gospel and what it says about them. Secondly, he ultimately wants them to start questioning the goodness of God and whether they can truly trust God. If he accomplishes this, the faith foundation can be cracked and that person exposed to oppression. Here are just a few indicators that can be used in a believer's life in the midst of trials and a healing process to make sure our faith foundation is on solid ground:

1.) *Are we more concerned about pursuing God and what He has done for us than what He has not done for us?* If we are living from a faith foundation we live daily from what God has done and will do rather than doubting Him and being focused on what He has not done or is not doing.

2.) *Are we giving people grace rather than easily being offended by others and caught in comparison?* If we are living from a faith foundation of the Gospel power in our life we should be un-offendable. We live from the truth of what God has done for us and how He sees us rather than giving someone and their words power over our emotions and identity.

3.) *Are we approaching God with a surrendered heart in covenantal relationship rather than with a demanding heart in a contractual relationship?* Living from a faith foundation is trusting in God and His promises regardless of our circumstances, not demanding He do something because we do something.

4.) *Are we living by faith asking God to increase our faith rather than feeling guilty for not having enough faith?* We know we are living from a solid faith foundation when our response to biblical exhortation is "Lord, increase my faith" instead of feeling shamed for not having enough faith.

This faith foundation is established by our trust in the promises of God and then we build a life of faith upon that foundation. What are the promises of God that we are to hold onto as part of our faith foundation? There is great confusion today about this question. Our foundation will be rocked if we take something from scripture that is not a promise for this life and expect it to be. The Bible is full of great promises and great truth principles. It is very important in establishing the new prosperous life of faith in Jesus that we learn to discern the difference and how to live by them.

God's promises that our faith foundation is to stand upon are all of His promises related to His work of salvation in our lives, the life of His Church and creation itself. For example Romans 1:16-17 and 10:9-10 are promises. Doubt is dangerous if we doubt these promises. What about all of God's truth principles within scripture? What about 1 Peter 2:24, "…By his wounds you have been healed"? Does God promise physical healing in this life? No, but He does promise to perfectly heal us at the end and for eternity. So, as part of our faith foundation we stand upon the good heart of God to heal and that He will perfectly heal one day, but we also activate our faith in going after healing in this life. Jesus has not guaranteed physical healing in this life, but He has made provision for us to go after it by faith. So, if for whatever reason the healing does not come in this life our faith foundation is not cracked because we stand upon God's promise that He will ultimately heal.

However, this does not let us off the hook to take the principles of scripture and press in by faith to see mighty miracles in this life. Jesus says in Matthew 17:19-21, "Then the disciples came to Jesus privately and said, 'Why could we not cast it out?' He said to them, 'Because of your little faith. For truly, I say to you, if you have faith like a grain of mustard seed, you will say to this mountain, 'Move from here to there,' and it will move, and nothing will be impossible for you.'" Is this a promise for our faith foundation or a truth principle for us to pursue by faith? This is a truth principle that can only be pursued when there is a solid foundation of faith and trust in the covenantal relationship with God. As friendship with God increases our ability to exercise our faith in these truth principles increases. When the faith foundation of trust is cracked we interpret many of God's promises and principles in a contractual way – if we do this, then God You should do that. That is not friendship with God. That is putting God in a box.

This brings us full circle back to our definition of true prosperity. True prosperity is living in tension between evil and suffering and the goodness of God by faith in the power and promises of the Gospel. It is where we learn to embrace the prosperity of the Gospel and stand firm on its faith foundation and build upon it a life infused with faith that fights suffering in this world. True prosperity is only found when our life firmly stands upon the gospel promises of God where our trust in Him stands strong regardless of the storms surrounding our life. It is this kind of foundation that God builds a vibrant prosperous life upon so we can take hold of His promises and principles and fight suffering in this world until Jesus returns to make everything right forever. Amen.

CONCLUSION
Don't Lose the Plot

A plot is critical to a good story. The plot is the "why" for the things that happen in the story. A story that loses its plot ceases to be a story. Our lives are like a story and need a plot to make sense of the big "why" questions in our world. Trying to live without a plot is lost-ness and does not end well. If we lose the plot or embrace a false plot we lose meaning and purpose and are bound to a deceptive vision of prosperity.

We lost the plot because we rejected the Author of the grand story and started trying to live our own story. We have lost the storyline and have gone after our own vision of prosperity. However, the Author is faithful to His story and stepped into our broken story and world and has called us back into His grand story. He has done everything needed to restore us to His story and the true prosperous plot.

There is no greater prosperity message in the world than the gospel of Jesus Christ!

I have tried to show throughout this book that true prosperity is living in tension between evil and suffering and the goodness of God by faith in the power and promises of the Gospel. We lose our place in the story when we swing to either the prosperity side or the suffering side and miss living in this tension by faith.

We have journeyed with Job through his story, which is a blueprint of the bigger story. We have gained insights from the three main movements of the grand narrative. First, we investigated *"prosperity without suffering"* and saw that from the beginning God has good things for His children and that we were made for eternal prosperity. But we also saw that suffering quickly entered the story and corrupted our pursuit of prosperity because of our rejection of God's plan. Through our investigation of this first main movement in the grand story we developed a biblical theology of prosperity. Secondly, we looked at *"suffering without prosperity"* and dove deeply into the harsh consequences of our rebellion and all the forms of suffering in the world and man's futile efforts to eradicate them or even understand them. It was through this process that we developed a biblical theology of suffering. Finally, we looked at *"prosperity through suffering"* where we brought together both our theology of prosperity and suffering and applied them to big life questions. We looked at how to apply this faith in tension approach and deal with the issues of wealth and poverty, health and sickness and deliverance and oppression.

There is actually a fourth movement to God's grand story and it is something of a restoration of the first movement, *"prosperity without suffering."* In reality it is not a fourth movement but the beginning of endless eternal movements as we live within the gracious prosperity of our loving Trinitarian Creator in a completely restored creation.

In closing, I leave you with a prayer and a promise:

"In prosperity may Thou grant perseverance to will one thing; amid distractions, collectedness to will one thing; in suffering, patience to will one thing." –Soren Kierkegaard

"He who did not spare his own Son but gave him up for us all, how will he not also with him graciously give us all things?" –Romans 8:32

Acknowledgements

First of all, I want to thank our wonderful church family at Crossroads Church Aspen and our growing church family beyond this valley for giving me the privilege to preach and teach God's truth. Most of this book has been a process of working out our salvation together.

Many thanks to Brett and Amy Moody for years of friendship and your support for this project and your faith to keep pressing in for all God has for us.

Many thanks to Jack and Leesa Deere for your friendship, theological insight and willingness to work through the manuscript.

Many thanks to Alex Dale and the Loudmark team. Your insight, creativity and partnership have been wonderful.

Finally, many thanks to Meshell and our kids, Megan, Mallory, Mckenna, Jonathan and Maggie for being willing to listen to Dad and more than anything to listen to your heavenly Father.

Notes

Chapter One
[i] *When Helping Hurts: How To Alleviate Poverty without Hurting the Poor…and Yourself* of Steve Corbett and Brian Fikkert, (Chicago, IL: Moody Publishers, 2012.) pg. 41.
[ii] John 17:5, Colossians 1:16, John 1:1, 1 Corinthians 8:6, Hebrews 1:2-4, 1 Corinthians 10:1-4, Luke 10:18, John 5:17, John 8:56,
[iii] Philippians 2:5-8, John 18:37, John 12:27

Chapter Two
[iv] Linda Stone, Q&A section on http://lindastone.net/qa.
[v] *Renovation of the heart, Putting on the character of Christ* by Dallas Willard, (Colorado Springs, CO. Navpress, 2002.) pg. 82.
[vi] www.chalmers.org/our-work/redefining-poverty/what-is-poverty
[vii] *The Disease of the Health and Wealth Gospels* by Gordon D. Fee, (Chapter 3, *The N.T. View of Wealth and Possessions*, Kindle Version).
[viii] *The Spirit of the Disciplines, Understanding How God Changes Lives* by Dallas Willard, (195 Broadway, New York, NY: Harper Collins Publishers, 1988.) pg. 194.
[ix] Ibid, pg. 203.
[x] *The Disease of the Health and Wealth Gospels* by Gordon Fee, Chapter two, *The Gospel of Perfect Health*, Kindle version, 1985, 2006.

Chapter Three
[xi] *The Conservative Heart, How to build a fairer, happier, and more prosperous America* by Arthur C. Brooks, (Harper Collins Publishers, 195 Broadway, New York, NY, 2015) pg.33-34.
[xii] Ibid, pg. 52.
[xiii] *The Disease of the Health and Wealth Gospels, The New Testament View of Wealth and Possessions* by Gordon D. Fee, Chapter Three, , kindle version.
[xiv] *John Piper and the Prosperity Gospel* by John Piper, Vimeo.

Chapter Four
[xv] *The Divine Conspiracy* by Dallas Willard, p108

Chapter Five
[xvi] CS Lewis, *The Problem of Pain* (New York: MacMillan, 1962), 81

[xvii] Frederick Beuchner, *Secrets in the Dark: A Life in Sermons* (New York: HarperCollins, 2007), 216

[xviii] C.S. Lewis, A Grief Observed (HarperOne, 2009), 26.

[xix] Dan Allender, *The Healing Path: How the Hurts in Your Past Can Lead You to a More Abundant Life* (Colorado Springs: Waterbrook Press, 1999), 14.

[xx] A.W. Tozer, Born After Midnight, page 21-22, Moody Publishers, Chicago IL, 1959, 1987

Chapter Six

[xxi] *This World: Playground or Battleground* by A.W. Tozer, Logos ebook, pg. 3.

[xxii] *Born After Midnight* by A.W. Tozer, (Moody Publishers, 820 N. LaSalle Boulevard, Chicago, IL, 60610) pg. 49.

[xxiii] *The Unseen Realm* by Michael S. Heiser (Lexham Press, 1313 Commercial St., Bellingham, WA 98225) pg. 87-88.

[xxiv] *The Unseen Realm* by Michael S. Heiser (Lexham Press, 1313 Commercial St., Bellingham, WA 98225) pg 63-65.

[xxv] *The Three Battlegrounds* by Francis Frangipane, (Arrow Publishing, Inc. P.O. Box 10102 Cedar Rapids, IA 52410) pg. 16.

Chapter Seven

[xxvi] Stephen Adei, *Wealth and Poverty*, by Stephen Adei, (The Africa Bible Commentary Grand Rapids: Zondervan, 2010), 788.

[xxvii] *Power, Poverty, and Prayer*, by Ogbu Kalu, (Studies in the Intercultural History of Christianity 122 New York: Peter Lang, 2000), 127-8.

[xxviii] *Human Trafficking: A Global Perspective*, by Louise Shelley (Cambridge: Cambridge University Press, 2010), 109.

[xxix] *Human Trafficking*, by Matthew K. Daniel, (South Asia Bible Commentary), 1145.

[xxx] Quoted in Paul John Isaak, *Luke*, (Africa Bible Commentary), 1246.

[xxxi] Mark 1:21-28, 5:1-20, 7:24-30, 9:14-29; Acts 5:1-11, 16:16-18, 19:11-20; 1 Peter 5:8; Revelation

[xxxii] *The Epistle to the Romans*, by Douglas Moo, (NICNT, Grand Rapids: Eerdmans, 1996), 511.

[xxxiii] *Romans 1-8*, by James D.G. Dunn, (Word Biblical Commentary 38, Dallas: Word Books, 1988) 505.

xxxiv *Paul's Letter to the Philippians*, by Gordon Fee, (NICNT, Grand Rapids: Eerdmans, 1995), 171-2.
xxxv *Psalms*, by Augustine Pagolu, (South Asia Bible Commentary), 685-6.
xxxvi *Accompany Them with Singing: The Christian Funeral* by Thomas Long, (Louisville: Westminster John Knox, 2009), 39-40.
xxxvii *A Theology of History* by Hans Urs von Balthasar, (San Francisco: Ignatius, 1994), 36-7.

Chapter Eight
xxxviii *The Problem of Pain* by C.S. Lewis (Harper, 2011) p.94.
xxxix Rom 8:18, 2 Cor 1:5, 6, 7; Col 1:24, 2 Tim 3:11, Heb 2:9, 10, 10:32, 1 Pe 1:11, 4:13, 5:1
xl James 5:10, 13, 2Ti 2:9, 4:5
xli Rom 4:19, 1 Cor 8:9, 2 Cor 11:29
xlii *A Twientieth Century Testimony* by Malcolm Muggeridge, (Nashville: Thomas Nelson, 1978), p.72.
xliii *Walking with God through Pain and Suffering* by Tim Keller (Penguin Books, 375 Hudson Street, New York, New York, 10014, 2013) p.5.
xliv *India: the grand experiment* by Vishal Mangalwadi, (Pippa Rann Books, Farnham, Surrey, UK, 1997) p.81.

Chapter Nine
xlv *Jesus and the Spirit, A Study of the Religious and Charismatic Experience of Jesus and the First Christians as Reflected in the New Testament*, by James D. G. Dunn, William B. Eerdmans Publishing Company, Grand Rapids, Michigan, 1975, p.353-354.
xlvi *Surprised by the Power of the Spirit, Discovering How God Speaks and Heals Today* by Jack Deere, (Zondervan Publishing House, Grand Rapids, Michigan, 1993) p.165.

Chapter Ten
xlvii *The Heart's Deepest Longing* by Peter Kreeft, (San Francisco, Ignatius Press, 1989), 12.
xlviii *The Gospel in a Pluralistic Society* by Lesslie Newbigin (Grand Rapids, Michigan, William b. Eerdmans Publishing Company, 1989), 16.
xlix *The Illusion of Technique* by William Barrett (Garden City, N.Y., Anchor Press/Doubleday, 1978) p. 219.
l *The Evangelical Case for Wealth Creation, Lausanne and BAM respond to Ron Sider* by Mats Tuunehag, Christianity Today, October 17, 2017.

[li] *The Good of Affluence, Seeking God in a Culture of Wealth*, by John R. Schneider, William b. Eerdmans Publishing Company, Grand Rapids, Michigan/ Cambridge U.K., 2002, p.36-37.
[lii] *The Good of Affluence, Seeking God in a Culture of Wealth*, by John R. Schneider, William b. Eerdmans Publishing Company, Grand Rapids, Michigan/ Cambridge U.K., 2002, p.3.
[liii] *The Good of Affluence, Seeking God in a Culture of Wealth*, by John R. Schneider, William b. Eerdmans Publishing Company, Grand Rapids, Michigan/ Cambridge U.K., 2002, p.115.
[liv] *Property and Riches in the Early Church*, by Martin Hengel trans. John Bowden (Philadelphia : Fortress, 1974), pp.26-27.
[lv] *The Good of Affluence, Seeking God in a Culture of Wealth*, by John R. Schneider, William b. Eerdmans Publishing Company, Grand Rapids, Michigan/ Cambridge U.K., 2002, p.189.
[lvi] *Social Capital, Corporate Purpose and the Revival of American Capitalism*, by Steven Pearlstein, Center for Effective Public Management at Brookings, January 2014

Chapter Eleven
[lvii] *The Beginner's Guide to Spiritual Gifts* by Sam Storms, (Bethany House Publishers, 11400 Hampshire Avenue South, Bloomington, Minnesota 55438, 2012) pg. 73.
[lviii] *The Beginner's Guide to Spiritual Gifts* by Sam Storms, (Bethany House Publishers, 11400 Hampshire Avenue South, Bloomington, Minnesota 55438, 2012) pg. 74.
[lix] *Hearing God, Developing a Conversational Relationship with God* by Dallas Willard, (Intervarsity Press, P.O. Box 1400, Downers Grove IL 60515, 2012) pg. 86.
[lx] *Practicing the Power, Welcoming the Gifts of the Holy Spirit in your Life* by Sam Storms, (Zondervan Publishing, 2017) pg. 30-31.

Chapter Twelve
[lxi] *When the Church Was a Family, Recapturing Jesus' Vision for Authentic Christian Community*, by Joseph Hellerman, (B & H Publishing Group, Nashville, TN, 2009) p.29
[lxii] *Former Facebook exec says social media is ripping apart society* by James Vincent, Dec 11, 2017 6:07am EST, theverge.com

Made in the USA
Columbia, SC
05 January 2023